Frontiers

Frontiers

A Short History of
the American West

ROBERT V. HINE & JOHN MACK FARAGHER

YALE UNIVERSITY PRESS / NEW HAVEN & LONDON

Designed by Nancy Ovedovitz and set in
Century Expanded type by Duke & Company,
Devon, Pennsylvania. Printed in the United
States of America by Hamilton Printing
Company, Castleton, New York.

Library of Congress
Cataloging-in-Publication Data
Hine, Robert V., 1921–
Frontiers : a short history of the American
West / Robert V. Hine and John Mack
Faragher.
p. cm.
Abridged ed. of: The American West. c2000.
Includes bibliographical references and index.
ISBN: 978-0-300-11710-3 (cloth : alk. paper)
ISBN: 978-0-300-13620-3 (pbk.: alk.paper)
1. West (U.S.)—History. 2. Frontier and
pioneer life—West (U.S.) I. Faragher,
John Mack, 1945– II. Hine, Robert V., 1921–
American West. III. Title.
F591.H673 2007
978—dc22   2006036192

A catalogue record for this book is available
from the British Library.

The paper in this book meets the guidelines for
permanence and durability of the Committee
on Production Guidelines for Book Longevity
of the Council on Library Resources.

10   9   8   7   6   5   4   3   2

Contents

Illustrations follow pages 56, 104, 152, and 200

Preface

 In alighting out for the West (that's the way Huck Finn put it) we intend to interpret the western story with little pretense of being comprehensive or completely objective. Instead we face with wonder the deep contradictions in our frontier history and try to make sense of them. Following the abundance of recent provocative work on the American West, we have highlighted the Native American side of the frontier, the significance of ethnicity in settlement, and the participation of women in the making of western history. There are many voices that speak directly from experience. There are rich galleries of illustrations, drawn from historical sources. Intended for the general reader, this book is a condensation of an earlier scholarly edition. Those seeking more detail should refer to that work, *The American West: A New Interpretive History,* or consult the list of "Further Reading" at the back of this volume.

We thank again the people listed in the Preface to our larger edition. For this shorter edition, we specifically thank Frank Turner, director of the Beinecke Rare Book and Manuscript Library at Yale University, and George Miles, curator of Yale's Western American Collection, for their assistance in selecting historic images and generously granting permission to publish them. We are grateful once more to the staff of Yale University Press and in particular to our editor, Chris Rogers. We also owe an unusually large debt to our astute copy editor, Jessie Dolch.

Long ago the two of us discovered our congruous mindsets, and the joint effort of producing this abridged edition has intensified and reinforced that happy congruity.

Dreams and Homelands

Centuries before they first sailed to the Americas, Europeans were dreaming of unknown lands to the west, places inhabited by "the fabulous races of mankind," with men and women unlike any seen in the known world. The people might be frightening, but their home would surely be a paradise, a golden land somewhere beyond the setting sun. Even centuries before, the Roman poet Horace wrote

> Through the thin dawn-mists of the West,
> Rich sunlit plains and hilltops gemmed with snow,
> The Islands of the Blest!

Similar visions inspired the great explorations of the early modern world. On his third voyage westward in 1498, as his ship coasted the shores of what today is known as Trinidad, Christopher Columbus convinced himself he was skirting the Garden of Eden. He was the first, but certainly not the last, European to seek paradise on Caribbean beaches. Dreams sent others in quest of the Fountain of Youth, the golden Cities of Cíbola, and the mystical isle of California, populated by beautiful but fierce Amazons. Centuries of "California Dreaming" inspired the conquest and colonization of the West.

During the epoch of European colonialism, with nation-states competing for the resources of the Americas, the dream took an imperial cast. "Westward the course of empire takes its way," Bishop George Berkeley of Ireland famously declared in the mid-eighteenth century, and the first generation of American nationalists adopted his rhetoric as their own. By then, pioneers were establishing the first American settlements west of the Appalachians. Westward ho! In the

1

nineteenth century American expansionists coupled the imagined West with the idea of American greatness and called the process Manifest Destiny.

But beyond the misty horizon of dreams was a world of human reality. Though European explorers believed they had discovered a new world, for thousands of years the Western Hemisphere had been home to peoples with histories and dreams of their own. Native Americans had developed more than two thousand distinct cultures, spoke hundreds of different languages, and made their livings in scores of dissimilar environments. Columbus, mistakenly thinking he had arrived in the East Indies, called the people of the Caribbean *los Indios*. Within a half-century, the word *Indian*, used to refer to all native Americans, had passed into English. Lumping together Aztec militarists, Hopi communalists, and Pequot horticulturalists, the term encompasses an enormous diversity among the native peoples of the Americas.

The Indians were descendants of ancient hunters who migrated from Asia to America some thirty to forty thousand years ago. Thereafter, even at the slow rates of population growth that characterize foraging peoples, it would have taken but a few thousand years to settle the whole hemisphere. Remarkably, the oral traditions of many Indian people depict a long journey from a distant place of origin to a new homeland. The Indian peoples of North America had embarked on their long journey toward the development of a set of regionally distinct cultures.

The foragers of the desert struck Europeans as materially impoverished. Nineteenth-century American pioneers, disdainfully labeled the Utes, Shoshones, and other desert peoples "Diggers" because they dug for edible roots. Colonizers may have thought of such people as inferior, but foragers themselves considered their way of life superior to any other. "There is no Indian who does not consider himself infinitely more happy and more powerful than the French," a chief of the hunter-gatherer Mi̇́kmaq people of Nova Scotia once told a Jesuit missionary.

In the myth of western conquest, all Indians were nomadic, but foragers and hunter-gatherers were actually far outnumbered by native peoples with other strategies for procuring a living. An early French visitor was amazed at the abundant harvests Timucua fishers took from the sea on what is now the Florida coast. In the Pacific Northwest the abundant salmon catch allowed the Tlingits, Haidas, and Kwakiutls to develop a rich and refined material culture, including grand clan houses with distinctive carved and painted totem poles and magnificent blankets woven of the wool of wild goats. Even more numerous than the fishers were the farmers living in central Mexico and the arid Southwest, one of four world sites where late-stone-age people invented the practice of growing their own food. Farming made possible a more elaborate social and cultural life, but it also encouraged and enabled the settlement of North America by Europeans. Without corn and potatoes—and other New World Indian crops such as tobacco, rubber, and short-staple cotton, each of which became the basis for important modern industries and markets—it is fair to say that the history of the modern world would have been far different.

Aside from Aztecs and other great farming chiefdoms along the Gulf Coast,

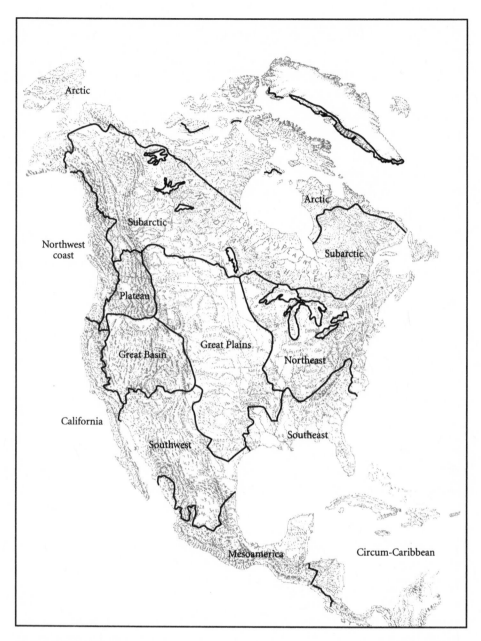

Native Culture Areas

no tribes had standing armies and certainly no bureaucracies. This was but one of several important differences between Indians and Europeans. Europeans had great difficulty understanding the authority of a tribal chief, whose performance among his people was often judged not by how much wealth and power he accumulated, but rather by how well he disbursed resources to clans and families. From the European perspective this respect for fairness made little sense. Indians found Old World traditions equally puzzling. A young Huron who visited France in the

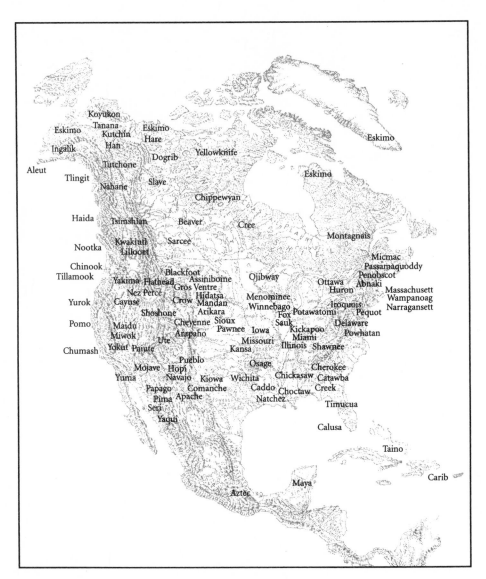

Tribal Locations

early seventeenth century reported his shock at the conditions he had found there. "Among the French," he told fellow tribe members, "men were whipped, hanged and put to death without distinction of innocence or guilt." He had seen a "great number of needy and beggars." He could not understand why the French people tolerated such conditions.

Native cultures had a very strong communal ethic and rarely allowed the individual ownership of land. Productive resources were considered common property. This pattern contrasted dramatically with the European tradition of private property, and colonists doubted that there could be individual responsibility without individual ownership. Sometimes colonial officials used these differences in cultural values to justify the dispossession of native communities, denying that Indians had any rights to the land at all.

Probably the most fundamental distinction between invading Europeans and indigenous Indian cultures was religion. There were, of course, religious differences among native cultures. But in the religion of most North Americans, human beings were thought to share a kinship with all other living things, and a pantheon of supernatural forces linked all of nature. If that chain was broken, the great cycles were damaged, and illness and disorder ensued. Native religion connected Indian people intimately with nature and encouraged a strong sense of belonging to their own places, their homelands. The Navajos sing in their Blessingway ceremony, "All my surroundings are blessed as I found it."

Europeans, by contrast, were less concerned with sacred places than with sacred time. The Christian emphasis on the Second Coming or a new millennium encouraged people to believe in progress, to believe that by picking up and moving to a new land they might better their future. The Bible taught Christians that they were separate and distinct from the rest of nature and were granted dominion over "every living thing that moveth upon the earth."

Despite what many of us may have learned in school or what we see in movies, the history of the frontiers of North America is not simply the story of warfare. It is first and foremost the story of where and how cultures meet. The colonization of the North American continent created a multidimensional world inhabited by peoples of diverse backgrounds, including many of mixed ethnic ancestry, the offspring of a process of interaction that spanned many generations. Frontier history tells the story of the creation and defense of communities, the utilization of the land, the development of markets, and the formation of states. It is filled with unexpected twists and turns. It is a tale of conquest, but also one of survival and persistence, and of the merging of peoples and cultures that gave birth and continuing life to America as we think of and experience it today.

The European invasion of North America created a frontier between natives and newcomers. The American frontier, declared Frederick Jackson Turner at the end of the nineteenth century, was "the meeting point between civilization and savagery." His phrase typified the arrogance of the victors in the centuries-long campaign of colonial conquest. Frontiers indeed were often the site of violent confrontations, as colonizers sought to conquer territory and Indians struggled to defend native homelands. But at the beginning of a new millennium, many Americans are less sure than Turner who exactly was the savage and who the civilized.

Frontier and *West* are two key words in the American lexicon, and they share an intimate historical relation. From the perspective of the Atlantic coast, the frontier *was* the West, and that could mean Kentucky or Indiana. *West* might remain as a regional nominative artifact—the Old Northwest, the Middle West—but *the* West moved on with the frontier. Where, then, is the West? The question has puzzled Americans, for its location has changed over time. A recent survey of western historians, writers, and editors found that about half believe the West begins at the Mississippi or the Missouri River, while others propose the eastern edge of the Great Plains or the front range of the Rocky Mountains. Most consider the Pacific Ocean to be its western boundary, but a sizable minority insist that the states of the "left coast" are not part of the West at all. "I wouldn't let California into the West with a search warrant," the late western historian Robert Athearn cracked. East is east and west is west. But consider other perspectives. For Latino settlers moving from Mexico, the frontier was *the North;* for Canadian métis moving onto the northern plains of the Dakotas or Montana, it was *the South;* for Asian migrants headed for California, it was *the East.*

Whatever its boundaries, the West has always been partly understood through the process of getting there—and the process of changing frontiers that keep redefining themselves even today. That may make the western story more complicated, but it also makes it more interesting and more relevant. The history of the frontier is a unifying American theme, for every part of the country was once a frontier, every region was once a West.

Chapter 1 **A New World Begins**

 The Indians who first met Columbus were the Taínos. On their island homes in the Caribbean (Cuba, Jamaica, Haiti, and Puerto Rico today) they cultivated corn and yams, made brown pottery and cotton thread, and fashioned deadly little darts from fish teeth and wood. But Columbus thought the Taínos had no weapons, a conclusion he based on a curious test. Handing them swords, he observed that they grasped the blades and cut their fingers. Steel had come to a people who previously had worked only with bone and stone. This surmise was typical for Columbus, who assumed the superiority of his own culture in all things. "They are all naked, men and women, as their mothers bore them," he condescended in his report to the Spanish monarchs. Columbus made his landfall in October 1492, when the prevailing Caribbean temperatures were balmy, and the natives he saw were attired in much the same costume as bikini-clad vacationers who flock to those beaches today. Although he could not understand the Taínos' language, Columbus assumed he could read their minds. When the natives lifted their hands to the sky, he wrote, it was an indication that they considered the Spaniards to be gods. It was only one of several possible explanations. Perhaps the Taínos were exclaiming, "Great God, what now!"

We can be more certain of what lay in the minds of the Spaniards. After noting the Indians' loving, cooperative, and peaceful reception, Columbus concluded that "all the inhabitants could be made slaves," for "they have no arms and are all naked and without any knowledge of war. They are fitted to be ruled and to be set to work, to cultivate the land and to do all else that may be necessary, and you may build towns and teach them to go clothed and adopt our customs."

Noticing the little gold ornaments the Taínos wore, Columbus contracted a bad case of gold fever. More than anything else, it was the possibility of setting the natives to work mining gold that would persuade the monarchs to finance a large return expedition. "The best thing in the world is gold," Columbus once wrote in his diary, "it can even send souls to heaven."

The conquistadors who followed Columbus were equally sure of themselves. They were also skilled in the arts of conquest because of their long experience fighting "infidels" on the Spanish peninsula. Muslims from Africa had flooded western Europe to a high-water mark in the eighth century, and thereafter the Christians slowly pushed back. These wars of the "Reconquest" directed the crusading propensities of many generations of young Spaniards. In 1492—that most extraordinary year—Granada, the last Moorish stronghold in Iberia, fell to the Christian warriors led by Isabella and Ferdinand of Castille and Aragon, and consequently their Catholic majesties turned their attention westward, across the ocean.

The invasion of America was marked by scenes of frightful violence. In the wake of Columbus, conquering armies marched across the islands of the Caribbean, plundering villages, slaughtering men, capturing and raping women. Once all the islands had been taken, the Spaniards turned to the mainland coast to the west. The people they encountered lived in far more complex societies than those of the Caribbean, with splendid towns and even libraries of handwritten, illustrated books. A Mayan reacted with surprise when he saw a Spaniard reading a European book. "You also have books?" he exclaimed. "You also understand the signs by which you talk to the absent?"

Responding to rumors of a land called Mexico in the interior, in 1519 a fleet of eleven ships with 530 Spanish soldiers departed from Cuba. Onboard were sixteen horses—"the nerves of the wars against the natives," as one Spanish chronicler called them—and numerous fighting dogs. Mexico, they thought, might be some powerful principality of the Great Khan of Cathay (China). Nearby must be fabled California, which was said to be located "on the right hand of the Indies . . . , very close to the region of the terrestrial paradise." Dreams die hard.

Leading this expedition was the archetypal conquistador, Hernán Cortés. An officer in Cortés's army of conquest, Bernal Díaz, described his commander as sexually attractive and physically strong, slow to anger but sometimes roused to speechless fury. He read Latin, wrote poetry, and was fond of gambling at cards and dice. Now he gambled for the highest stakes in the New World. Shortly after his arrival on the Mexican coast, near present-day Veracruz, he ordered the ships dismantled. The game was winner take all, and the Virgin Mary was on his side.

Even as they landed, Cortés and his men were being observed by spies of Moctezuma II, the ruler of the Aztecs of central Mexico, an empire that exploited the peoples of several dozen surrounding city-states. Moctezuma's men recorded the strangers' movements in a set of detailed drawings and reported: "Their flesh is very light, much lighter than ours. They all have long beards, and their hair comes to their ears."

The Aztecs dominated the surrounding region from their capital at Tenochtitlán, which was built and maintained with the tribute collected from their conquests. One of the sixteenth-century world's greatest cities, it rested on an island in the midst of a large lake and was resplendent with stepped pyramids, stone temples, golden vessels, and causeways with cleverly engineered irrigation canals. The Aztecs were as certain of themselves as were the Spaniards. "Are we not the masters of the world?" Moctezuma remarked to his council when he first heard of the landing of the Spaniards.

At this point, the Aztecs might easily have crushed the several hundred Spaniards, who were struggling to survive amid the sand dunes and mosquitoes of the Gulf Coast. But Moctezuma was undecided about the right course. Confident of the enormous power of his empire, he indulged his desire to see with his own eyes the strangers from another world.

How Cortés conquered an empire that could at any time raise thousands of well-trained fighting men remains something of a mystery. One explanation emphasizes Aztec doubts about the invaders. For several years there had been evil omens—comets, heavenly lights, monstrous two-headed births, foaming lake waters. Very much like Europe's kings, Moctezuma held his office in trust for sacred authority, and as he and his high priests worried over these signs, there came the news of the strange appearance of the invaders from across the ocean. Didn't they ride on weird creatures larger than deer? Were not the heads of the men covered with iron, and did they not use strange rods that spit fire and killed? It was an ominous year, and perhaps Cortés had come to fulfill a prophecy.

But certainly there was more to it than the Aztec preoccupation with signs and omens. Cortés proved masterful at the art of diplomacy, and his first assistance came in the form of one of the cleverest women of history, a young Aztec named Malíntzin, who is best known as La Malínche, the Hispanicized version of her native name. Sold into slavery as a child, she was given to Cortés by a local chief and made the decision to align herself with the Spaniards. Possessing an enormous talent for languages, she quickly mastered Spanish and became Cortés's indispensable interpreter. But she also proved a master interpreter of Aztec intentions, and in the Aztec images of the conquest, Malínche is often shown by Cortés's side.

Malínche was a powerfully complex character, and the Mexican people have never ceased arguing over the meaning of her actions. On the one hand, her name symbolizes the betrayal of native culture, synonymous with the worst traitor. Because she became Cortés's mistress and bore him a son, other Mexicans see her as the mother of *la raza*, the new people who arose out of the blending of Indian and Spanish, native and European. Thus she symbolizes not only betrayal, but also the mixing of cultures and peoples that is the foundation of modern Mexico. Malínche stands for the process of interchange in the frontier cultures of the Americas.

Just as Cortés exploited Malínche's alienation from her people, so he brilliantly exploited the resentments of the Aztec's many subject peoples. He was able to persuade the Tlaxcalans, a small republic that lived under the heavy heel of Aztec domination, to join him, and thus thousands of Indian warriors marched with the

Spaniards over the mountains to the great city of Tenochtitlán. The conquest of Mexico would largely be the work of Indians fighting Indians—a powerful lesson Europeans learned from Cortés's victory.

When Cortés and his Spanish-Tlaxcalan army arrived at Tenochtitlán, Moctezuma gave Cortés and his lieutenants the use of large quarters near his own palace and tried to enter into dialogue with his counterpart. But when Cortés knocked down an Aztec religious shrine and set up a Catholic altar in its place, Moctezuma was shocked. Cortés was certain in his convictions. After all, Aztec priests practiced rituals of human sacrifice, inflicting a terrible death on captives by cutting open their chests and tearing the pulsing hearts from their living bodies. Yet Aztec priests also subjected themselves to frightful self-torture, slashing their own bodies with obsidian blades and piercing their tongues and penises with cactus thorns to draw the blood that was the ultimate sacrifice to the gods. The Aztecs were, in short, as thoroughly committed to their own religious beliefs and practices as the Spaniards.

Eventually, in 1520, the Spaniards seized Moctezuma and massacred a group of young men engaged in religious observance. That precipitated a revolt, and the Aztec army besieged the Spaniards in their quarters in the center of the city. After seven days, the Spaniards made a bold attempt to flee by night, during which two-thirds of the Spanish troops died. Dressed in heavy armor stuffed with gold and precious stones looted from Moctezuma's treasure house, many drowned in the canals. So clogged did the channel become with their bodies, it was said, that those who managed to escape did so by running across the backs of the dead. After the battle the Aztecs dredged the canal and brought up the dead in order to retrieve the treasure.

But the Spaniards returned, reinforced by troops from Cuba as well as thousands of Indian allies who now grabbed the opportunity to overthrow the Aztec overlords. During the intervening year, Tenochtitlán had been struck by an epidemic of smallpox brought by the invaders. Some contemporaries estimated that this disease reduced the population by half. It was then that Cortés attacked the city. The invaders fought their way to the central pyramid where the last battle took place. Many thousands, perhaps tens of thousands, died, including Moctezuma. The Aztec leaders were captured and tortured to reveal the location of the state treasure, which the Spaniards plundered.

The successors of Columbus established a feudal institution known as the *encomienda*. This system placed Indian workers at the disposal of Spanish lords, who set them to work building the new capital of Mexico City on the ruins of Tenochtitlán, dredging the streams for alluvial gold, and working the fields. There were reports that rather than accept this form of slavery, many Indians killed themselves, after killing their children. Native peoples resisted the conquest in many ways. One chronicler of the conquest told of a particularly ironic torture some Indians invented for captured Spaniards with a hunger for gold. Heating the metal to its melting point, they would pour the molten stuff down the throats of their prisoners.

Some Spaniards protested the horrors of the conquest and worked to obtain justice for the Indians. Principal among them was the Dominican priest Bartolomé de Las Casas. The Christian mission in the New World was to convert the Indians, he argued, and "the means to effect this end are not to rob, to scandalize, to capture or destroy them, or to lay waste their lands." Centuries before the nations of the world recognized the concept of universal human rights, Las Casas had proclaimed that "the entire human race is one." He became a towering moral figure in the early history of the Americas.

Those seeking to justify the conquest argued that the Indians were savages who practiced horrible vices. It was widely reported, for example, that Indians used drugs and were sexual libertines or sexual deviants. But the most common complaint was that they were cannibals. In the earliest books devoted to the conquest, the Caribs (a people of the Lesser Antilles and the neighboring South American coast, from whose name the Spanish derived not only the word *Caribbean* but also the word *cannibal*) were shown devouring the flesh of captured Spaniards.

Las Casas considered such claims slanderous. The charge of sexual deviance he dismissed as "a falsehood," and he compared the native use of drugs to communion in the Catholic Church, pointing out that it was part of a ceremony of divination. He even made an effort to explain Aztec human sacrifice in its own terms. "It is not surprising that when unbelievers who have neither grace nor instruction consider how much men owe to God," he explained, "they devise the most difficult type of repayment, that is, human sacrifice in God's honor." The Church, he argued, should aim to correct such practices through enlightenment, not punishment.

The controversy over the treatment of the Indians finally came before the royal court of Spain. Impressed by Las Casas's argument, the Spanish monarchy declared that henceforth it would be official policy that the Indians be considered fully human and treated fairly. But these ideals, overwhelmed by more typical patterns of colonial exploitation, were never realized in practice. As Cortés once said, "I came to get gold, not to till the soil like a peasant." Dreams of riches easily obtained easily corroded ideals.

The most enduring contribution of Las Casas came not in his contribution to policy but in his history of the conquest. *The Destruction of the Indies*, published in Spain in 1552, is one of the most influential books in the history of the early modern world. Las Casas blamed the Spaniards for the deaths of millions of Indians and indicted them for what today we would call the crime of genocide. Other European powers later used these arguments to condemn Spain while covering up their own dismal records of colonial conquest. Subsequent scholars, doubting Las Casas's estimates of huge population losses, criticized his work as part of a "Black Legend" of the Spanish conquest.

Scholars dispute the size of the indigenous population of the island of Hispaniola at the time of the conquest. Estimates range from several hundred thousand to several million. But there is no dispute over the fact that fifty years after Columbus's landing, only a few hundred native people remained alive. The Taínos virtually disappeared. Faced with a severe labor shortage, the Spaniards began importing African slaves, and by 1560 Africans had become the majority population, ruled by a small elite of European colonists.

The destruction of the native population of mainland Mexico was one of the greatest demographic calamities in human history. Many thousands died in the fighting, or as the consequence of the destruction of their communities, but by far the greatest loss of life resulted from the introduction of Old World diseases. Pre-Columbian America seems to have had few contagious epidemic diseases, and Indian peoples had no protective antibodies. A shipload of colonists from Spain carried smallpox to Hispaniola in 1516, and the expedition of Cortés brought it to Mexico, where it seriously undermined Aztec society. Disease, which frequently preceded conquest, was the secret weapon of the European invaders and helps to explain their success. The outstanding difference between the European colonial experience in the Americas and elsewhere—in Africa and Asia, for instance—was the extraordinary reduction in the native population.

Yet the rate of Spanish immigration to the New World remained relatively low, so Indians continued in the majority, and by the end of the sixteenth century the native population of Mexico had begun to rebound from its disastrous collapse. In addition to Europeans, Africans, and Indians, a fourth demographic group had taken shape. Since the great majority of European immigrants to the New World were young, single, and male, a pattern of sexual relations and cohabitation among colonists and native women quickly developed, and soon a large population of mixed ancestry, known as *mestizos*, arose. By the eighteenth century the mestizos made up nearly a quarter of the population of the area known as New Spain, and by the nineteenth century they were the majority.

Conquistadors and colonists continued to expand the frontiers of New Spain, which first stretched from the Isthmus of Panama to Mexico in the New World. Fanlike, they spread northward, creating the northern borderlands of New Spain, the region that would become the southern tier of the United States. Many remarkable stories come from this time. One began in 1528 when an ill-fated colonizing expedition was wrecked along the Gulf Coast of Texas. A handful of survivors trekked westward, living among the Indian communities they encountered on their journey. It ended after seven long years when the last men left alive chanced upon a Spanish expedition seeking Indian slaves in the far northern Mexican province of Sonora. One of the survivors, Álvar Núñez Cabeza de Vaca, wrote an account of his adventures in which he told of a North American empire of Cíbola, with cities larger than the cities of Mexico, where the king took his siesta under a tree of golden bells. This heady myth was based on nothing more firm than the adobe pueblos of New Mexico, but the report inspired Spanish attempts to penetrate the mystery of North America.

Two Spanish efforts set off to conquer the northern borderlands. The first, launched from central Mexico, was aimed at the future American Southwest. Francisco Vásquez de Coronado—in command of three hundred Spaniards, both cavalry

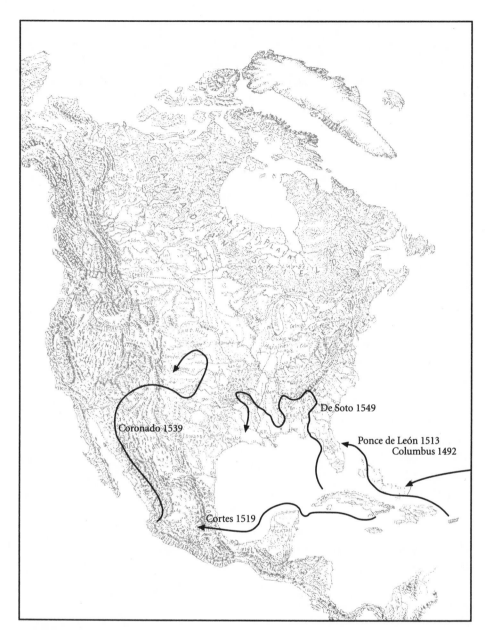

The Spanish Invasions

and infantry, as well as eight hundred Tlaxcalan warriors—moved north along a well-marked Indian trading route that connected central Mexico to the northern region known as Aztlán—the legendary homeland of the Aztecs. Coronado was in search of Cabeza de Vaca's golden Cities of Cíbola.

From a base camp along the Rio Grande he sent out expeditions in all directions. Although men from these expeditions were the first Europeans to see the Colorado River and the Grand Canyon, they saw no evidence of the Cities of Cíbola.

Coronado himself took his army as far north as the Great Plains and was among the first Europeans to see great herds of buffalo—Coronado called them "shaggy cows"—but he found no gold. He and his discouraged army dragged themselves back to Mexico, and for the next half-century Spain lost interest in the Southwest.

When the Spaniards did return, it was not as conquistadors but as Catholic missionaries. The densely settled farming communities of the Pueblo Indians may not have offered much wealth to plunder, but they did offer a harvest of souls. During the 1580s Franciscan missionaries began to proselytize among the Pueblos, but within a few years rumors began drifting south of rich silver mines along the Rio Grande. Gold and silver mining were major industries in northern New Spain, and men were always restless to make new strikes. Many times over the next four centuries rumors of gold would spark new colonization in the West.

In 1598 an expedition left New Spain under the command of Juan de Oñate, a member of a wealthy mining family. Oñate's party consisted of 130 predominantly mestizo and Tlaxcalan soldiers and their families, along with some twenty Franciscan missionaries. They encountered varying degrees of resistance, with the most found at the town of Acoma, or the "sky city," built high atop a commanding mesa in present-day New Mexico. Laying siege to the town, the attackers climbed the rock walls and killed some eight hundred men, women, and children. They also herded more than five hundred off into slavery.

It was easier to conquer, however, than to make gold from desert sand. Oñate was soon recalled to Mexico. Without mines to exploit, Spanish interest in the region subsided once again. But then the Church persuaded the monarchy to subsidize "New Mexico" as a special missionary colony. In 1609 a new governor founded the capital of La Villa Real de la Santa Fe de San Francisco de Asís ("the royal town of the holy faith of Saint Francis of Assisi")—now known simply as Santa Fe—and from this base the Franciscans penetrated all the surrounding Indian villages.

Their mission was the cultural conquest of the Pueblos. But the missionaries entered an Indian world they found difficult to understand. Both Spanish and Pueblo society were divided into separate domains for men and women, but the cultural meanings of the division were quite different. The Pueblos reckoned descent through the mother's line, with women exercising nearly complete control over their households. "The woman always commands," wrote one Franciscan, "not the husband." Men and women, wrote another, "live together as long as they want to, and when the woman takes a notion, she looks for another husband and the man for another wife." Accustomed to the norm of the patriarchal family, the friars found this system incomprehensible.

The two cultures also had very different understandings of sexuality. Sexual intercourse was to the Pueblos a symbol of the powerful force bringing the separate worlds of men and women together, and was thus their symbol for community. Public displays of intimacy shocked and disgusted the priests. The Pueblos, for their part, were astounded by the celibacy of the Franciscan missionaries, for it marked the priests as only half-persons. Indeed, the Franciscans struck the Pueblos as preoccupied with sex. At Taos Pueblo a priest humiliated men by grabbing their testicles and twisting until the victims collapsed in pain. One Taos man complained in court that a priest had "twisted his penis so much that it broke in half."

The Indians of the outlying towns—the Acomas, the Zunis, and the isolated Hopis—were the most successful at resisting Christian conversion and retained more of their old customs, including the system of matrilineal kinship. But the Pueblos of the Rio Grande valley were dramatically affected by Spanish and Christian patterns, and over time the power of women and of the lineage of the mothers faded. As one Pueblo tale put it, "when Padre Jesus came, the Corn Mothers went away."

By the mid-seventeenth century this northern-most outpost of the far-flung Spanish empire in the New World was populated by about three thousand mostly mestizo colonists clustered in a few settlements along the Rio Grande. Surrounding them were an estimated fifty thousand Pueblos in some fifty villages. Despite the large imbalance between the number of colonists and natives, the Indian population was in precipitous decline, again largely because of European epidemic diseases. As Indian numbers fell, the exploitation of their labor became less profitable, and colonists began instead to extend their own land holdings, their agriculture, and particularly their stock-raising activities. The result was increasing conflict with Pueblo communities, who considered those lands their own. The conflict escalated to crisis amid a severe drought that brought widespread suffering during the late 1670s. Missionaries chose this as the moment to escalate their attacks on native religion, invading underground ceremonial chambers and destroying sacred artifacts. The governor of New Mexico had three holy men executed and dozens more whipped for merely practicing their religion.

One of those humiliated men became the leader of a movement to overthrow the colonial regime. In August 1680, implementing a secret plan with superb timing, warriors led by a man known as Popé of San Juan killed four hundred colonists, including several dozen priests, whose mutilated bodies they left strewn upon the altars. The victorious Pueblos turned the governor's palace in Santa Fe into a communal dwelling. On its elegant inlaid stone floors, Pueblo women now ground their corn. The corn mothers had returned. Santa Fe became the capital of a Pueblo confederacy with Popé in charge. He forced Christian Indians to the river to scrub away the taint of baptism, and ordered the destruction of everything Spanish. But most Pueblos found it difficult to turn back. The colonists had introduced horses and sheep, fruit trees and wheat, new tools and new crafts that the Indians found useful. Although they could accept a world without Jesus, they could not imagine a world without iron, or sheep, or peaches. Old ways and new ways had gotten too mixed up to pull apart easily.

The Pueblo Revolt was perhaps the most successful native uprising in American frontier history. It slowed, but it did not stop, the Spanish advance. Some years after Popé's death, in 1692, the Spanish began a violent reconquest that in six years of fighting reestablished colonial authority. Yet over the next generation the colonists and the natives reached an implicit understanding. The Pueblos observed Catholicism in the missionary chapels, while the missionaries tolerated the practice of traditional religion in the Indians' underground kivas. Royal officials guaranteed the inviolability of Indian lands in exchange for the Pueblos' pledge of loyalty to the Spanish crown. Native workers voluntarily turned out for service on colonial lands, and colonists for their part abandoned the system of forced labor. Colonist and Indian communities remained autonomous, but they learned to live with one another.

In New Mexico and elsewhere in their New World colonial empire, the Spanish established a *frontier of inclusion*. Their colonial communities were characterized by *mestizaje*, or ethnic intermixing that included a great deal of intermarriage between male colonists and native women. Hundreds of thousands of Indians died of warfare and disease, but thousands of others passed their genes on to successive generations of mestizos. The children of Old World fathers and New World mothers became the majority population of New Spain. Thus while the coming of the Spaniards to the Americas was characterized by the destruction of peoples, it also resulted in the birth of new ones.

Chapter 2 **Contest of Cultures**

 Ships from ports in England, France, Spain, and Portugal probably plied the waters of the great fishing grounds of the North Atlantic years before Columbus made his first voyage to the Caribbean. Thus the woodland Indians on the shores of the Atlantic may have been the first to see Europeans. They watched with curiosity the strange "little islands" of ships from beyond the sunrise, as the Míkmaqs of Nova Scotia later told of them, which seemed to have trees and branches on them and a "number of bears" crawling about.

The first European to record making contact with the native people of the northeastern coast of the North American continent was Giovanni da Verrazano, a gentleman from Florence sailing for the French. In 1524, along the coast of Maine, he encountered a troublesome people who shot arrows at his shoreside exploring party. But they made it clear they wanted to trade for knives, fishhooks, or edged metal. These Indians were experienced enough to be wary of Europeans, yet also understood the value of their technology.

Ten years later the Indians of the Saint Lawrence valley marveled at two ships that came sailing up their river. The vessels were mastered by French navigator Jacques Cartier, whose king was ready to compete with imperial Spain. Cartier had come to seek the Northwest Passage to India and to establish French claims to lands "where it is said that he should find great quantities of gold."

Cartier visited the village of Hochelaga (later the site for the city of Montreal), which he noted was composed of "some fifty houses." These were the famous "longhouses" of the Iroquois, each a communal dwelling headed by a clan mother. Women controlled domestic and village space. The women "are much respected," a French observer wrote. "The Elders decide no important affair without their advice." Men were in charge of "outside" space, of hunting, warfare, and diplomacy.

The beautiful fur coats of the Indians caught Cartier's attention. Back home there was a strong demand for pelts of all kinds for winter wear. The growing European population had depleted their own wild game, so here was the potential for a profitable trade. The stereotype of ignorant Indians trading valuable furs for cheap trinkets is not accurate, as on this early frontier of the Atlantic coast, Indians were in the commanding position. Because of heavy competition among traders, they frequently could demand very good exchange rates. They had a sharp eye for quality and insisted on superior goods of their own specification—heavy woolen cloth, for example, in their favorite colors of deep blue, dark red, and steel gray. In the seventeenth century, the trade blankets of the British Hudson's Bay Company, still renowned for their high quality, were designed to Indian specifications.

Cartier and his crew spent the winter of 1535–36 in Hochelaga. His hosts were remarkably cooperative and helpful. They suggested, for instance, a potion of boiled bark that cured almost magically an epidemic of scurvy threatening to wipe out the company. The bitter cold, however, was beyond relief. Mountainous snowdrifts lay against the ships in the harbor, their bulwarks encased in ice four inches thick. Once the ice broke, Cartier sailed for home. It was not until the dawn of the seventeenth century that the French would permanently colonize the Northeast.

But in the meantime, trade continued and grew increasingly important. Thus the early connections between Europeans and Indians in the Northeast took on a different character from those of northern New Spain, emphasizing commerce rather than conquest. Both, of course, were colonial relationships, with negative consequences for native people. From the beginning, trade was stacked in favor of Europeans. As manufactured goods became essential to their way of life, Indians gradually grew dependent on European supplies. And as elsewhere, Europeans introduced new diseases, which soon began to ravage northeastern native communities. Furthermore, intense and deadly rivalry broke out among tribes over access to hunting territory. By the end of the sixteenth century the Saint Lawrence valley had become a no-man's land for Indians, opening the way for European settlement.

In 1608 Samuel de Champlain established the first permanent French settlement in the New World at a place on the northern shore of the Saint Lawrence he called Québec. Champlain understood the importance of good relations with native tribes, and he forged an alliance with the powerful Huron people living north of Lake Ontario. The Hurons were traditional enemies of the five nations of the Iroquois Confederacy (the Mohawks, Oneidas, Onondagas, Cayugas, and Senecas—known to Europeans as the League of Five Nations) to their south. Good relations with some Indians meant war with others, and Champlain joined the Hurons in an attack on the Iroquois. Thus the French initiated their American empire by allying themselves with a powerful Indian force, demonstrating once again the importance of native people in the making of continental history.

As an industry, the fur trade of New France rivaled cattle raising and mining in New Spain. And just as the ranches and mines of Mexico depended on native labor, so the trapping of beaver and otter in New France relied on the work of the Indians. Champlain understood this simple necessity and therefore sent his agents and traders in canoes to negotiate with Indians and to live in their villages, learning native languages and customs.

But the French had trouble attracting colonists. In the early 1700s, a century after its founding, the population of New France numbered only fifteen thousand (New Spain, by contrast, included at least one million colonists and mestizos). Québec, the administrative capital, was small by Spanish colonial standards, and the settlement of Montreal remained little more than a frontier outpost. Because of the importance of the fur trade, the communities of the Saint Lawrence looked west toward the continental interior rather than east across the Atlantic. It was typical for the sons of colonists to take to the woods in their youth, working as agents for fur companies or as independent traders. The contact between French traders—the *coureurs de bois* or "runners of the woods"—and Indian peoples resulted in much cultural exchange, as Indians adopted aspects of European material culture and Europeans took up the lifeways of Indians. Like the Spanish, the French established a frontier of inclusion, although it developed its own unique character.

Some of the traders married Indian women. For some, such a relationship was the fulfillment of an erotic fantasy associated with colonialism. "A young woman is allowed to do what she pleases," one Frenchman wrote, "let her conduct be what it will. . . . A young woman, say they, is master of her own body, and by her natural right to liberty is free to do what she pleases." To be sure, exploitation was often a component in these relationships. Prostitution, unknown among the Indians before the colonial era, soon became a prominent institution at every fur trading post and fort. Numerous traders took Indian women as lovers but then abandoned them without a word or the least consideration for any children they left behind. But there was opportunity for exploitation on both sides. Indian women established liaisons with traders in order to bring valuable commercial connections to their families, their clans, or to themselves personally. Most of the native cultures of the Northeast were matrilineal, and women expected rather weak marital connections. Moreover, polygamy and divorce were fairly commonplace.

So for the most part, intermarriage seems to have been mutually advantageous. The Indian wife of a trader or trapper prepared furs and skins for market, cooked, and helped to carry packs. Most of the connections made between traders and Indian women seem to have been stable, permanent, and constant, lasting for years, with a great deal of commitment on the part of the men to their children. Many traders remained in Indian country and raised mixed families.

Out of this process of intermixing, which the French called *métissage*, a new people developed, the *métis*, or "people in between." Many conservative colonial officials disapproved of this trend, criticizing the métis as neither fish nor fowl, yet métis proved themselves useful. Often bilingual, sometimes trilingual with highly developed skills of moving across cultural boundaries, these people became guides, interpreters, and often traders in their own right. As early as the 1620s, métis coureurs de bois were living among the Indians of the Great Lakes, and a generation later they were on the upper reaches of the Mississippi.

In 1673 Governor Louis de Frontenac authorized Jacques Marquette, a Jesuit priest, and Louis Joliet to travel two-thirds of the way down the Mississippi to the Arkansas River, testing the Spanish colonial frontier. Then in 1682 Robert Cavelier, Sieur de La Salle, leading a bickering but courageous expedition, traveled all the way to the river's mouth on the Gulf of Mexico. There in the swampy delta he planted a cross, turned a spade of earth, and claimed all land drained by those waters for France.

New France became a giant crescent—the interior heartland of North America embracing the two immense river systems of the Saint Lawrence and the Mississippi joined by the five Great Lakes. Its dimensions were nearly as breathtaking as the sweep of New Spain, whose northeastern borders it overlapped. The French, too, founded a few settlements along the Gulf of Mexico, most importantly at New Orleans in 1718. Except for these ports, however, the French turned inward to the land they named Louisiana for King Louis XIV.

The French also had religious aspirations: they wished to see Indians converted to the Catholic faith. In 1611 the first Jesuit missionaries arrived in New France. The Jesuits often accompanied traders into Indian country, and sometimes they led the way. At first, Indians looked upon the "Black Robes" as culturally inferior. They wore inefficient and sexually ambiguous clothing, and they seemed uninterested in women, which Indian men found incomprehensible. The Indians had great difficulty understanding the concept of celibacy or other sexual mores of the missionaries. To a missionary preaching against the sin of divorce, a Huron man expressed a point of view with which most modern Americans would agree: "You make no sense. My wife does not agree with me, and I cannot agree with her. She will be better suited with another who does not get on with his present wife. Do you wish us four to be unhappy the rest of our days?"

The Jesuits began to succeed in their missionary work only when they started allowing Indians to build bridges between their own customs and Christianity. "One must be very careful before condemning a thousand things among their customs, which greatly offend minds brought up and nourished in another world," one insightful Jesuit observed. Unlike the Spanish Franciscans, who linked conversion to the full acceptance of European cultural norms, the Jesuits succeeded because they introduced Christianity as a supplement to the Indian way of life.

Several other factors led to Jesuit success. Most important was the enormous social and cultural dislocation caused mainly by disease. During the 1630s the Hurons, for example, were struck by a horrible smallpox epidemic. In a few years, as many as half the Hurons, who numbered in the tens of thousands, perished. Some of them blamed the Jesuits for sapping their spiritual power by practicing their strange rites. For others, however, the plagues caused them to lose faith in their own religion because traditional healers were unable to handle these massive

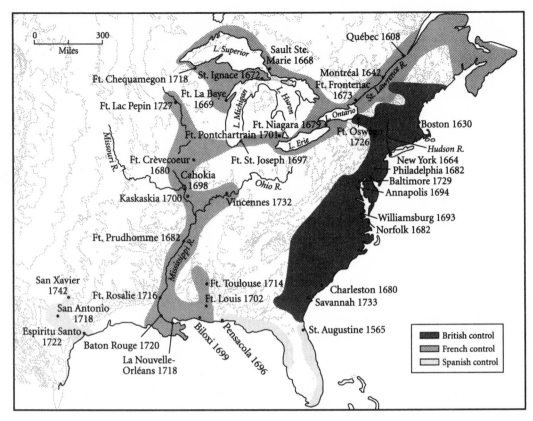

Three North American Empires in the Eighteenth Century

outbreaks of deadly disease. In the aftermath of the epidemic, Jesuit conversions picked up dramatically. The missionaries were particularly successful among Huron women. Just as these women were free to choose European lovers and husbands, so also they could choose to follow Jesuit priests. The Jesuits consciously appealed to them through the cult of the Virgin Mary, the veneration of female saints, and the sisterhood of nuns. By the 1640s the Jesuits had succeeded in converting some six thousand Hurons, about 40 percent of the nation.

As a rule the French Jesuits lived and worked with the natives on their own ground, in contrast with the Spanish Franciscans who attempted to take Indians from their villages and concentrate them at missions. But note that both considered Indians as human beings with souls worth saving. By no means would all subsequent inheritors of the North American continent agree with this assessment of native people.

The English first turned toward the New World in the mid-sixteenth century during the reign of Elizabeth I. A consensus developed among the queen's closest advisers that the time had come for entering the colonial competition. A first attempt at colonization came in 1585 when Sir Walter Raleigh sponsored the establishment of a base of English soldiers and mercenaries on the Outer Banks of North Carolina. The colony Raleigh christened Virginia, in honor of the virgin Queen, was located on an island the local Algonquian people called Roanoke. It was a dismal failure. At first, the Indians fed the English, but when stores grew short, the colonists mounted a surprise attack, killing several of the leading men and beheading the chief. Soon thereafter they abandoned their settlement and returned to England, leaving a legacy of violence and hatred in their wake. In 1587 Raleigh established a new colony at Roanoke, this time composed of sixty-five single men and twenty families. The plan was that this settlement of farmers would live in close association with the native people of the country.

But the Algonquians had learned from their first encounter with the English, and they killed one of the colonists as he fished for crabs. Knowing that the mission hung in the balance, Governor John White sailed home for reinforcements in the colony's single seaworthy vessel. War with Spain broke out during his absence, and three long years passed before he returned. He found the settlement in ruins and the colonists gone without a trace, except for the word *Croatan* (the name of an obscure island) carved in a tree. Roanoke became known as the "Lost Colony." The ultimate fate of the colonists remains one of the great enduring mysteries of the English colonial frontier.

The war between England and Spain suspended any further efforts at English colonization, but at its conclusion in 1604, King James I, Elizabeth's successor, issued a number of royal charters for the colonization of the mid-Atlantic region by several companies. The joint-stock company was basic to English colonization. It sold shares of stock, and the money raised met initial costs without financial assistance from the monarch. The stockholder was liable only for the amount he invested, and if the venture failed, he could not be sued for his remaining resources. Raleigh had discovered how much failure could cost a single investor when he lost £40,000 in the Roanoke disaster. A company would have distributed the loss among many small investors.

In 1607 a group of one hundred colonists in the employ of the Virginia Company built a fort named Jamestown on Chesapeake Bay. It was to become the first permanent English settlement in North America. The Chesapeake was already home to an estimated twenty thousand Algonquian villagers, most of them united in a chiefdom led by a powerful ruler named Powhatan. He envisioned an alliance with the English colonists, both as protection against the Spanish slave raiders who periodically visited his territory and as allies in his struggle to extend his sovereignty over outlying tribes. He also looked forward to establishing commercial relations. As was the case among the Tlaxcalans in Mexico and the Hurons of Canada, the Algonquians of the Chesapeake attempted to use Europeans to pursue ends of their own.

For their part, the Jamestown settlers saw themselves as latter-day conquistadors. Abhorring the idea of physical labor, they survived the first year only with Powhatan's assistance. "In our extremity the Indians brought us Corne," wrote

Captain John Smith, the colony's military leader, "when we rather expected they would destroy us." When the English demanded more than Powhatan thought prudent to supply, events took a familiar turn. Smith inaugurated an armed campaign to plunder food from surrounding villages, and Powhatan retaliated by trying to starve the colonists out. He now realized, he declared to Smith, that "your coming is not for trade, but to invade my people and possess my country." The English came, in other words, not in the mode of the French but in the pattern of the Spanish. During the terrible winter of 1609–10, scores of English colonists starved and a number resorted to cannibalism. By the spring, only sixty people remained of the more than five hundred sent by the Virginia Company.

Determined to prevail, the company sent out from England a large additional force of several hundred men, women, and livestock, committing themselves to protracted conflict with the Indians. By 1613 the colonists had succeeded in establishing firm control over the territory between the James and York rivers. In an attempt to negotiate a peace, Powhatan sent his daughter Pocahontas, who had become fluent in English, to be his ambassador at Jamestown. As in Mexico, the role of mediator would be played by an Indian woman. John Rolfe, a leading Jamestown settler, was smitten by her and wrote, "My heart and best thoughts are and have been a long time so entangled and enthralled in so intricate a laborynth when thinking of her." But alas, they could not marry, for she was "an unbelieving creature." Pocahontas removed that obstacle by converting to Christianity, and they were married. Theirs was the best known of many intimate connections between Indians and Englishmen during those early years. There was even hope that the couple would beget a Christian line of succession for Powhatan's Chesapeake chiefdom. But the plan ended in 1617 when Pocahontas died at the age of twenty-two while visiting England.

Yet John Rolfe himself provided the key to Virginia's future by developing a hybrid of hearty North American and mild West Indian tobacco, and soon the Jamestown colony was shipping cured tobacco to England. Tobacco first had been introduced to English consumers by Francis Drake in the 1580s, and despite King James's description of the habit as "loathsome to the eye, hateful to the nose, harmful to the brain, dangerous to the lungs," by the 1610s a craze for smoking had created strong consumer demand. Tobacco made the Virginia colony a success. Soon the company began to send over large numbers of indentured servants to work the tobacco fields. Gradually, a society of English families began to take shape in Virginia, and the need to integrate Indians into the population as workers disappeared. In contrast to the Spanish and French, who built societies based on the inclusion of Indian people, the English began to establish a *frontier of exclusion*, pushing Indians to the periphery rather than incorporating them within colonial society.

The English thus pressed the Algonquians for further concessions of land on which to plant their profitable crop, leading to an uprising that began on Good Friday, March 22, 1622, and completely surprised the English. Nearly 350 people, a quarter of the colonists, died before Jamestown was able to mobilize its defenses.

Yet the colony managed to hang on, and the attack stretched into a ten-year war of attrition. The war bankrupted the Virginia Company, and in 1624 the king converted Virginia into a royal colony. But the tobacco economy boomed, leading to a doubling of the English colonial population every five years from 1625 to 1640, when it numbered approximately ten thousand. Native populations, in the meantime, were decimated by warfare and disease. Numerical strength thus shifted in favor of the English.

English tobacco farmers took control of coastal Virginia. But a state of war continued to exist to the westward between colonists and native peoples. In 1675 the wealthy backcountry planter Nathaniel Bacon and his neighbors launched a series of violent raids against Indian communities they deemed obstacles to the expansion of their farms. Virginia governor William Berkeley attempted to suppress these unauthorized military expeditions, so infuriating Bacon and his followers that in the spring of the next year six hundred of them turned their fury against the colonial capital of Jamestown. Berkeley fled across the Chesapeake while Bacon pillaged and burned the capital. Soon thereafter, Bacon died of dysentery and his rebellion collapsed. But Bacon's Rebellion of 1676 would go down as the first movement of frontier agrarian dissent in American history. Bacon had issued a manifesto demanding not only the destruction or removal of all Indians from the colony but an end to the rule of aristocratic "grandees" and "parasites" as well. Western farmers tested the limits of Indian endurance and the strength of controls on the eastern seaboard.

Many Indians fled westward. Colonial authorities required those who remained to sign formal treaties granting them small reserved territories. By the 1680s, when the English population numbered more than fifty thousand, only a dozen tribes of about two thousand Indians remained in the Virginia region.

In the northern colonies of New England the English carried out a similar policy of exclusion, although in almost every other way the history of the northern frontier colonies was quite different. Coastal New England seemed an unlikely spot for English colonization, for in the second decade of the seventeenth century the French dominated the Indian trade as far south as Cape Cod, while the Dutch controlled access to the Delaware, Hudson, and Connecticut rivers. A twist of fate, however, provided the English with an opening. From 1616 to 1618, a widespread epidemic of some unknown infectious disease ravaged the native peoples of the northern coast. Whole villages disappeared, and the trade system of the French and the Dutch practically collapsed. The native population of New England as a whole dropped from an estimated 120,000 to less than 70,000, and the surviving coastal societies were so crippled that they were unable to provide effective resistance to the establishment of English colonies.

When in 1620 a group of English religious dissenters landed at the site of the Algonquian village of Patuxet, the future settlement of Plymouth, they found it abandoned, with the bones of the unburied dead scattered before them. They fell on their knees to thank God for "sweeping away great multitudes of natives" to "make room for us." But the Pilgrims, as later generations of Americans would know these colonists, themselves had arrived stricken with scurvy and weakened by malnutrition, and over the first New England winter nearly half of them perished. Like the settlers of Jamestown, the Pilgrims were rescued by Indians. Massasoit, the leader of the native Wampanoag people, hoped for an alliance with the newcomers against his powerful neighboring enemies, the Narragansetts, so he offered food and advice in the early months of 1621. The translator in these negotiations was a native man named Squanto who had been kidnapped by the crew of an English vessel in 1614 and taken to Europe. He succeeded in returning five years later, only to find his village of Patuxet wiped out by the plague. Knowledgeable in the ways of the Europeans, and speaking beautiful English, Squanto became an invaluable adviser to Massasoit. He secured seed corn for the colonists and taught them how to cultivate it.

The Algonquians of New England found these Englishmen concerned less with commerce and more with the acquisition of land for their settlements. The Puritans believed they had the God-given right to take "unused" lands—those not being used by natives for farming—and depopulated village sites were prime targets. "The country lay open," wrote Puritan leader John Winthrop, "to any that could and would improve it." Potential conflicts among settlers over title, however, made it necessary to obtain legal deeds from Indians. The English used a variety of pressure tactics to push them into signing quitclaims. For instance, they would fine Indians for violations of English law, such as working on the Sabbath, and then demand land as payment. Disorganized and demoralized, many of the coastal Algonquians soon placed themselves under the protection of the English; it was one of the very few survival strategies open to them. (Yet they endured, and in the late twentieth century many of them engineered a revival based on casino gambling.)

Indian peoples who lived inland, however, remained a formidable presence. They effectively blocked Puritan expansion until they, too, were hit by a smallpox epidemic that spread with devastating consequences from the Saint Lawrence River south to Long Island Sound in 1633 and 1634. The epidemic occurred at the same time that hundreds of new English colonists were crowding into coastal towns. "Without this remarkable and terrible stroke of God upon the natives," recorded the minutes of one Puritan town meeting, "we would with much more difficulty have found room, and at far greater charge have obtained and purchased land." In the aftermath of the epidemic, colonists established a number of new inland towns along the lower Connecticut River.

English expansion was contested, however, by the Pequots, who lived on the coast near the mouth of the Connecticut River and were principal trading partners of the Dutch. In 1637 the Puritans, joined by the Narragansetts, attacked the Pequots, destroying their main settlement and killing most of its slumbering residents, including women and children. The Pequot War was an act of terrorism, intended to send a message to the other tribes of the region.

For the next four decades English colonists and the remaining Algonquian

Indians of New England lived in close, if tense, contact. A number of Puritan ministers conducted a series of brief experiments in Indian conversion. Roger Williams, who had broken with the Puritans and established a colony for dissidents in Rhode Island, had a special relationship with the Narragansetts. Overflowing with zeal to bring Christ to the Indians, he occasionally lived with them in their "filthy, smoky holes," struggling to learn their language. The Narragansetts trusted him because he maintained that Europeans had no right to land except with prior Indian agreement. Another colonist, clergyman John Eliot, learned Indian languages, translated the Bible into Algonquian, evangelized among the tribes, and succeeded in bringing together fourteen villages of "Praying Indians." These self-governing communities were the closest the English came to imitating the Franciscan or Jesuit missions of New Spain and New France.

All the while, however, the gradual but inexorable expansion of the colonial population continued. Immigration from England fell off, but the fertility of colonial women was extraordinarily high. As one New Englander claimed, he and his fellow colonists enjoyed a biological edge over native peoples through their capacity "to beget and bring forth more children than any other nation in the world." Population growth in turn produced a hunger for new land, creating pressures for further expansion into Indian territory.

The English-Indian conflict boiled over in early 1675 in what became known as King Philip's War, after the English name for the Wampanoag leader Metacomet. Although the Wampanoags remained formally allied with Plymouth Colony, they were forced to concede authority over an ever increasing proportion of their tribal lands. Metacomet reluctantly concluded that he had no alternative except armed resistance. But before he could act, the colonists invaded, attacking and burning villages. Escaping into the New England interior with a guerrilla army, Metacomet led a general Indian uprising. Towns throughout New England were destroyed. "The English man hath provoked us to anger & wrath," one native fighter declared. "We have nothing but our lives to lose but thou hast many fair houses, cattell & much good things." By the beginning of 1676, however, the Indian struggle was collapsing. Defeated in a climactic battle, Metacomet was killed, his body mutilated, and his head placed on a pike, which was marched triumphantly through the Puritan towns. His wife and son, among hundreds of other captives, were sold into West Indian slavery.

The wars between the natives and the Puritans deeply influenced the way Americans would think about the frontier. Puritans interpreted their victories as part of God's plan. "Thus the Lord was pleased to smite our Enemies in the hinder Parts, and give us their land for an Inheritance," wrote Captain John Mason, after he torched the sleeping Pequots. While invoking the name of God is hardly unprecedented, here are the origins of what a later generation would call Manifest Destiny.

At the conclusion of the war, some four thousand Algonquians and two thousand English colonists were dead. Dozens of English and Indian towns lay in ruins.

Measured in relation to population, it was one of the most destructive wars in all American history. The Puritan colonists rounded up hundreds of Praying Indians and concentrated them on desolate islands in Boston harbor. John Eliot worked hard to protect his converts, but to little avail. Although a few isolated native Christian communities remained after the war, most of the converts who survived fled west or north. With few exceptions, Englishmen seemed to see only two alternatives for dealing with the Indians: removal or extermination. Yet communities of Narragansetts, Pequots, and other small tribal groups survived into the twentieth century, as anyone who has gone to the Pequot casino of Foxwoods in Connecticut knows. These several thousand native residents have an alternative perspective on the history of New England. In the homeland of Metacomet, his descendants claim that because he was denied a proper burial, his ghost still rises at night and walks among the Indian spirits.

Chapter 3 The Struggle of Empires

Along the Atlantic coast, between Virginia and New England, relations between Indians and European colonists took a more positive turn. The first Europeans in the region were Scandinavians—Finns, Swedes, and Danes—who came to the short-lived colony known as New Sweden, founded in 1638. Their loose organization and local autonomy fostered a cultural fusion between native and settler cultures that proved one of the most notable and least understood developments of early American history. The natives were both farmers and hunters, with women raising gardens of corn, beans, and squash and men hunting for furs, hides, and meat. This division of labor by gender was much like the one Swedish and Finnish settlers practiced. Scandinavian women quickly adopted the crops of native women, and those women in turn welcomed European metal hoes as well as pigs and chickens. Just as quickly, Scandinavian men took to the surrounds and hunting methods of the local Algonquians, being receptive to learning the calls, disguises, and decoys that worked for the Indians. For their part, Indian men readily incorporated into their hunting routines European steel knives, firearms, and linen hunting shirts, which were much more comfortable in wet weather than buckskin. The Delaware valley was what geographers call a *cultural hearth*, an originating place, for a unique woodland way of life that combined traits from both the Indian and European worlds.

The most ubiquitous symbol of pioneer America, the log cabin, emerged in the Delaware valley and could serve as a symbol of this composite culture. The pioneers of New Sweden, particularly the Finns, brought to North America the tradition of log construction with axes. Other settlers quickly picked up the method, for with the resources of the American woods and a few tools, several men could erect a rough shelter in a day, a solid house in a week. But the Indians also quickly learned these construction techniques and probably did as much as colonists to spread the practice of building with wood across the frontiers of North America.

New Sweden was attacked and taken by the Dutch in 1655, then by the English in 1664. In 1682 William Penn established the Quaker colony of Pennsylvania. No account of frontier history should omit Penn, who towers as a symbol of generous understanding with native people. To a degree not previously known in the colonization of North America, he tried to deal fairly with the Indians, not permitting colonization to begin until he negotiated the right to settle and purchased the land. Indeed, the composite woodland culture of the Delaware valley continued to flower because of the relative peace that Penn and his Quaker followers brought to this distinctive mid-Atlantic frontier.

By the first decades of the eighteenth century, the English colonies were expanding rapidly, doubling every quarter-century. The 250,000 colonists of 1700 would explode to more than 1.3 million fifty years later. Several factors were at work, the extremely high levels of fertility prominent among them. Rebecca Boone, wife of frontier hero Daniel Boone, for example, bore ten children, and the couple was surrounded by sixty-eight grandchildren in their old age! Such high fertility was combined with relatively low mortality. Blessed with fertile lands and the productivity of Indian agricultural techniques, famines simply did not occur in North America. Death rates were 15 or 20 percent lower than in Europe, with a low level of infant mortality.

Immigration also continued to contribute to the population boom. Large movements of Germans and Scotch-Irish to the fringes of English settlement had an immense effect on the American frontier. By the second decade of the eighteenth century, Germans by the thousands were streaming out of the Rhineland as the result of depressed farm conditions, war, and New World advertisements. They were Pietists, pacifists, and good farmers, and they sought fertile land in the interior. In their native language, the Germans were "Deutsch," so some came to be known as the Pennsylvania Dutch in the New World. Wherever they went, they were found to be a people willing to endure hardships if the future promised harvests and well-filled barns.

The Scotch-Irish, who began pouring into western areas about the same time, colored the frontier even more. They were fighters, hunters, and marksmen and bred leaders like Andrew Jackson, John C. Calhoun, and Sam Houston. They had been transplanted from Scotland to northern Ireland and came to America with pronounced antipathies to Catholicism and Anglicanism. Therefore, it is not surprising that once here they moved as far away from the seaboard colonists as possible. But the coastal regions were becoming crowded anyway. By the 1720s, the Scotch-Irish began to push into the backcountry, down the great Shenandoah valley, running southwest along the eastern flank of the Appalachians. This was the first of the great pioneer treks that took Americans into the continental interior, and the Shenandoah was the site of British America's first "west." Within a generation, settlers could be found all along the front range of the Appalachians, from Pennsylvania south to the Carolinas. They laid claim to the lands of Indian peoples, who found themselves pressed to the mountain walls.

Although the population in Canada climbed from fifteen thousand in 1700 to more than seventy thousand by mid-century, it was relatively puny compared with the English colonial behemoth. In the absence of large numbers, French colonial policy in North America aimed at blocking British expansion by a system of trade networks and alliances with Indian peoples. The French worked to strengthen their great crescent of military posts and isolated settlements extending down the Saint Lawrence to the Great Lakes, and then reaching the whole length of the Mississippi River to the Gulf of Mexico. The scattered French settlements in the western country anchored this colonial crescent at strategic locations such as Detroit, Saint Louis, and New Orleans. In these French frontier communities, the continued intermarriage between colonial men and native women meant that groups of métis lived in every French settlement. Choosing a path of mutual accommodation, the French and Indians established some of the most interesting and distinct communities in all of North America.

The colonial period of North American history was marked by a series of bloody wars involving French, Spanish, and English colonists, punctuated by periods of armed and uneasy peace. Indians played a role in all of these conflicts, European national rivalries fanning ancient tribal hostilities. Such wars decimated many Indian peoples but strengthened others. By the late seventeenth century, for example, the Iroquois Confederacy was one of the most important empires in North America. Neither Indians nor Europeans understood the colonial wars as racial conflicts of "red man" versus "white man," but rather as a kind of free-for-all, with every group fighting for itself, allied as circumstance and interest demanded. Indian fought Indian and colonist fought colonist at least as much as Indian fought colonist.

Many of the North American wars had European origins, but they also had colonial aims. What English colonists called King William's War began in 1689 in a dynastic quarrel among European monarchs but was fought in America over access to the rich fur grounds of the north and west. It ended with a European treaty of 1697 that established an inconclusive peace. Only five years later, during Queen Anne's War, as English colonists called the next violent conflict, frontier antagonisms once again provided a focus for the fighting. Indians played an important part on both sides. This war officially ended in 1713, but English slave traders encouraged their Indian allies among the Creek Confederacy to continue attacks against natives allied with Spanish Floridians and French Louisianans. Over the next quarter-century, these raids destroyed the last of the Spanish mission stations of Florida. Thousands of mission Indians were captured and sold into slavery in the Caribbean, and thousands more were killed or dispersed.

The Creeks would resettle Florida. They joined with fugitive African American slaves from South Carolina as well as other Indians in the area to form a new mixed group known as the Seminole nation. The word *Seminole* itself is an interesting linguistic example of cultural interchange. It originated in the Spanish *cimarrón*, meaning "wild" or "untamed," which colonists in Florida used to refer to fugitive slaves living with the Creeks. The Muskogee language of the Creeks has no *r* sound, so when the Indians used the word, they pronounced it "cimaloe," which eventually became Seminole.

Renewed struggles over royal succession in the 1740s resulted in renewed warfare between Great Britain and France. What North Americans called King George's War ended in a stalemate in 1747. The Iroquois Confederacy supported the British, but, like other native peoples, they were unhappy because they felt under siege. As one of their chiefs, a man named Canasatego, declared: "We are now straitened, and sometimes in want of deer, and liable to many other inconveniences since the English came among us, and particularly from that *pen-and-ink work* that is going on at the table." Here he pointed to the scribe who was taking down his speech. "Pen-and-ink" frauds remained much on the Indians' minds. Most notorious was a series of seizures of Delaware lands by the colony of Pennsylvania, notably the "Walking Purchase" of 1737. Under terms negotiated by William Penn a half-century before, the Delawares agreed to cede lands vaguely bounded by the distance a man could travel in a day and a half. The Indian understanding was that this was to be a walk taken at the "common" pace, pausing at noon for a midday meal and a pipe. But Pennsylvania authorities prepared a cleared path for a group of specially trained "walkers" who ran and covered more than sixty miles in the specified time. The runners turned this vague provision into a huge tract encompassing the entire upper Delaware and Lehigh valleys and dispossessing a large number of Indian communities. Overturning William Penn's legacy of fair dealing, the Walking Purchase was a disturbing sign of things to come.

Another omen was the Indians' growing dependence on European traders and their goods, which included tools, weapons, and clothing, but also liquor—much liquor. Alcohol abuse among the Indians was one of the signs of the disorientation that colonialism introduced. Liquor was illegally manufactured in New England distilleries from contraband sugar smuggled in from the West Indies. During the eighteenth and nineteenth centuries, the alcohol trade to the Indians was much like the modern cocaine business, with the traders acting like drug lords. By the mid-eighteenth century, violent drunken scenes had become commonplace features of Indian life in eastern North America.

The struggle between Britain and France for control of North America reached its climax in what a later generation of Americans would call the French and Indian War. The Ohio Country—the great trans-Appalachian watershed of the Ohio River—became the primary focus of British and French attention. British traders began to challenge the French with goods of superior quality, and the rich land of the interior became a prime target of frontier land speculators and backcountry settlers. The French feared that the loss of the Ohio would threaten their entire North American empire. To reinforce their claims, in 1749 the French sent a heavily armed force of Canadians and Indians down the Ohio to warn off the British, and in 1753 they began constructing a series of forts that extended south from Lake Erie to the forks of the Ohio River, the junction of the Allegheny and Monongahela rivers. In response, the British strengthened existing forts and built new ones along the frontiers, and the king conferred an enormous grant of land on the Ohio Company, organized by Virginia and London capitalists. The company made plans to build a fort of its own at the forks of the Ohio.

The coming conflict did not merely involve competing colonial powers. In addition to its native inhabitants, the Ohio Country became a refuge for Indian peoples who fled from the colonial coast. Most of these Indians opposed the British and were eager to preserve the Appalachians as a barrier to westward expansion. They were also disturbed by the French moves into their country, but unlike the British, French outposts did not become centers of expanding agricultural settlements. Indian diplomats understood that it was in their interest to perpetuate the existing colonial stalemate. Their position would be greatly undermined in the event of an overwhelming victory for either side.

In 1754 the governor of Virginia sent Colonel George Washington, a young militia officer, to expel the French from the region granted to the Ohio Company on the western frontier. But confronted by a superior force of Canadians and Indians, Washington was forced to surrender his troops. From their base at Fort Duquesne at the forks of the Ohio, the French now commanded the interior country. The next year General Edward Braddock of the Scottish Coldstream Guards led westward toward the fort more than two thousand British troops and fifty Indian scouts from Virginia. Among them was Colonel Washington. The French and their Indian allies ambushed them, and in the worst defeat of a British army during the eighteenth century, Braddock lost his life.

Braddock's defeat was the first of a long series of setbacks for the British. As a result, Prime Minister William Pitt, an enthusiastic advocate of colonial expansion, committed the British to the conquest of Canada and the elimination of all French competition in North America. Pitt dispatched more than twenty thousand regular British troops across the Atlantic, and in combination with colonial forces he massed more than fifty thousand men against French Canada. These measures succeeded in reversing the course of the war. A string of British victories culminated in the taking of one of the western frontier's key posts, Fort Duquesne, in 1758, which was renamed Fort Pitt and later Pittsburgh.

The decisive British victory came in 1759. British forces converged on Québec, the heart of French Canada. Approaching down the Saint Lawrence River, British general James Wolfe faced the French, commanded by the Marquis de Montcalm. Wolfe and his men devised a scheme worthy of a wilderness scout: a night maneuver up a cleft in the bluffs two miles behind the city. At dawn on September 13, 1759, the French on the Plains of Abraham behind Québec discovered a British force of forty-five hundred men, as large as their own. In a day's hard fight, Montcalm was killed and Wolfe was shot three times. As Wolfe died, he was told the battle was won. In effect, at that moment England supplanted France in North America. At approximately the same time, England also conquered India, thus becoming the greatest imperial power the world had yet known.

The bells were loud in London and silent in Paris. New France was no more. In *Candide* (1759), Voltaire could describe Canada as a few acres of worthless snow, but England could afford to smile as its firms took over the lucrative western fur trade. In the Treaty of Paris, signed in 1763, France gave up all its North American possessions, ceding its claims east of the Mississippi to Great Britain, with the exception of New Orleans, which, along with its other trans-Mississippi claims, it passed to the control of Spain. In exchange for the return of its Caribbean and Pacific colonies, Spain ceded Florida to Britain. The imperial rivalry in eastern North America that began in the sixteenth century now came to an end with what appeared to be the final victory of the British empire. All territory east of the Mississippi was now claimed by the English—thousands of green valleys and fair forests for those who bore the long rifles and carried the maps.

When the Ohio Indians heard of the French cession of the western country to Britain, they were shocked. And a new set of British policies soon shocked them all the more. The British military governor of the western region, General Jeffrey Amherst, in one of his first official actions, banned the long-used diplomatic protocol of gift-giving to Indian chiefs and tribes, demanding that they learn to live without "charity." Because Indians were completely dependent on the British for supplies, including the ammunition they needed for hunting, many were left in a starving condition. In this climate, hundreds of Ohio Indians became disciples of an Indian visionary named Neolin ("The Enlightened One" in Algonquian), known to the English as the Delaware Prophet. The core of his teaching was that the Indians had been corrupted by European ways and needed to return to their traditions. Neolin's ideas prepared the way for war chiefs who laid plans for a coordinated attack against the British in the spring of 1763. The principal figure among them was a proud Ottawa named Pontiac, a renowned orator and political leader who was thoroughly incensed by Amherst's policies. In May 1763 the Indians simultaneously attacked all the British forts in the west, killing more than two thousand settlers in a conflict called Pontiac's Rebellion.

General Amherst proposed that his officers "Send the *Small Pox* among those Disaffected Tribes of Indians" by distributing infected blankets from the fort's hospital. This early form of germ warfare spread the epidemic from the Delawares and Shawnees to the southern Creeks, Choctaws, and Chickasaws, killing hundreds of people. Although Pontiac fought for another year, most of the Indians sued for peace, fearing the complete destruction of their villages.

Yet the British made a significant concession to the Indian nations. In accordance with wartime agreements with their Indian allies, the king assumed jurisdiction over Indian lands and issued the famous Royal Proclamation of 1763, which set aside the trans-Appalachian region, the western frontier, as "Indian country" and required the specific authorization of the crown before the purchase of these protected Indian lands on the other side of what was called the Proclamation Line. British authorities promised to maintain commercial posts in the interior west for Indian commerce and to fortify the border to keep out land-hungry settlers. Indians were pleased with the proclamation, but land speculators and backcountry British Americans were outraged.

In fact, the British proved unable and ultimately unwilling to prevent westward migration. Within a few years of the war, New Englanders were moving west into the region known as Vermont; New Yorkers were pushing ever closer to the homeland of the Iroquois; and hunters, stock herders, and farmers from Pennsylvania, Virginia, and North Carolina were crossing west over the first range of the Appalachians, establishing pioneer communities in what are now West Virginia and eastern Tennessee. The press of population growth and economic development turned the attention of investors and land speculators to the West.

No longer able to play the balancing game between rival colonial powers, Indian options were reduced to a choice between compliance and resistance, and weakened by the recent war, they chose to sign away their rights to land. In 1768, the Cherokees ceded a vast western tract on the waters of the upper Tennessee River, while the Iroquois gave up their claim to possession of the Ohio valley, hoping to deflect the tide of western English settlement away from their own homeland.

Western backcountry pioneers wanted to do as they pleased—cut timber, trap furs, speculate in land, plant farms on the rich soil. They supported whoever stood to help them and fought against restrictions such as the Proclamation Line, but not because they wanted the government to get out. They petitioned strenuously for government assistance against the Indians; if the colonial governments refused it, they became furious, as Nathaniel Bacon had, and took the law into their own hands. Pioneers were conservative, Tory, Whig, liberal, Democrat, Republican, radical, rebel—whatever they had to be to protect their own interests.

On the western fringes of Pennsylvania, a largely Presbyterian log cabin cluster called Paxton looked askance at the Quakers who controlled the colony. How could those effete Philadelphia pacifists and notorious coddlers of savages know the needs of westerners? Thirty miles from Paxton lay a village of Conestoga Indians—poor, peaceful descendants of a tribe that had long lived in submission. There were rumors, though, that the Conestogas were spying on Paxton, and that was enough to raise a lynch mob.

In December 1763 a small band of men calling themselves the Paxton Boys massacred twenty Conestoga men, women, and children. When other Indians fled to Philadelphia for protection, the Paxton Boys marched on the capital. Philadelphia officials, genuinely alarmed, sent out the militia and dispatched negotiators led by Benjamin Franklin. Franklin had already written an essay expressing his sympathy with the Indians and calling the Paxton Boys "Christian white savages." But he satisfied the angered settlers that their cause would be heard by the colonial assembly and the governor; so, leaving a long written remonstrance, the farmers trudged home to Paxton. They complained that the government showed a "manifest Partiality for Indians," forcing the farmers to fend for themselves. They wanted more effective political representation and the abolition of property qualifications for voting. In the background lay the economic indebtedness of western farmers to eastern financiers. Altogether, the uprising in Pennsylvania was an agrarian revolt not unlike that of Nathaniel Bacon, and it had mounted to the point of threatening the colonial establishment.

Backwoods revolt broke out again in 1767 in South Carolina when a wave of murders, thefts, and general anarchy threatened order. Miscreants were often captured, but when tried in Charleston, they were almost as often pardoned. Settlers began to take the law into their own hands. The governor was upset and called them "licentious spirits," but the settlers called themselves Regulators, suggesting that they would restore order to the frontier. One thousand of them signed an agreement to protect one another. They roamed the backcountry, pursuing suspected criminals, whipping and hanging some, and bringing some in to be tried in the proper manner. Often their violent and bloody methods were as notorious as those of their quarry, whom they frequently blamed for their misdeeds. Like the Paxton Boys, the backcountry Regulators clothed criminal savagery in the cloak of political legitimacy. But, perhaps more important, they sought better representation in the colonial legislature, better courts in the frontier areas, more schools and jails, more regulation of taverns and public houses, more restrictions on hunters and lawyers (both of whom they found offensive), and even distribution of Bibles at public expense. Four thousand men signed a remonstrance covering most of these points.

The South Carolina Regulator movement is sometimes paired with the actions of the Paxton Boys as an example of frontier rebellion. Both groups were agrarian dissenters. The men from Paxton, however, functioned like a lynch mob, attacking a minority and then using the occasion to carry their grievances further. The Regulators were vigilantes, allegedly responsible members of society trying to clean up local corruption. Both lynch mobs and vigilantes would appear and reappear in only slightly varied guises on every American frontier.

Thousands of miles from the violence tearing through the eastern woodlands, on the fog-bound coasts of the northern Pacific, what we now call Alaska, New World natives and Old World colonists were locked in yet another bloody confrontation. Driven by the search for valuable furs, Russians conquered Siberia and in the 1740s moved across the icy sea to the Aleutian archipelago, homeland of the Aleuts, hunters of sea mammals and perhaps the most amphibious people on the face of the earth. Hundreds of fur traders followed the Aleutian chain to the mainland and soon were sending home a steady supply of furs, valued in the millions of rubles, from what they called, with the arrogance of colonizers, Russian America.

The Russian expansionists of the eighteenth century employed methods as brutal as any colonial power in North America. Traders held Aleut villages hostage, forcing the men to trap and the women to perform sexual service. At first, native resistance was sporadic and local, but it soon broadened into large-scale revolt. The Aleuts had no military tradition, but in 1762 the natives of a number of villages effectively coordinated an uprising that destroyed a whole fleet of Russian ships. In 1766 a force of Russians returned to crush the rebel Aleuts, destroying dozens of native villages and carrying out deliberate "reductions" of the native population.

By the end of the century the Aleut population had fallen from a high of twenty-five thousand to perhaps six thousand. The causes were familiar: warfare, alcoholism, disease. But sexual relations and intermarriage between Russian men and Aleut women created a substantial group of mixed-ancestry people called *Creoles*—the equivalent of the French métis and the Spanish mestizos—who assumed an increasingly prominent position in the northern Pacific fur trade as navigators, explorers, clerks, and traders.

The Spanish responded fearfully to the activity of Russians, French, and English in North America. In the early eighteenth century, concerned over French designs in the lower Mississippi River valley, officials of New Spain began building a string of Franciscan missions among the Indian peoples of Texas. And responding to the Russian threat, in 1769 officials in Mexico ordered Gaspar de Portolá, governor of Baja California, to begin planting missions along the Alta California coast. The next year Portolá established his headquarters at the fine bay of Monterey to defend the empire against the Russian push he believed was imminent.

In both Texas and California, the mission was an important frontier institution. Today, the old missions, with their quaint adobe walls and cracked tiles, fascinate tourists. But these visitors seldom perceive the reality of the mission as an institution: a tough, pioneering agency that served as church, home, fortress, town, farm, and imperial consulate. Two missionaries with three or four soldiers could create an orderly town out of several thousand Indians, often from diverse and mutually hostile clans. The primary aim of the mission was to Christianize people who had not yet heard the true word of God.

But the mission also shared the aims of economic development and social discipline. It was an arm of the state, and as such could help transform Indians into subjects of the crown. These Indian colonials would be unified through education and language. The Indians learned Spanish readily, and imperial unification through a common tongue was not a farfetched idea; a century or so later it worked well enough for the British in India. The mission introduced breeds of cattle and agricultural products such as grapes and citrus, laying economic foundations that are still apparent today. It is not surprising that colonial administrators were willing to support the missions from their royal treasuries, though in fulfilling their principal purpose, the conversion and reeducation of Indians, the missions were only marginally successful.

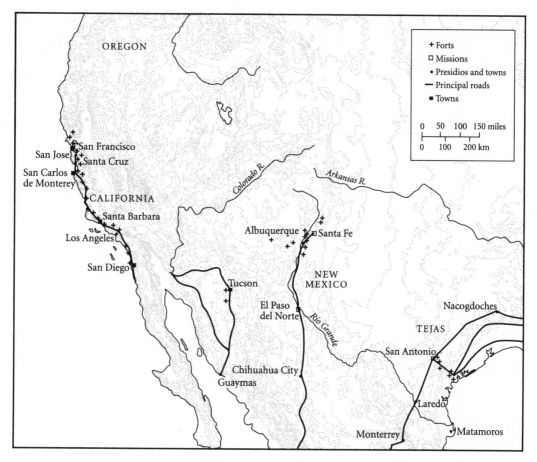

The Spanish North in the Eighteenth Century

    In Alta California the system was directed by the Franciscan Junípero Serra, who, with his fellow Franciscans, founded twenty-one missions from San Diego to Sonoma. Secular officials, meanwhile, established a half-dozen garrisoned presidios and pueblos, including San Francisco in 1776, and Los Angeles in 1781, which was settled by a group of mestizo and mulatto colonists from Sinaloa. But the number of Spanish colonists in California never exceeded thirty-five hundred. It was Indian labor, both at the missions and in the towns, that herded the cattle, sheep, and horses; irrigated the fields; and produced a flourishing California economy.

    At the end of the eighteenth century, the missions of Alta California housed more than twenty thousand "neophytes" (as the padres called them), but native mortality was high, and historians estimate that their numbers had already fallen by about a third. They suffered from changes in diet and confinement in close quarters, and died of dysentery, fevers, and venereal disease. We cannot tell how much death resulted from the harsh discipline of the padres—shackles, solitary confinement, and whipping posts. There were native rebellions from the very beginning. In 1775 the villagers around San Diego rose up and killed several priests, and the history of many missions is punctuated by revolts, although the arms and organization of Spanish soldiers were usually sufficient to suppress uprisings. One form of protest was flight; sometimes whole villages escaped to the inaccessible mountains.

Looking backward from the twentieth century, some historians have called the missions charnel houses and compared them to Nazi concentration camps. But this view is as misleading as the picture of Indians as silly sheep and the padres as gentle but effective shepherds. The modern anthropologist Alfred L. Kroeber came closest to proper balance when he wrote, "It must have caused many of the fathers a severe pang to realize, as they could not but do daily, that they were saving souls only at the inevitable cost of lives."

Chapter 4 The Western Land and Its Markers

Relative to population, the West during the American Revolution suffered greater losses than any other part of the country. Compared with some ten war-related deaths for every one thousand people in the thirteen coastal colonies, there were better than seventy per thousand in Kentucky. Though not unified on the politics of revolution—there were both Tories and Patriots on the frontier—backcountry Americans could agree on the Indian menace, and the Revolution continued the conflict between settlers and Indians for control of the West. The British held an essential advantage because they kept the tribal allies they had won, chiefly the Iroquois, in their long fight against the French, although disease, alcohol abuse, and economic dependency had terribly weakened them.

A principal British supporter among the Mohawk was Thayendanegea, whose English name was Joseph Brant. At the Indian academy later known as Dartmouth College, Brant had proved himself a brilliant scholar. As the first fighting broke out at Lexington and Concord, Brant went to London at the request of British authorities to negotiate an anti-Patriot alliance between the Six Nations of the Iroquois Confederacy (the confederacy had admitted the Tuscororas as partners in 1722) and the British. He toured the capital in the company of no less a Londoner than James Boswell and sat for his portrait in oils by no less a painter than George Romney. Brant led Indian armies to victories over the Patriots, and his name came to summon more fear to western hearts than any Indian since Pontiac. When Cornwallis surrendered at Yorktown in 1781, and the fighting in the East came to an end, it accelerated in the West as Brant mounted a new set of offensives.

By 1783 the western Indians had every reason to think they were winning the war. Thus when word came of peace between the Americans and the British, they were thunderstruck. They were even more shocked when the details of the treaty became known: the Americans had won the right to the entire trans-Appalachian country, a region the British had reserved for the Indians since the Royal Proclamation of twenty years before. The British had abandoned their Indian allies in the West.

When the thirteen colonies achieved their independence, they took from under the British crown three million Euro-Americans and uncounted Indians living on 541 million acres, an area roughly seventeen times the size of England. The western territory, the trans-Appalachian lands, those beyond the generally accepted boundaries of the new states, covered about 230 million acres, nearly half of the new country. There were serious questions about this western territory: Did it belong to the Indians, to the respective states, or to the new national government, the Confederation Congress? In what manner should the lands be distributed? How were they to be governed? These questions may seem abstract, but they were wrung from human dreams—the dream of homelands, the hope of owning land and prospering from laboring upon it, the promise of liberty and independence.

The Indian residents of the West, none of whom considered themselves defeated, naturally assumed that they held their traditional lands. But the United States assumed that victory over the British meant victory over their Indian allies as well. The national government claimed the *right of conquest*—the seizure of the lands and property of all who had fought against the Revolution. In 1784 commissioners of the Confederation Congress forced segments of the Six Nations to sign a new treaty ceding a large portion of their homeland. The next year they forced the same terms on the Ohio Indians, eliminating aboriginal title to the lands in the southeastern portion of the western frontier that would become the state of Ohio. Even Indian nations that had fought with the Patriots, tribes such as the Oneidas of the Iroquois Confederacy, suffered similar losses. The arrogant way in which the Americans treated the Indians guaranteed that bloody warfare would continue in the West.

The British king, through his charters, had given the land to the colonies, so it might have followed that the individual states, counterparts of the colonies, would take possession of it. Understandably inclined to this position were the seven states—Massachusetts, Connecticut, New York, Virginia, the Carolinas, and Georgia—with colonial charters granting them boundaries running westward beyond the Appalachians (in some cases all the way to the "South Sea"). But the six landless states without such charters—Pennsylvania, New Hampshire, Rhode Island, Delaware, Maryland, and New Jersey—demanded that Congress assume authority over the western lands for "the good of the whole." This dispute lasted for four years, delaying ratification of the Articles of Confederation until 1780, when Congress finally passed a resolution promising that any ceded western territory would "be disposed of for the common benefit of the United States, and be settled and formed into distinct republican States, which shall become members of the Federal

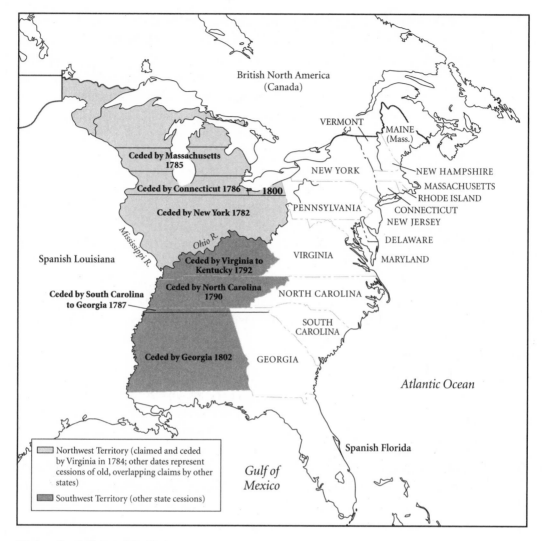

Western Land Claims of the States

Union, and have the same rights of sovereignty, freedom and independence as the other States." By 1790 all the states but Georgia had surrendered their pretensions to western territory, thus creating a vast public domain under the control of the Confederation Congress.

Now there was the problem of what to do with the western land. On this question the Confederation Congress did not start from scratch. The colonies had used various systems of land distribution. In the flinty hills of New England, for example, colonial governments granted land not to individuals but to congregations and community groups, preferring to keep settlement compact and contiguous. Yankee pioneers generally continued to practice prior survey and compact settlement. In the South, with single-crop plantation agriculture (tobacco, rice, and later cotton), pioneer planters typically sought out large tracts that they found appealing, even if it was relatively far from the nearest settlement, and requested a grant from the colonial government. Unlike the communal tradition of the Yankees, the southern pioneer assumed the obligation for independent development. The law that Congress wrote, the Land Ordinance of 1785, pragmatically drew from both traditions. From New England it borrowed the idea of prior survey and orderly contiguous development, and from the South, the practice of allocating land directly to individuals.

Yet what was most notable about the Land Ordinance was its invention of a new and revolutionary system of measuring and bounding the land. Traditionally, surveyors described each parcel by the distinctive lay of the countryside and the successive property lines of previously surveyed lots. This time-tested method, however, could produce big problems when used to survey vast new territories. The haphazard and hurried survey of Kentucky, for example, which took place amid the chaos of the Revolution, resulted in considerable conflict, even violence, over confusing boundaries and titles, and it was with this cautionary tale in mind that Congress broke with tradition. All the land in the western territory, the Land Ordinance declared, would be partitioned "into townships of six miles square." A great grid of "Principal Meridians" and "Base Lines" would divide the whole American West into numbered ranges of townships, with each township divided into thirty-six square-mile sections, each section further divisible into half-sections and quarter-sections, as well as quarter-quarter-sections of forty acres. Every farmer's field would be instantly identifiable by its range, township, and section numbers. Owing much to Enlightenment rationalism, this system had all the advantages and disadvantages, clarity and distortion, of any rational approach to human affairs. The national survey would assure clear boundaries and firm titles, highly important in wild new lands. But it would press upon the land a uniformity that took no account of contrasting valleys, different climates, or individual people who might wish for other arrangements.

The Land Ordinance also created the system for converting western lands to private ownership. Thomas Jefferson argued for giving western land away "in small quantities" to actual settlers. "I am against selling the lands at all," he declared. The people on the frontier were poor and would simply ignore the law and "settle the lands in spite of everybody." Jefferson understood the mentality of western settlers (and his thinking anticipated the Homestead Act of 1862), but he was out of step with most other leaders. Instead of giving the land away, as Jefferson advised, in the Land Ordinance of 1785 Congress decided to auction it off in chunks no smaller than 640 acres, and at a price no less than one dollar per acre. This was well beyond the means of most farmers, but Congress was not interested in equality of opportunity for western settlers; instead, it cared about providing a revenue base for the national government and for giving eastern elites the best shot at the western land. The ordinance did reserve the revenue of one section in each township for the maintenance of public schools. Narrowly defeated was an attempt to set aside another section for the support of religion.

Although Jefferson's plan was rejected, there were great hopes for the role the West would play in the development of the new nation. In what was perhaps the best-selling American book of the decade, *Letters from an American Farmer* (1782), the French immigrant J. Hector St. John de Crèvecoeur announced that America would find its destiny in the West. "Scattered over an immense territory" and "animated with the spirit of an industry which is unfettered and unrestrained," Americans were building "the most perfect society now existing in the world." The limitless West was the best guarantee that the American people would maintain their economic independence, the foundation of republican government. Jefferson echoed these sentiments, writing in 1787 that Americans would remain virtuous as long as they maintained their roots in the agricultural soil. But he recognized a darker side to Crèvecoeur's vision. Once the western lands were exhausted, he wrote, Americans would "get piled upon one another in large cities, as in Europe, and go to eating one another as they do there."

The surveyors headed west in late 1785 as soon as the Iroquois and the Ohio Indians ceded lands, but running the lines and marking the township boundaries proved to be slow and torturous work. Impatient to begin the flow of badly needed revenue, in 1787 Congress ordered a public auction in New York City of the first surveyed ranges. The results were extremely disappointing, producing nothing like the expected windfall. While skeptical eastern capitalists sat on their hands, however, western settlers were proving Jefferson right by simply moving onto choice tracts north of the Ohio River and claiming ownership by the right of occupancy.

Faced with frontier squatting, the disappointing initial sale of western lands, and the crying need for revenue, Congress now charted a different course that seemed to contradict its own land law. In 1787 a number of congressmen were approached by a lobbyist named Manasseh Cutler, a restless Yale-educated minister with an eye roving from heaven to a quick business dollar. Cutler proposed a huge western land grant for a group of wealthy New England capitalists known as the Ohio Company of Associates. They wanted a grant of one-and-a-half-million acres of lush, green Ohio hills and valleys but were unwilling to pay the dollar-an-acre price mandated by the Land Ordinance. Instead, Cutler proposed a convenient dodge for the conscience of the Congress. Let them pay in depreciated Revolutionary currency, worth only eight or nine cents on the dollar. As a result, the Ohio Associates wrested from the government a principality in exchange for a pittance.

A considerably more outrageous western land scam took place in Georgia, the only state continuing to claim trans-Appalachian lands. In 1795 land speculators bribed members of the state legislature into granting them an enormous tract in what would later become the states of Alabama and Mississippi. Georgia's authority over that territory was dubious at best. The lack of secure title, however, did not bother the speculators, who quickly sold their "rights" to thousands of gullible investors. After the sale was declared a fraud by no less an authority than

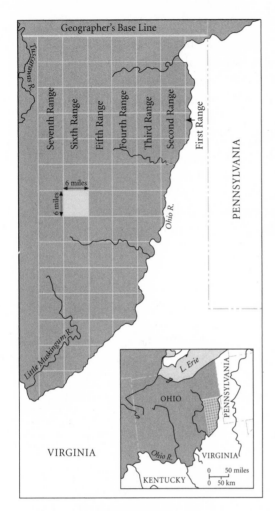

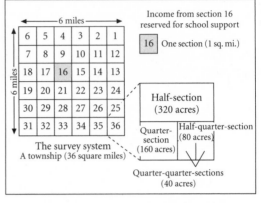

The Survey System

President Washington, the Georgia legislature recanted and caused even more controversy, as thousands of naive speculators throughout the country faced the loss of their entire investment. In an attempt to limit its liability, Georgia finally ceded its western claims to the federal government in 1802 after Congress voted to award the speculators more than $4 million (about $70 million in 2005 values). The Ohio and Georgia affairs testified to the victory of speculators over actual settlers in the land policy of the early republic.

Still unresolved was the question of the political relationship of the new western settlements and the established states. Again, Thomas Jefferson attempted to create a democratic colonial policy. His plan would have divided the western public domain into distinct territories, each granted immediate self-government and republican institutions with rapid admission to statehood. But the continuing Indian warfare, the squatter problem, and a general wariness about the unruliness of western society persuaded Congress to reject Jefferson's plan. The Northwest

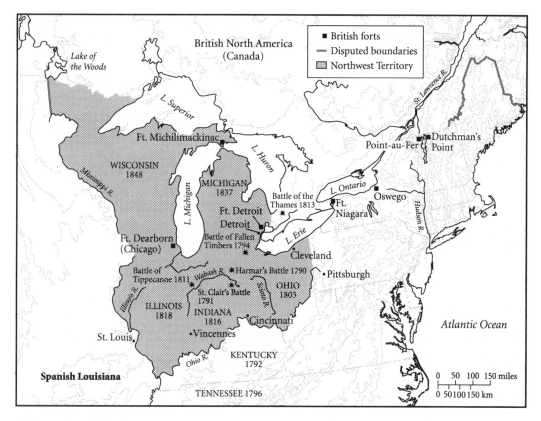

The Northwest Territory

Ordinance of 1787 divided the territory "northwest of the river Ohio"—called the Northwest Territory or the Old Northwest (present-day Ohio, Indiana, Illinois, Michigan, Wisconsin, and northeastern Minnesota)—into a number of separate districts. The Congress, not the settlers, would choose the territorial officers, and the governor would enjoy absolute veto power. These provisions were strict and authoritarian, even anti-democratic and imperialist, but nevertheless this ordinance included the promise that when any district grew to include sixty thousand residents, it could be admitted to the Union on equal terms with the existing states.

The Northwest Ordinance has been called, rather extravagantly, one of America's greatest contributions to political theory. It not only provided for an orderly abolition of territorial or colonial status for the new states, it outlawed involuntary servitude north of the Ohio River. Yet the Northwest Ordinance represented no triumph of democracy or self-government. The limitations on self-government reflected eastern fears of violent mobs and frontier roughnecks. Still, with the exception of Texas and California (and Nevada, for which the minimum population regulation was overlooked), over time all the western states were admitted to the Union in accordance with this ordinance.

Easterners never fully understood westerners and always held ambiguous attitudes toward them. "Heathen" Indians or Mexican "greasers" were beyond the pale, of course. But the antipathy often extended to those who lived in the American backwoods as well. Some emphasized people of the frontier as magnificent, self-reliant hunters roaming the untrod forest wilderness. Others saw only lowdown, shiftless, lazy riffraff. Some of these ambiguities are apparent in the life and legend of Daniel Boone.

Boone was born on the Pennsylvania frontier in 1734, and when he was fifteen he migrated with his parents to the North Carolina backcountry. There, he married a hearty pioneer woman named Rebecca Bryan. By all accounts she was a strong and commanding woman who in midlife stood nearly as tall and as broad as her husband and could handle an ax or a gun as well as most men. In the typical frontier division of labor, she managed the household and raised their family of ten children, but she and the kids also did practically all the farming, while Boone devoted himself to his occupation as a professional hunter and woodland guide, a pursuit that took him ever westward in pursuit of game. By the late 1760s he had found his way to the beautiful bluegrass valleys of Kentucky and fallen in love with the western country. Boone brought his family and others to settle the bluegrass.

After the Revolution, Kentucky schoolmaster John Filson published a promotional tract praising Kentucky as the new "land of promise, flowing with milk and honey." Thousands of settlers headed west through the Cumberland Gap in the Appalachians. The stories they told about Kentucky, previous settlers had told about Pennsylvania, Virginia, and North Carolina. Like the one about the fertility of the soil—corn would yield twenty bushels to the acre if it was planted and cultivated carefully, ten bushels if it was planted and neglected, and seven bushels if it wasn't planted at all. Like hundreds of others, Daniel Boone staked claims to thousands of acres of bluegrass prairie. The desire to engross land was typical. But the claims of Boone proved defective, and growing unhappy, he and his large extended family crossed the Mississippi and settled in Spanish Missouri in 1799. He lived the rest of his life near Saint Charles on the Missouri River, working as a hunter until he died in 1820.

Americans would have remembered none of this except for the fact that John Filson included a stirring account of Boone's adventures in his book on Kentucky, presenting him as a pathfinder, "an instrument ordained to settle the wilderness." But others saw him differently. A missionary in North Carolina complained that Boone did "little of the work" around his farm but left it to his wife and children. Boone and pioneers like him were refugees, "placing themselves at a distance from the deceit and turbulence of the world," as literary romantic Henry Marie Brackenridge wrote in 1814. But others argued that he was a misanthrope, a man who, as one critic put it, wanted "to live as remote as possible from every white inhabitant." Thus Boone could be different things to different people—a lazy drifter or a truly free man.

During the 1780s and early 1790s there was no respite from the fighting in the West. The cause of the fighting was no mystery. From just a few hundred American settlers at the beginning of the Revolution, by 1785 the population of Kentucky stood at thirty thousand; it grew to nearly ninety thousand by the time it was admitted as a state in 1792. Without waiting for the official opening of lands of the Northwest Territory, and making no distinction between the public domain and Indian homelands, pioneers began squatting and settling illegally. Combined with the arrogance of the new nation's right-of-conquest theory, the Indians of the Ohio valley received a clear message: the Americans were about to dispossess them completely of their lands.

The Indians east of the Appalachians had lost their lands, one Iroquois chief declared, because they had fought one another instead of uniting, as the Americans had. Let us profit by their example, he counseled, "and be unanimous, let us have a just sense of our own value. And, if after that, the Great Spirit wills that other colors should subdue us—let it be—we then cannot reproach ourselves for misconduct." Thus as Americans were uniting under a new constitution, an Ohio Indian confederacy was agreeing to the principle that all Indians, whatever their tribe, held their lands in common, and that unanimous consent of all would be necessary to cede any part of it. They demanded that the United States accept the Ohio River as the boundary between the Indians and the Americans.

When George Washington assumed office as the first president of the new federal government, the troubled West was the most pressing problem facing him. The western Indian confederacy seemed unified and determined. Great Britain continued to maintain a force of at least one thousand troops at northwestern posts like Detroit, from where they managed the fur trade and supplied the Indians with guns and ammunition. Spain also encouraged and supplied native resistance to the expansion of American settlements in the South, refusing to accept the territorial settlement of the Treaty of Paris and claiming that the northern boundary of Florida extended all the way to the Ohio River.

Washington and Secretary of War Henry Knox knew that the attempt to enforce an American right of conquest had failed, and in desperation they put together a new approach that would set the terms and the tone of American Indian policy during the first half-century of the young republic. Actually, the language of the Northwest Ordinance of 1787 had first signaled this departure. "The utmost good faith shall always be observed towards the Indians," it read, "their lands and property shall never be taken from them without their consent; and in their property, rights, and liberty, they shall never be invaded or disturbed, unless in just and lawful wars authorized by Congress." This amounted to a rejection of the right-of-conquest theory of Indian relations and recognition of the independent character of Indian tribes. It became law in the Indian Intercourse Act of 1790.

To be sure, there were enormous contradictions in America's Indian policy. On the one hand was the pledge to protect Indian homelands. On the other was the program to survey, sell, and create new political institutions in those very same lands. In the long term, Indian tribes would successfully appeal for the return of lands taken by states or private individuals in violation of federal law. But in the short term, violent conflict, not "utmost good faith," would characterize Indian-American relations in the Ohio Country, where the growing population of settlers pressed violently against the rich farming lands held by Indian villagers. The Ohio confederacy proved unable to restrain and coordinate the passions of its many members. Chiefs could not control their young warriors as Indians struck back at Americans with equal violence.

In 1790 President Washington, himself a large investor in western lands, sent an expeditionary force to the Ohio Country led by General Josiah Harmar to suppress the Indians, but Little Turtle, brilliant war chief of the Miamis, badly defeated him. In 1791 the Americans once again invaded the Ohio Country, this time with a large but poorly trained army under the command of the governor of the Northwest Territory, Arthur St. Clair. The Indian forces led by Little Turtle subjected them to another terrible and humiliating defeat. With more than nine hundred American dead and wounded, this would go down as the single worst defeat of an American army by Indian warriors, a far more serious loss than the famous defeat of George Armstrong Custer at the Little Big Horn in 1876.

Knowing that he required a dramatic victory in the West, Washington now committed more than 80 percent of the federal government's operating budget to a massive campaign against the western Indians and appointed General Anthony Wayne to subdue the Ohio Indian confederacy and secure the Old Northwest. The battle of Fallen Timbers, fought on August 20, 1794, was a decisive defeat for the Indians and an important victory for the United States. The native confederacy fell apart. Hundreds of Indians joined kin who had already left the Ohio Country and emigrated west across the Mississippi. Many of those who planned to remain now prepared to come to terms with the Americans.

The representatives of twelve Indian nations, led by Little Turtle, ceded a huge territory encompassing most of present-day Ohio, much of Indiana, and other enclaves in the Northwest Territory, including the town of Detroit and the tiny village of Chicago. The strengthened American position in the West—as well as the rising threat of revolutionary France—encouraged the British to settle their differences with the Americans and withdraw from American soil. The next year the United States resolved its boundary dispute with Spain, which agreed to grant Americans free navigation of the Mississippi River with the right to deposit goods at the port of New Orleans.

Defeated in wars of conquest, and suffering from the effects of colonization, the Indians of the trans-Appalachian West now had to learn to live under the dominating authority of the United States. Different peoples chose different paths, but many included forms of spiritual revitalization. When native cultures seem overwhelmed, a prophet often emerges who offers a message of cultural salvation. In the late eighteenth century, this happened first among the Iroquois.

Their frustration stemmed from their reduced homelands, mere fractions of the land they once held, and the previous half-century's awful toll on their people. Before the Revolution the British estimated Iroquois strength at about ten thousand, but by 1800, after the bloody warfare of those intervening years, their numbers had fallen to only four thousand. Alcoholism was a major problem, and they faced economic depression as their hunting territory was severely constricted. "It appears to me," one Iroquois testified with tears rolling down his cheeks, "that the great Spirit is determined on our destruction."

Iroquois leaders took different positions on the way forward. The Seneca leader Cornplanter came to believe in accommodation. "We are determined to try to learn your ways," he told a missionary. But Cornplanter was opposed by Red Jacket, the leader of the Seneca traditionalists, who pointed out to a missionary that even though "you are sent to instruct us how to worship the Great Spirit, we also have a religion, which was given to our forefathers, and has been handed down to us, their children. We worship in that way." The conflict between *progressives* and *traditionalists* that tore at Iroquois communities in the 1790s continues in many Indian communities to this day.

Another response came in the person of Handsome Lake, who had been an Iroquois war chief during the Revolution. But in the aftermath of defeat, like many other warriors, he despaired and became an alcoholic. After a long bout of drinking in 1799, he fell into a coma and his family thought him dead. But he finally awakened and began to preach a glorious message of renewal. His words were taken up by hundreds of followers, and within a generation the teachings of Handsome Lake had become a major force of reform within the Six Nations. Urging a return to the ancient rites and rituals of the people, Handsome Lake seemed to be a traditionalist. But he also advocated that Iroquois men forsake hunting and take up farming, and that women give up their traditional power within Iroquois society.

Handsome Lake's followers thus tried to emulate their American neighbors in many things, but they gathered in traditional longhouses for their services. The "Longhouse Religion," as it came to be called, combined Iroquois spirituality with the values of Quaker Christianity: temperance, nonviolence, and frugality, with an emphasis on personal good and evil. The Bible found a place within the longhouse alongside more traditional Iroquois oral texts and teachings. Although the Longhouse Religion did not solve the Iroquois problem of living as a colonized people, it restored their self-respect and gave them the means to revitalize their culture.

Another Indian prophet arose in the Ohio Country. He was a Shawnee, and like Handsome Lake, a dissolute alcoholic who in a drunken stupor had once poked out his own eye. One day in 1805 he collapsed into a trance so deep that his family feared he had died. But he awoke and told them that the Master of Life had sent him back from the dead to lead the Indians to redemption. He took the name Tenskwatawa, meaning "The Open Door." Among Americans he became known as the Shawnee Prophet. Tenskwatawa condemned alcohol as "the white man's poison." He told his followers that they must abandon white ways—including clothing, tools, and weapons—and return to the traditions of the people. In a brilliant adaptation of Christian imagery, he preached that all the Indians who followed him would be wonderfully rewarded in the afterlife, but that all the bad Indians would join the Americans in a hell of fire and brimstone. By 1809 Tenskwatawa's large following was living in a new multitribal Indian community named Prophetstown at a place called Tippecanoe near the Wabash River in the heart of the western frontier.

Joining the Prophet at Tippecanoe was his brother Tecumseh, a traditionalist Shawnee chief who adopted his brother's religious vision and used it to fight Indian leaders who wished to make accommodation with the Americans. Tecumseh was a remarkable man, a brilliant orator with a powerful understanding of the Indians' tragic history. He worked to rebuild the Ohio confederacy, left in ruins after the battle of Fallen Timbers. "Let the white race perish!" he thundered.

In 1810 Tecumseh and a delegation of chiefs and warriors from Prophetstown came to the headquarters of William Henry Harrison, governor of the Northwest Territory. The Great Spirit, he told Harrison, intended the land to be "the common property of all the tribes," and it could not be sold "without the consent of all." Harrison feared the growing power of Tecumseh and the Prophet, and in the fall of 1811, while Tecumseh was organizing resistance in the South, he attacked Prophetstown. "What other course is left for us to pursue," wrote Harrison, "but to make a war of extirpation upon them?"

As the United States and Great Britain moved closer to war over maritime problems in the Atlantic, the British again adopted the policy of using the western Indians to destabilize the young republic. They supplied Tecumseh and his followers with weapons and encouraged them to think that the British supported the creation of an Indian republic in the Great Lakes region. In 1812 the United States once again went to war against the British. If the outcome of that war was a wash for the United States and Great Britain, it was a disaster for the Indians of the Northwest Territory. The hopes of the traditionalist followers of Tecumseh turned to ashes when they were defeated at the battle of the Thames, northeast of Detroit. Compounding the damage, Tecumseh himself was killed. Tenskwatawa lived until the 1820s, but he had lost his power as a prophet. Thus the equilibrium of the western coexistence of whites and Indians was again broken by warring Europeans.

The Cherokees provide a final example of the revitalization movements that swept through the Indian nations of the trans-Appalachian West during the first decades of the nineteenth century. After the Revolution, the Cherokees were devastated. As among the Iroquois, the conflict among the Cherokees had taken on aspects of civil war, with the people divided and fighting each other. Patriots had invaded the Cherokee towns and burned them to the ground. Hundreds were killed.

In the aftermath, the leadership of the Cherokee nation was claimed by men of mixed ancestry such as Major Ridge and John Ross, the sons of native mothers and American traders. To a greater extent than any other Indian nation or tribe in North America, the Cherokees took the early Indian policy of the United States at its word and fulfilled its most extravagant expectations. With the assurance of federal protection of their homeland and their sovereignty, the Cherokees took up the whites' economic system—farming and owning slaves, then selling their goods in the market—and began to accumulate homes and possessions. They even modeled their government on the institutions of the United States. Violating their traditional ethics of sharing, the new leadership practiced real capitalism.

Perhaps the best symbol of this Cherokee renaissance was the invention by a man named Sequoyah (his English name was George Guess) of a written phonetic system for spoken Cherokee—the first writing system to be invented by a North American Indian. Sequoyah was a traditionalist who had removed west to the Arkansas Country, and he was seeking a way to communicate with kith and kin back home. His syllabary proved easy for Cherokees to learn, and it immediately caught on. Within a few years of the syllabary's development, a majority of Cherokees had learned to read and write using Sequoyah's system. Literacy rates among the Cherokees were higher than among their American neighbors. "Guess's alphabet is spreading through the nation like wildfire," wrote an admiring missionary. The nation set up its own newspaper, the *Cherokee Phoenix*, published in both English and Sequoyan.

In a remarkable talk given before a white audience in 1826, Elias Boudinot, the Cherokee editor of the *Cherokee Phoenix*, addressed himself to the revitalization and renaissance of his people. "There is, in Indian history, something very melancholy," he told them. "We have seen everywhere the poor aborigines melt away before the approach of the white population." But the Cherokees intended to write a new chapter. "I can view my native country, rising from the ashes of her degradation, wearing her purified and beautiful garments, and taking her seat with the nations of the earth." How would the United States answer? "I ask you," he concluded, "shall red men live, or shall they be swept from the earth? . . . Must they perish? . . . Let humanity answer."

Chapter 5 The Fur Trade

 Nothing proved more important to the American nation than the frequent addition of large tracts of the North American continent. The history of American expansion is unparalleled in the modern world, and after the gain of trans-Appalachia at the close of the Revolution, expansion continued with President Thomas Jefferson's famous Louisiana Purchase. Louisiana irrevocably turned the nation's eyes westward, brought it incalculable natural wealth, and ensured the emergence of the United States as a world power. It was the beginning of a continental empire.

At the close of the French and Indian War, France had ceded control of Louisiana to Spain. The boundaries of this huge cession were vague, but they were generally understood to begin at the Mississippi on the east (but including the delta with the city of New Orleans), following the northern border of Spanish Texas on the south, extending to the sources of the Mississippi on the north, and reaching the crest of the Rocky Mountains on the west. The Spanish periodically closed the port of New Orleans to American shipping. Westerners were certain that the economic development of the West depended on continued access to the Gulf via the Mississippi, so after long negotiations, Spain agreed in 1795 to reopen the port to the United States. But soon, American concerns shifted to France. Napoleon Bonaparte had New World imperial dreams of his own, envisioning a revived empire that would unify France's Caribbean colonies with mainland Louisiana. In 1800 Napoleon invaded and defeated Spain and dictated a secret peace treaty transferring Louisiana back to French control. A few months into his presidency, Jefferson became aware of the secret terms and sent an American delegation to France to negotiate for the purchase of New Orleans, meanwhile dropping broad threats of the consequences of renewed French imperialism in North America.

Napoleon did not abandon his imperial plans because of hollow American threats, but rather because of the revolt of Haiti's slaves against their French masters, led by the revolutionary François Dominique Toussaint, who took the name L'Ouverture, "The Opener." With fierce guerrilla tactics, as well as an opportune outbreak of yellow fever, L'Ouverture decimated the French armies sent by Napoleon. By early 1803 it had become clear that the Haitians had won their independence, and Napoleon decided to cut his losses. His attention had begun to center on Europe, and even for a man as ambitious as Napoleon, conquering one continent at a time was enough.

In April 1803 the American negotiators in Paris were shocked when French foreign minister Talleyrand suddenly asked, "What will you give for the whole?" The Americans cautiously asked what the boundaries of "the whole" might be. "Whatever it was we took from Spain," the minister answered with a shrug. The Americans offered $15 million (the equivalent of more than $250 million in 2005 values), an incredible deal, only slightly more than they had been prepared to offer for New Orleans alone. "You have made a noble bargain for yourselves," Talleyrand declared at the conclusion of the negotiations for the Louisiana Purchase. "And I suppose you will make the most of it."

Jefferson intended to do just that. His long interest in far western exploration now assumed new meaning, even urgency. He planned a western expedition, commanded jointly by Meriwether Lewis and William Clark, which became the most illustrious exploring party in American history. Aside from Jefferson's scientific intentions, most important were the expedition's economic objectives, for the incorporation of this vast tract of continent into the nation hinged on finding a way to exploit it. Jefferson hoped that his explorers would open an easy route across the continent by waterway, even though beyond the Rocky Mountains some of it would cross foreign soil. Such a route could redirect the lucrative fur trade of western Canada into American channels. Corollary gains would include more effective ways to take advantage of the sea otter trade of the northern Pacific coast. The friendship of the native nations was essential to these goals, and thus Indian diplomacy was also high on the agenda of the explorers.

In the spring of 1804 the Corps of Discovery pushed off from its base camp on the Illinois side of the Mississippi River, across from the mouth of the Missouri. The forty men made up a motley crew: backwoodsmen, métis, and Lewis's black slave York. It took them all summer to go up the Missouri River to the earth lodge villages of the Mandan and Minnetaree Indians in what is now central North Dakota. But just before reaching the Mandan towns, the expedition tensely encountered a band of Lakotas, more generally known as Sioux. The Mandans requested American help in defending against Sioux raids, and the Americans were sympathetic. "We were ready to protect them," wrote Clark. Thus from the first moment the expanding Americans entered into the world of the plains, they willingly counterpoised themselves against one of the most powerful of the nomadic peoples.

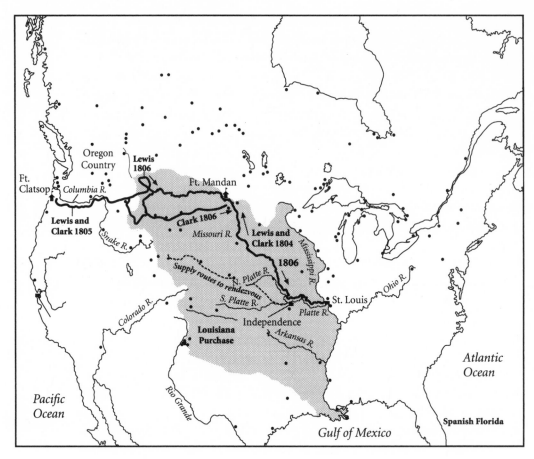

The Louisiana Purchase and the Fur Trade

The Americans found French traders living among the Mandans and Minnetarees with Indian wives and métis children. Frenchmen had been visiting them since at least 1738. Lewis warned the French off, announcing, "This is now American territory." But a number of the resident traders hired on to the expedition as interpreters, and one, Toussaint Charbonneau, offered the interpretive skills of one of his wives, a fifteen-year-old Shoshoni captive named Sacajawea. "The sight of this Indian woman," wrote Clark, convinced the Indians "of our friendly intentions."

The company constructed Fort Mandan and spent the winter among the villagers, becoming part of its social life. There were dances and joint hunts, long talks around the fire, and for many men, pleasant nights spent in the arms of Mandan women. When the party left in the spring, Clark wrote (with his usual atrocious spelling) that the company were "generally helthy except for Venerials Complaints which is verry Common amongst the natives and the men Catch it from them."

The winter the Americans spent with the Mandans and Minnetarees introduced them to the complicated world of the Great Plains, a world that had been transformed over the preceding century, especially by horses stolen from the Spanish settlements. Indians were soon breeding horses in great numbers, enabling hunters to exploit the huge buffalo herds of the plains much more efficiently and thus develop a new way of life. Here is another of those fascinating ironies of frontier history. The first settlers of the Great Plains during the colonial era were not Europeans but Indians. And the mounted warrior of the plains, the ubiquitous and romantic symbol of native America, was in fact not an aboriginal character at all, but one born from the colonial collision of cultures.

Using charts and maps drawn with the help of their native friends, the company followed the Missouri and its tributaries to the continental watershed ("the distant fountain of the waters"). Obtaining crucial horses from Sacajawea's Shoshoni relatives, they reached the Snake River and followed it to its junction with the Columbia. Finally, in the rainy November of 1805 they stood on the shores of the Pacific Ocean. After a hard and depressing winter, they largely retraced their route, and in September 1806 the hardened band returned, twenty-eight months after it had left.

Lewis and Clark brought back an incredible amount of scientific information, including descriptions and specimens of hundreds of species of fish, reptiles, mammals, birds, plants, and trees. Their journals featured Lewis's long-winded philosophizing on the future route of empire, and the notes on his diplomacy with the Indians, who on several occasions might have wiped the expedition from history. Clark left a record of frontier know-how. The journals also detail the endurance of Sacajawea, who bore a baby along the way, a boy Clark loved and subsequently adopted. They document snow blindness and snakebite, and the one death that occurred from a burst appendix, a malady that would have been fatal anywhere. Their journals have inspired generations of Americans.

Was the trip worthwhile? The captains made contact with dozens of Indian tribes and distributed more than one hundred impressive silver peace medals. Despite the troubles with the Sioux, they found most Indians eager for better trading connections. But the commercial objectives of the expedition were only partly realized. It failed to find what Jefferson had declared to be its most important object: an easy water route linking the Atlantic and the Pacific that could be used for trade and commerce. The route that Lewis and Clark charted over the Rockies was impossibly hard going and practically useless.

In the long view, the most important accomplishment of the trip was locking Louisiana territory securely into the minds and plans of the nation, and associating the distant Oregon Country so closely with it that Americans thereafter assumed it was their own preserve. Although another generation passed before American settlement poured into that part of the continent, the expedition aroused popular interest in the Far West. No other exploration was so influential, wrote historian Bernard DeVoto: "It satisfied desire and it created desire: the desire of a westering nation."

The Lewis and Clark expedition also set a pattern, establishing a precedent for a strong government role in the development of the American West. Theirs was the first American exploration mounted and pursued with government encouragement and financing. Historians have tended to overlook the basic preparations for westward expansion that the government undertook—surveying the land, marking the routes, building the wagon roads, clearing the rivers for navigation, dredging the harbors along the coasts, planning and digging canals, subsidizing railroads, suppressing the protests of Indians, and in general standing close beside the pioneers as they toiled to the Pacific.

After three centuries of operation, the fur trade continued to be one of the largest and most important commercial enterprises in North America. Although the trade depended on local Indian labor, it was controlled by two large companies whose directors sat in London and Montreal. The Hudson's Bay Company, which the British monarchy chartered in 1670, exclusively coordinated a far-flung network of field directors and workers (*engagés*). So great was the power and prestige of the company, it was said, that the initials HBC stood for "Here Before Christ."

The HBC was locked in competition with a newcomer, the North West Company, a Montreal partnership including French-Canadian and Highland Scots traders, that the British government chartered in 1784. The Nor'Westers had a special spirit and manner about them, less bound by protocol and formula than Hudson's Bay men, more willing to risk all and venture far in pursuit of furs. With all its color and flair, the North West Company was as natural a magnet for restless energies as the life of a cowboy would later be. One young spirit, John McLoughlin, as a boy in Québec watched Nor'Westers swagger through the streets. Barely out of his teens, he became an apprentice Nor'Wester and entered the world of rivalry between the two companies.

To curb the competition, the British government forced the two companies to combine, and in 1821 the Nor'Westers were absorbed into the HBC. Convinced of McLoughlin's good judgment and devotion, in 1824 the company named him to the general superintendency of the far western Columbia River District. Ensconced in the Oregon Country, McLoughlin's flowing mane of prematurely white hair came to symbolize honesty and decency. He married a métis woman, and together they had four children. McLoughlin was representative of those traders who never wavered in their commitment to their native wives, and his children were proud of their métis heritage. For more than twenty years McLoughlin majestically dominated the region from his post at Fort Vancouver on the Columbia River.

The mouth of the Columbia had been the great western target of the only American who in the first decade of the nineteenth century rivaled the prosperity and power of the Canadian traders. John Jacob Astor was a stout, arrogant man who transferred his meager business in musical instruments to furs and made his original fortune organizing and exploiting the trade of the Northwest Territory. He eventually became the richest man in America, with assets at the time of his

European explorers believed they had discovered a new world, but for thousands of years the Western Hemisphere had been home to peoples with dreams and histories of their own. Petroglyph, Canyon de Chelly, New Mexico, photograph by Richard Erdoes (c. 1965).

The Pueblo people of the Southwest inhabit the oldest continuously occupied communities within the United States. American Indians came from more than two thousand distinct cultures, spoke hundreds of different languages, and made their livings in scores of dissimilar environments. Zuni Pueblo, New Mexico, photograph by Timothy H. O'Sullivan (c. 1873).

Illustrating an edition of Columbus's report of his discoveries, published the year after his return, this first image of the colonial encounter depicts King Ferdinand directing the expedition from Spain and naked Indians of the Caribbean fleeing in terror. From Giuliano Dati, *La lettera dellisole che ha trouata nuovamente il Re dispagna* (1493).

A different interpretation of a colonial encounter, produced by artists among the Tlaxcalans, native allies of Hernán Cortés. Cortés is depicted meeting Montezuma II and other Aztec leaders at their capital of Tenochtitlán, assisted by his translator and consort Malínche. Lithographic copy of a sixteenth-century tapestry, *Homenaje á Cristóbal Colón. Antiguedades Mexicanas* (1892).

Engraved copies of watercolors John White made of the Indian villages of Secota *(left)* and Pomeooc *(right),* located in what is today coastal North Carolina. White produced some of the most accurate depictions of American Indians before the nineteenth century. From Thomas Hariot, *A Briefe and True Report of the New Found Land of Virginia* (1590).

"The Cruelties us[e]d by the Spaniards on the Indians," from *An Account of the First Voyages and Discoveries Made by the Spaniards in America* (1699), an early English translation of the history written by Bartolomé de Las Casas.

French colonial leader Samuel de Champlain joins the Hurons in making war on their traditional enemy, the Mohawks. The French initiated their North American empire by allying themselves with a powerful native confederacy. From *Les voyage du sieur de Champlain* (1613).

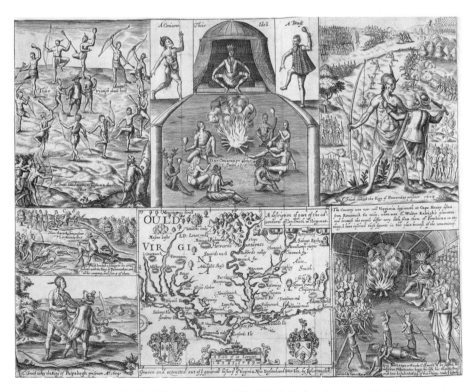

Engraving depicting John Smith's adventures in Virginia, including (bottom right) his rescue from death by Pocahontas. In contrast to the "frontier of inclusion" of the Spanish and French, the English established a "frontier of exclusion." From Smith, *A General History of Virginia, New-England, and the Summer Isles* (1624).

French fur traders, known as "coureurs de bois," lived among Indian communities and adopted many aspects of their culture, part of the French "frontier of inclusion." From a French sketchbook, "Drawings of Canadian Beaver Hunting" (c. 1730).

Cooperation between Swedish colonists and Indian residents of the Delaware valley led to the development of a unique woodland way of life combining both native and European traditions. From Thomas Campanius Holm, *Kort beskrifning om provincien Nya Swerige uti America* (1702).

One of the earliest depictions of a log cabin, a building tradition that Scandinavian colonists of the Delaware valley brought to North America. It was adopted not only by other European settlers but by Indians, who helped to spread the tradition across the continent. From Georges-Henri-Victor Collot, *Voyage dans l'Amerique Septentrionale* (1826).

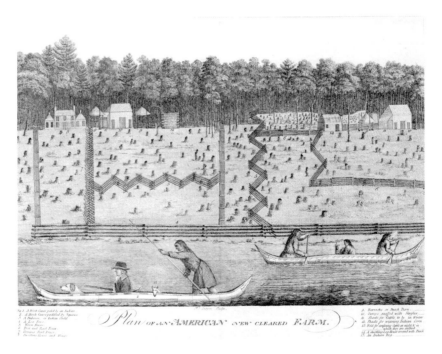

Late eighteenth-century engraving illustrates the frontier pattern of fencing fields and planting corn amid the stumps of cleared forests. From Patrick Campbell, *Travels in the Interior Inhabited Parts of North America* (1793).

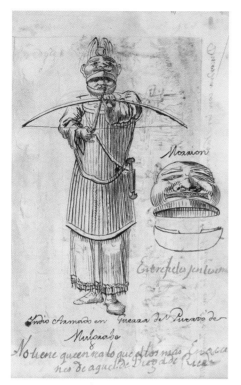 

Armed warrior *(left)* and ordinary villager *(right)* of the Northwest coast, drawn by Tomas da Suría, an artist attached to a Spanish exploring expedition led by Alejandro Malaspina. The Northwest was one of the last North American regions to be colonized. From Tomas da Suría, manuscript sketchbook (1791).

Russians trading with the Aleuts of the Aleutian Islands. Despite the good relations this image suggests, Russian traders were among the most brutal colonists in North America. From Greigorii Ivanovich Shelikhov, *Puteshestvie G. Shelokhova* (1812).

Indians gambling at Mission San Francisco de Asís on San Francisco Bay. Indian labor was critical to the success of the Spanish colony of California. From Louis Choris, *Voyage pittoresque autour du monde* (1822).

Engravings by the American artist Benjamin West depicting negotiations between the Ohio Indian confederacy and the British at the end of the French and Indian War *(left)*, and the subsequent return of colonial captives *(right)*, including many children who had become emotionally attached to their adoptive Indian parents. From William Smith, *An Historical Account of the Expedition against the Ohio Indians* (1766).

death in 1848 of some $20 million (about $490 million in 2005 values). Astor's was the first of the great American fortunes, and it was built on furs.

Astor was quick to exploit the Louisiana Purchase by forming the American Fur Company. He dreamed of a western empire controlled from a post on the Columbia River, where pelts from the interior could be shipped to the Orient. In 1811 he sent from New York a ship, the *Tonquin*, as well as an overland expedition to meet at the mouth of the Columbia and construct the fortified post of Astoria.

That coastal area had been fiercely contested among the Spanish, British, and Russians. The impressive and wealthy Indian societies along the coast were testimony to the potential riches Europeans envisioned. There were sea otters in the waters, beavers in the streams, whales and limitless supplies of salmon, great stands of spruce and pine, as well as thousands of Indian consumers who promised a brisk commerce in trade goods. In 1790 the viceroy of New Spain, who considered this coast part of his jurisdiction, had sent a warship north to warn off intruders. At Nootka Sound, located at latitude 50°, the Spanish seized two British trading vessels and their crews and arrested a British captain. The Spanish monarchy proved unwilling to pursue the conflict, however, and in the Nootka Convention of 1790 Spain agreed to jointly share the coastline with the British.

Over the next ten years trading vessels from all over the world plied these waters, exchanging goods for furs with the native chiefdoms along the coast. This aggression, of course, was worrisome to the Russian-America Company, which controlled the coastline to the north. With their trained force of Aleut hunters, the Russians were making fabulous profits from the trade in sea otters, tea, and silk between Alaska and China; but they were in danger of hunting the animals to extinction in the waters off Alaska. They pushed south to establish their own claims. By 1811, when the Astorians arrived, the Russians controlled the northern coast.

Astor thus confronted opponents on all sides. His dream quickly turned into a nightmare. Captain Jonathan Thorn, in command of the *Tonquin*, turned out to be murderous, if not mad. He was a kind of Captain Bligh, quick-tempered, haughty, and cruel. Once on the scene, he provoked the Indians into a surprise attack on the ship. In the resulting melee, the captain and so many of the crew were killed that the ship became helpless. During the vicious final bloody scene, a single remaining white man waited until the largest possible number of Indians were aboard and then blew up the ship, killing himself and at least one hundred natives. Meanwhile, Wilson Price Hunt, in charge of the overland expedition, had faced almost every obstacle the wilderness could raise. Voyageurs plotted and deserted, Indians grew hostile, horses ran off, men were lost, boats were wrecked. Toward the end, they splintered into isolated, struggling groups. Hunt himself reached Astoria in the cold February of 1812, ten months after leaving the Missouri settlements.

But it was the War of 1812 that delivered the coup de grâce to Astoria. When a British warship challenged Astoria, Astor's employees simply signed over the deed to the North West Company. Soon the British abandoned the settlement for a better location upriver known as Fort Vancouver. It would be thirty years before another generation of Americans would lay a new claim to the Oregon Country, one based not on furs but on farms.

The first Americans to successfully challenge the Canadians and exploit the great fur-bearing regions of the West came not from the East, as did Astor, but from Saint Louis. When that small western town became part of U.S. territory with the Louisiana Purchase, the most important traders there were the Chouteau family. Led by the widowed matriarch Marie Thérèse, the Chouteaus made a fortune in the Missouri valley Indian trade during the period of Spanish sovereignty. Over the next half-century Marie and her sons, René Auguste and Jean Pierre, would raise much of the capital for the expanding western fur trade.

One of the Chouteaus' local rivals, Manuel Lisa, half French, half Spanish—and half grinning alligator—had moved up the river from New Orleans as a boy of eighteen. When Lewis and Clark returned, he immediately set into motion plans to organize and exploit the newly discovered lands. Lisa persuaded John Colter, who had scouted for Lewis and Clark, to guide his traders into the mountains, and Colter became the first American to explore the Yellowstone River country. In 1808, in partnership with other Saint Louis traders, including the Chouteaus, Lisa organized the Missouri Fur Company. It proved a highly profitable operation. One happy season Lisa made $35,000—this in an age when a successful merchant might clear $1,000 in an entire year.

In the early 1820s, the day's fashion called for broad-brimmed, stovepipe beaver hats, and with style dictating, the fur trade boomed. One of the men who chose this time to invest was William H. Ashley, lieutenant governor of the new state of Missouri. On March 22, 1822, he advertised his intention to bankroll an expedition of one hundred "enterprizing young men" to the sources of the Missouri River. The project was an enormous success, and the fabulous cache of beaver brought back the first year made Ashley a rich man.

The alumni of Ashley's first brigade included some of the most notable characters in the history of the West. Mike Fink, the "ring-tailed roarer" of Mississippi flatboatmen, may have been the original frontier braggart. "I'm a land-screamer," he shouts in a typical tale. "I can out-run, out-dance, out-jump, out-dive, out-holler, and out-lick any white thing in the shape o' human that's ever put foot within two thousand miles o' the big Massassip." Among a collection of scoundrels, Fink might have been the worst, a man novelist Don Berry described as "a lying, sadistic, foul-mouthed braggart, a treacherous and murderous psychopath." But along with the likes of Daniel Boone and Davy Crockett, Mike Fink quickly found a place in the Valhalla of frontier heroes.

Ashley's group also included old Hugh Glass, another veteran of the frontier. Glass's character may not have been strikingly better than that of Fink, but he illustrates the courage and stamina of these men. While out trapping once, he was attacked by a mother grizzly bear protecting her cubs; she tore open his throat and left his body covered with bleeding lacerations. Abandoned for dead by his two companions, Glass pulled himself to a spring, sustained himself on berries and the carcasses left by wolves, and dragged himself across nearly one hundred miles of present-day South Dakota until he was rescued by friendly Indians. For a year he searched for his faithless companions like an avenging angel. One put himself out of reach because he had joined the army, and Glass didn't want to kill a soldier. And Glass spared the other because he was only a boy of seventeen.

That boy's name was Jim Bridger. He would become one of the best-known of the mountain men, working for all the important outfits, organizing companies himself, building posts and forts, scouting for explorers and generals. He came to know the northern Rockies better than any man alive, his mind a veritable atlas of peaks, passes, and meadows. He married three successive Indian women (the first two died, one in childbirth), and with the last, a Shoshoni named Mary, he settled in Westport, Missouri, and arranged to have all his children educated in missionary schools and convents.

Perhaps the most remarkable of Ashley's remarkably "enterprizing young men" was a clean-cut, serious, blue-eyed boy who neither swore nor smoked. Jedediah Strong Smith spent only a decade in the West, but he firmly left his stamp upon it. In 1824 Indians guided him to the great South Pass across the Rockies, and Smith's discovery allowed American trappers to exploit more easily the far side of the Continental Divide. Two years later he traveled over the great southwestern desert to California and became the first American to cross the Sierra Nevada east to west. Smith's physical endurance allowed him to cover the West like a real Paul Bunyan, with steps too large to be believed.

But what really set Smith apart was his moralism and religious dedication. Instead of tramping the wilderness, he felt he should be helping the poor, "those who stand in need," wherever they were. But the wilderness turned him in on himself, intensifying his guilt. "O, the perverseness of my wicked heart," he once wrote. Such a vague search for personal fulfillment may have appeared often enough on the frontier to explain some of the restlessness. Smith probably never resolved his frustrations. He died alone on the southern plains in 1831, his mouth undoubtedly still unprofaned but his body punctured with Comanche lances.

Ashley restructured the American fur trade of the Rockies through a set of innovations he instituted after some of his men were killed by Indians along the Missouri River trading route. Avoiding the river altogether, he sent his men overland to the mountains, pioneering a path across the plains that would later become the Overland Trail. His mounted brigades wintered in their own mountain camps, doing their own trapping. Rather than investing in fixed posts in the style of the Hudson's Bay Company, Ashley used the same overland route to supply his men by pack and wagon train, meeting them at a predetermined summer "rendezvous," which he opened to any and all "free trappers." This annual rendezvous took place each summer for the next fifteen years. No other assemblies in American history

—except the Mardi Gras of New Orleans—matched the color and excitement of the rendezvous. Fur trading companies would agree on a location, any one of a thousand green meadows, a year in advance. There for a week in July or August, the poorest season for trapping, the trappers would straggle in, their mules top-heavy with the season's harvest of skins, converging on the merchant caravans from the east. Indians would come, too, to barter furs or just to watch. And there was plenty to see.

Like sailors home from sea, the trappers were ready for a wild debauch. They drank barrels of Saint Louis whiskey and "Taos lightning" (*aguardiente*—brandy flavored with red peppers). They bargained with Indian women. There were fights among drunks, duels among the sober, and gambling everywhere—over horse races and footraces, at cards and dice. The lilt of a French-Canadian song ("A la claire fontaine") might melt into a Highland fling or a Mexican fandango. A big rendezvous could attract more than one thousand trappers and traders. Imagine sundown behind the Teton ridges, hundreds of teepees and tents, the smoke of wood fires rising above the cedars, the sounds and smells!

In the flush years of the late 1820s, traders, if not trappers, took in handsome returns at the rendezvous, ranging to several hundred percent. In 1825 Ashley brought home furs worth nearly $50,000, and in 1826 he made enough to retire with a fortune. In 1832 the company took back 168 packs of beaver pelts worth $85,000, more than $1.9 million in 2005 values.

Many of these men were loners, patriarchs of the mountains, ruling over none but their lone, free self. If freedom is defined as the absence of external restraint, then they were supreme examples of free men, and in American thought and legend, they have often been so considered. But if freedom is a state of mind, it is arguable that men like this were maladjusted, and their aversion to society was based on a restless pursuit of something they could neither find nor define. Jedediah Smith, once hallucinating from thirst and hunger, said he dreamed not of gold nor honor, but of family, friends, and home. A quest for freedom that becomes a relentless prod to move on was shallow, at best.

But there was another side to the experience of the mountain men, a side of deepening connections to a human world. Historian Bernard DeVoto imagined that the trapper serenely pulled the wilderness round him "like a robe." If so, the robe was of Indian design. This "white Indian" worked and lived intimately with real Indians. He traded with them and picked their brains; he fought with and against them and appreciated their courage. He recognized their cruelty and he often shared in it. To the mountain man, the Indian warrior could be both friend and enemy. At times, he esteemed the Indian less than he did the beaver, at times more highly than he did the wind spirits on the peaks. The Indian woman he knew as both prostitute and tender wife. He understood how vital the woman was to the Indian economy, and that her role as camp-keeper and hide-tanner was no less important to him. He knew that she could increase his opportunities through kin and tribe. In short, the mountain man knew Indians too well to generalize about them. Like any other group of people, he realized the native people were a mixed lot. Indeed, a life in the fur trade was all about mixing.

The trappers did their jobs so well that there was danger that the beaver would become extinct. Intensive competition threatened to kill the golden goose. We can only guess at the total number of beaver killed. In 1800 more than 245,000 beaver skins were exported from eastern ports alone. A little later one English ship carried more than 21,000 pelts to Canton. Extrapolating from such shreds of evidence, and assuming a continuous rate of destruction, we must conclude that the beaver might not have held out at the same level of trapping. What saved it was a decline in the market for its pelt. Fashions changed. "I very much fear beaver will not sell well," Astor wrote from Paris in 1832; "it appears that they make hats of silk in place of beaver." With his acute nose for business, two years later he sold his western operations to the Chouteaus, shifting his investments into the booming New York real estate market. It was a sign of the times. The last real summer rendezvous took place in 1840; the following year only a few wagons met a handful of dispirited trappers. The trade continued, focusing on other kinds of fur, with less frantic activity and greater control by large companies. Fortunately, by the 1850s, large numbers of beaver tails once more slapped the waters of the upper Missouri country, but few free trappers heard them.

Chapter 6 From Texas to Oregon

Settlement was the key to America's conquest of the continent. Common folks craved a piece of land, and such expectations were far more powerful than soldiers in establishing the sovereignty of the United States over the West. A Connecticut Yankee named Moses Austin joined crowds of them pushing across the Appalachians to Kentucky in 1797. "Ask these Pilgrims what they expect when they git to Kentuckey," Austin noted in his diary, "the answer is Land. Have you any? No, but I expect I can git it. Have you any thing to pay for land? No. Did you ever see the country? No, but Every Body says its good land." The first federal census in 1790 counted fewer than one hundred thousand Americans west of the Appalachians. Fifty years later there were more than seven million, better than 40 percent of the nation's population. Propelling this surge was the enormous growth in total American population, which through the republic's first seventy-five years nearly doubled every twenty years. Neither Mexico nor Canada experienced explosions of such proportions.

Pioneers did not go unaided, of course. One of the principal contributions of the federal government was to explore the land of the trans-Mississippi West and assess its potential for settlement. In 1806, even before the return of Lewis and Clark, President Jefferson dispatched a second major expedition under the command of Lieutenant Zebulon Pike to reconnoiter the southern reaches of the Louisiana Purchase. Pike blundered into New Mexico where Spanish dragoons arrested him. They escorted the Americans south to Chihuahua where officials closely questioned Pike before finally conducting him back home through the northern province of Tejas (which Americans knew as Texas). In his report Pike compared the southern plains to "the sandy deserts of Africa." The only future he could imagine for those "immense prairies" was to leave them "to the wandering and uncivilized aborigines of the country."

Pike's opinion soon would be seconded by another American explorer of the West, Stephen H. Long of the Army Corps of Topographical Engineers. The account of his expedition across the plains to the Rocky Mountains in 1819 and 1820 concluded that the region was "almost wholly unfit for cultivation" and included a map on which the present states of Oklahoma, Kansas, and Nebraska were labeled the "Great American Desert." For the next forty years that phrase became the commonsense way of referring to the Great Plains.

Pike was more favorably impressed with Texas. He wrote of its fertile soil, luxurient grasslands, and "general urbanity and suavity of manners" among the *Tejanos*—the native-born Mexicans. But a few years after Pike's departure, the Texas he admired lay in ruins. During Mexico's rebellion against Spain in the 1810s, the province became a target for American adventurers known as *filibusters*, a word derived from "freebooter," but these pirates operated on land. As a result of the fighting, by 1820 the population of Texas had been reduced by half.

Unless the province was strengthened, Spanish authorities knew that it was only a matter of time before it would fall victim to American aggression. Unable to attract migration from central Mexico, they proved receptive to an idea proposed by the entrepreneur Moses Austin, who had prospered in Missouri. After a visit to Texas in 1820, Austin applied for a large grant of land on which he would settle three hundred American families. Clearly, inviting Americans was taking a risk, but Austin promised to settle a different kind of American, and the Spanish reasoned that unless the province was developed it would inevitably fall to the United States anyway. In 1821 they approved Austin's plan, granting him two hundred thousand acres of rich Texas soil.

Moses Austin died of pneumonia, but his son Stephen F. Austin carried on with the Texas enterprise on land the new Mexican government confirmed by a generous grant. His lands stretched along the rich bottoms of the Colorado and Brazos rivers, rolling gently down to the Gulf Coast. These were among the richest alluvial lands in all the West. Settlers were given the choice of claiming 177 acres of farmland or 4,428 acres for grazing—not surprisingly, most of Austin's colonists chose ranching. The herds of cattle that fattened on these ranges and the cotton that flourished in these soils were soon major exports, almost all of which went to the United States.

The Mexican government made three more grants to Austin, allowing him to colonize an additional nine hundred American families. Austin adopted the perspective of a patriarch. "I feel almost the same interest for their prosperity that I do for my own family," he wrote of his colonists. Meanwhile, other Americans simply drifted into Texas and squatted on the best land they could find. Austin excluded these squatters from his own "family." By 1823 the fifteen hundred settlers in the Austin colony had been supplemented by at least three thousand squatters in

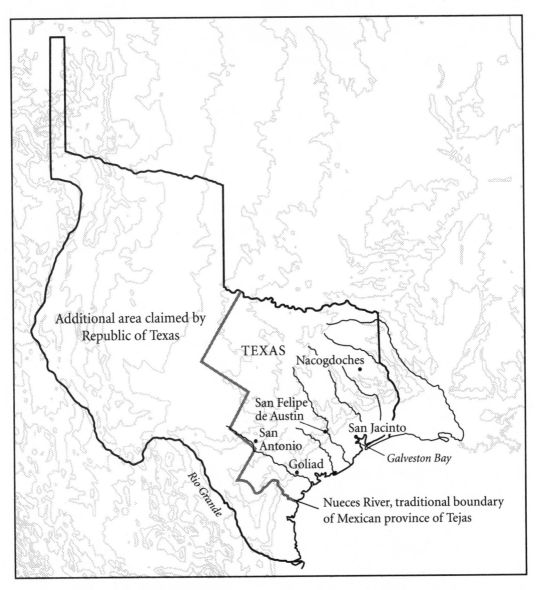

Texas before the Mexican War

the east Texas region bordering Louisiana. The *Texians*, as the Americans called themselves, were rapidly outnumbering the Tejanos, who were concentrated in the southern half of the province.

One of the fundamental principles of the Mexican independence movement was the abolition of slavery and the equality of all citizens regardless of color. Attracted by these ideals, a small number of free African Americans emigrated from the United States to Texas during the 1820s. Several free black heads of household were granted land by the Mexican government, and at least two African American settlers moved to the Austin colony. But the number of free blacks was insignificant compared with the thousands of slaves who came with the white settlers. Slavery was one of the founding institutions of the whole region of the Old Southwest—the present-day states of Tennessee, Alabama, Mississippi, Louisiana, Arkansas, and Texas. Black labor cleared the pine forests and drained the swamps, opening plantations and making cotton production the engine of the region's economy. Planters on this frontier were infamous for driving their slaves beyond the point of endurance, and slaves in the upper South trembled at the thought of being "sold down the river." Travelers in the Old Southwest often encountered slave traders with their human livestock. Edwin L. Godkin overtook a group struggling through a Mississippi swamp and wrote, "The hardships the negroes go through who are attached to one of these emigrant parties baffle description." Westering without hope—this version of American pioneering has not received sufficient attention, but it, too, is an essential part of our frontier history.

Slavery lent its full measure to the violent character of frontier life. Samuel Townes was one of many southwestern masters who drove their slaves hard. Impatient that his black women were picking less than half the cotton of the men, he insisted that his overseer "make those bitches go to at least 100 [pounds a day] or whip them like the devil." Combining the everyday violence of slavery with the unsettled social conditions of the frontier—large numbers of unattached men, excessive drinking, and endemic Indian-hating—produced a lethal brew. Visitors were horrified by the dueling, fistfighting, and brutal practical joking.

It was the dawning "age of the common man"—for white men, anyway—and new rough-and-tumble characters were emerging as political heroes. David Crockett of Tennessee provided a prototype. Working his way up the local political ladder in the 1820s, Crockett cultivated the persona of a backwoods bumpkin who consistently bested his highborn opponents by using native wit and wisdom. During his successful run for Congress, Crockett once addressed a rally, "Yes, fellow citizens, I can run faster, walk longer, leap higher, speak better, and tell more and bigger lies than my competitor, and all his friends, any day of his life." The crowd roared its approval, and Crockett's astounded opponent soon dropped out of the race.

Crockett and others might speak the boisterous language of frontier democracy, and even win elections, but the Southwest was quickly becoming a society of great inequality. By the 1820s the *nabobs*—the elite class of planters—included some of the wealthiest Americans of the day. But the vast majority of whites were *nobodies*—small aspiring planters with a handful of slaves, or hardscrabble farmers subsisting on the thin soils of the pine barrens or grazing cattle on the prairie grasses. As the nabobs grew richer, they gobbled up the farms of the nobodies. Thus the need for new frontiers, where opportunity still beckoned for "the little man." And thus did an army of nobodies push off for Texas.

The arrival of Americans in Texas—many of them with slaves—caused great concern in Mexico, so in 1824 a new Mexican constitution reaffirmed the abolition of slavery. In Texas the slaveowners momentarily panicked, but with the support of leading Tejanos, local authorities created a paper fiction called "contract labor," allowing planters to hold their slaves in bondage for ninety-nine years. It was an uneasy solution to a sensitive problem.

The 1820s also brought change to the Mexican province of New Mexico. In 1823 Missouri Indian trader William Becknell blazed a wagon route from Missouri to Santa Fe. By mid-decade hundreds of wagons were heading down the Santa Fe Trail each spring, and soon the value of American imports into New Mexico averaged $145,000 annually (the equivalent of $2.7 million in 2005 values). Traders from the United States hauled tools and household utensils, bolts of fabric and the latest fashions. The markup was fabulous. Wagon freighting on the Santa Fe Trail continued to be important until rail connections with the Southwest were established in the 1880s. Mexican money and Mexican mules did much to transform frontier Missouri. The silver peso was, for several decades, the principal medium of exchange in the West, much preferred to the highly unstable and inflated paper currency issued by state banks. And the stubborn but nearly indestructible Mexican mules that came back with the traders soon became the most important work animal of the nineteenth-century West.

The Santa Fe trade demonstrated the mutual benefits of strengthened connections between the United States and Mexico. It was cause for little concern among Mexican officials. But Texas was more worrisome. In an attempt to protect their border province, in 1830 the Mexican congress passed a Colonization Law banning further immigration from the United States. But the Southwest was experiencing an epidemic of "Texas Fever." Hundreds of cabins in Alabama, Mississippi, and Louisiana stood deserted, signs nailed to their doors printed with the initials *GTT*—"Gone to Texas." Over the next five years, despite the new law, the Texian population rose from seven thousand to nearly thirty thousand, and by 1835 Tejanos were outnumbered seven to one.

Texians were divided into two political factions. Austin's group, known as the Peace Party, argued for Texas continuing in the Mexican union with more autonomy, the complete legalization of slavery, and the elimination of all barriers to free trade with the United States. These moderates were opposed by a War Party that demanded the secession of Texas from the Mexican federation and its annexation by the United States. William Barret Travis, a volatile and ambitious young lawyer from Mississippi, became the rallying point for this group. Like many other settlers, Travis had come to Texas to escape creditors and a failed marriage, leaving his wife behind to nurse their infant son and fend off the bill collectors. In 1835 Travis and a group of hot-headed followers forced the surrender of a Mexican garrison supervising the collection of import duties at Galveston Bay. The actions of the War Party were condemned by the moderates, who placed their faith in Austin.

Austin was in Mexico City making the case for the Peace Party, but he fell under the growing Mexican suspicion of all Americans. He was thrown into jail and kept for eighteen months in a small, windowless cell. When finally released, he was a convert to independence. But by then a more volatile breed of Texian was in the saddle. First, there was David Crockett, who had recently lost his congressional seat. "I told the people of my district that if they saw fit to reelect me, I would serve them faithfully," he told a crowd. "But if not they might go to hell, and I would go to Texas. I was beaten, gentlemen, and here I am." Then there was Samuel Houston, a giant of a man with an equally giant charisma. He had served two congressional terms in Tennessee and began a promising term as governor. But when his first marriage ended mysteriously after less than a year, he resigned, fled west, and eventually relocated in Texas. Houston and Crockett hoped to make a new start on this new frontier. They arrived just in time for a revolution.

The attack on the garrison at Galveston Bay convinced Mexican authorities that the Texians were in revolt. Rebellion against central authority was simmering in other provinces as well, so President Antonio López de Santa Anna issued a decree abolishing all state legislatures and placing the central government directly in charge of local affairs, essentially transforming himself into a dictator. With an army of four thousand, Santa Anna marched north, crushing all opponents in his path.

Texians, joined by a number of leading Tejanos, now took up arms, and Sam Houston was named commander-in-chief of the motley army. They besieged San Antonio and at the cost of much destruction forced the withdrawal of the Mexican troops stationed there. The Tejano supporters of the rebellion were on dangerous ground. Mexican authorities condemned them as traitors, and many Texians also suspected them of disloyalty. Considering San Antonio indefensible, Houston ordered his troops north, leaving only a small detachment under the command of William Travis to hold the city. At the approach of Santa Anna's army, most Tejanos fled, and the Texians—including James Bowie and David Crockett—fortified themselves in the ancient mission ruin of the Alamo.

Tejanos were in the Alamo as well—a group of armed horsemen under the command of Captain Juan Seguín, son of a prominent provincial leader. Travis might have led a retreat—there was no strategic significance to holding the Alamo when Santa Anna could simply have swept north, leaving a regiment to keep the Texians boxed up. But instead, he dispatched Seguín and his men with an urgent appeal to Houston for support and issued a "liberty or death" proclamation swearing not to give an inch. Probably thinking to terrorize the Texians, Santa Anna decided he would destroy the Alamo and all its defenders. His siege ended in a five-hour assault on March 6, 1836, that cost the lives of some 600 Mexican soldiers and 187 Texians. Santa Anna had their bodies burned so there would be no memorial. Yet the slogan "Remember the Alamo" became the emotional fulcrum that helped keep doubters in the camp of independence and potential deserters in the ranks. At the little village of Washington-on-the-Brazos, an emotional meeting of delegates declared Texas an independent republic.

Then Santa Anna made a disastrous error, dividing his army in order to further intimidate the people by burning and plundering the country. Seizing the opportunity, Houston and nine hundred Texians surprised Santa Anna and a rump force of twelve hundred at the San Jacinto River. Taking their revenge for the Alamo, the Texians slaughtered more than six hundred of the disorganized Mexicans. Santa Anna was captured and, under duress, signed a treaty granting Texas independence.

The Texian-Tejano alliance survived the revolution, but just barely. Houston was elected president of the Texas republic, and Juan Seguín, who led a troop of Tejano cavalry at the battle of San Jacinto, served three years in the Texas Senate. But bitter anti-Tejano sentiment gradually developed among Texians in the aftermath of the war. Seguín did his best to protect the Tejano community, but it was a losing battle. "White folks and Mexicans were never made to live together," a traveler declared in the 1850s. By that time entire Tejano communities were being uprooted and expelled, and San Antonio had been "half-deserted" by its Spanish-speaking population. As Seguín wrote, he became "a foreigner in my native land."

The United States recognized the independent Republic of Texas on March 3, 1837. Texas condoned slavery, and the problem of slavery and race was immediately thrust into the national and congressional debate over the admission of Texas to the union of states. Texas would remain on the back burner until American expansionists could find a way to subsume this controversy within a general enthusiasm for making the nation continental.

As cotton production expanded throughout the South, and the price of land skyrocketed, many white southerners demanded the final liquidation of all Indian title within their borders. The focus was on Georgia. In 1802 the state agreed to relinquish its lingering claim to lands in the Old Southwest in exchange for a federal promise to extinguish all remaining Indian title within its boundaries. But the Cherokees resisted all federal attempts to broker an exchange of their homeland in the northern highlands of Georgia for lands west of the Mississippi. By 1825 the "Cherokee problem" had become the driving issue in the state's politics. In the words of a popular tune of the day:

All I want in God's creation
Is a pretty little wife and a big plantation
Away up yonder in the Cherokee Nation.

It was not "virgin land" the Georgians wanted. It was the land the Cherokees had improved for the booming cotton economy. Cherokee leaders had modernized tribal government, and in 1827 they adopted a republican constitution and declared themselves an independent nation. Along with the other tribes of the South—the Creeks, Choctaws, Chickasaws, and Seminoles, commonly referred to as the Five Civilized Tribes—the Cherokees were the great success story of American Indian policy. Their very success, however, exposed the unresolved contradiction at the heart of that policy. Few political leaders of the United States were prepared to accept an outcome in which Indians adopted many of the customs of the dominant society but retained independent cultures and polities.

The crisis came in 1829 when American prospectors found gold in the northern Georgia hills, precipitating a frantic rush that by year's end had some ten thousand miners scouring the watercourses of the Cherokee homeland. Cherokee people call this event the "Great Intrusion." Andrew Jackson had just become the first westerner to be elected president. He took the position that it was farcical for the federal government to treat Indian nations as if they were sovereign and independent states. Thus assured of presidential sympathy, Georgia sent the Georgia Guard to protect American miners and squatters and intimidate the Cherokees. Almost simultaneously, Jackson presented Congress with his Indian Removal Act, a comprehensive plan for the relocation of all eastern Indians to west of the Mississippi. The passage of the Removal Act in 1830 made it clear that the federal government would ignore the accomplishments of nations such as the Cherokees in order to respond to the demands of land speculators, miners, and white settlers.

Federal commissioners soon pressured the Choctaws, Chickasaws, and Creeks into signing treaties of removal. The Cherokees, however, remained adamant in their opposition. With the assistance of missionary and lawyer friends, they brought suit in federal court against Georgia's infringement of their sovereignty. The case soon found its way to the Supreme Court. Chief Justice John Marshall concluded that the Cherokees constituted "a distinct community, occupying its own territory, with boundaries accurately described," within which "the laws of Georgia can have no force." The Cherokees were elated, but Jackson reacted differently. "The decision of the Supreme Court has fell still born," he wrote, and predicted that the court "would find that they cannot coerce Georgia to yield to its mandate." Indeed, encouraged by Jackson, Georgia ignored the Court's ruling. The president was perfectly willing to violate the Constitution in order to get rid of the Indians.

The Cherokees now faced an impossible choice. If they remained in Georgia, they would surely lose their lands as well as their political identity. If they agreed to removal, they might maintain that identity, but at the cost of surrendering the homeland they had fought for two centuries to hold. One faction among the leadership, led by Major Ridge and Elias Boudinot, decided that further resistance was useless. But the majority, led by Chief John Ross, rejected the views of the so-called Treaty Party. In 1835 Georgia authorities arrested Ross and his supporters, and while they languished in prison, federal commissioners negotiated an agreement with leaders of the Treaty Party. They agreed to relinquish the Cherokee homeland for $5 million (about $110 million in 2005 values) and the promise of permanent lands on the Arkansas River, west of the Mississippi. From prison, Ross denounced this "fraud upon the Cherokee people," and former president John Quincy Adams declared that the treaty would endure as "an eternal disgrace upon the country."

A small group of Treaty Party supporters left for the West, but most Cherokees refused. Finally, in the spring of 1838 seven thousand army troops under the command of General Winfield Scott began systematically rounding them up. Eighteen thousand Cherokees were herded into concentration camps where they suffered from malnutrition and dysentery. Hundreds, perhaps thousands, died of

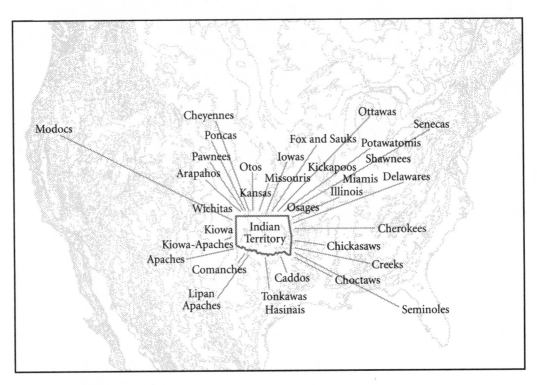

Indian Removal

disease. Despite his bitter opposition to removal, Chief Ross felt compelled to take charge of the exodus. Nearly every family lost a loved one during the forced march westward of more than one thousand miles, known as the "Trail of Tears" or, in a translation from the Cherokee, the "Trail Where They Cried."

There were other violent episodes of Indian removal. The most infamous was the campaign to remove the Seminole people of Florida. The problem here was the presence in the Seminole nation of many African Americans, including runaway slaves. Southerners were not so much interested in Seminole lands—which were mostly the swamps of central Florida—but were dedicated to reclaiming fugitive slaves and enslaving the other African Americans who lived among the Indians. A few Seminole chiefs signed a removal treaty in 1832, but the majority refused to abide by it. When the army moved into central Florida in 1836 to enforce the removal order, the war chief Osceola struck back and inflicted a humiliating defeat. The war dragged on for years, with the United States unable to root out the Seminoles from the swamps. Acknowledging defeat, the army offered Osceola safe conduct to a peace negotiation, then treacherously captured him and threw him into prison, where he eventually died. By 1842 the majority of Seminoles had been harried into moving west, and despite the fact that hundreds remained in the Everglades, the federal government finally called off the operation, which had become extremely unpopular. What did this war accomplish? The removal of some three thousand Seminoles to Indian Territory, but at the cost of $20 million and the lives of more than fifteen hundred American soldiers and untold numbers of Seminoles.

Under the terms of Jackson's removal policy, thousands of Indians from the states of the Old Northwest were also forced to leave the trans-Mississippi West. Many of them had been extremely successful in the ways of the whites, becoming landowners, farmers, stockraisers, even businessmen, while still maintaining their distinct cultural identity. For the most part there was little violence, although the Indians resisted removal for as long as they were able. A brief but brutal war occurred when Black Hawk, leader of the Sauk and Fox, led two thousand followers back across the Mississippi into Illinois, precipitating a general panic among settlers. Black Hawk and his people fled to Wisconsin, where they were cornered by the outraged militia. At the massacre of Bad Ax River, dozens of Indians were slaughtered, including many women and children.

Emigrant Indians found that native peoples of the plains resented their presence, and the emigrants frequently were required to defend themselves against fierce attack from western tribes. But in time, Indian settlers successfully transplanted their communities to the river valleys of the trans-Mississippi West, and gradually their settlements expanded as they started new farms and plantations. Within a few years the Five Civilized Tribes were shipping cotton, grain, and livestock to markets in neighboring states. The emigrant Indians reestablished their governments, built towns, opened schools, and generally became carriers of Anglo-American culture onto the plains, fifty years before the arrival of white settlers.

While Indians were settling the eastern fringe of the Great Plains, many Americans were focusing on coastal Oregon. As early as the 1790s New England Yankees had become aware of the commercial potential of the Pacific Northwest. Great sailing ships returned to Boston harbor smelling of tea and spice, their holds spilling out rich profit from a trade that began with barter among the coastal Indians for sea otter furs, which were carried to China and traded for prized oriental goods. John Quincy Adams, delegate at the negotiations concluding the War of 1812, knew how lucrative this Pacific trade could be and pressed for fixing the boundary between the United States and Canada at the forty-ninth parallel. If boundaries were further extended to the Pacific, his country would have sole possession of present-day Oregon and Washington. The British refused. Since the Nootka Convention of 1790, they had considered themselves sovereign along the coast between California and Russian America.

The claims of the United States to the Pacific Northwest were weak compared with those of the British, or even the Russians, both of whom had established substantial outposts along the coast at Fort Vancouver and New Archangel, respectively. The Americans pointed out that in 1792 an American captain, Robert Gray, had named the region's great river, the Columbia; that in 1804 Lewis and Clark had traversed and mapped the same river; and that in 1811 the American trading post of Astoria had been the first imperial settlement on its banks. Yet these claims meant little against the effective occupancy of the Pacific coast by other powers. No matter. Adams, an avid expansionist when he became secretary of state in 1817, was determined to extend American sovereignty to the Pacific. "Our proper dominion," he confided in his diary, is "the continent of North America. . . . The United States and North America are identical."

Adams pursued his goal through effective diplomacy. He threatened the British with a Russian-American alliance and was able to win acceptance of a northern boundary at the forty-ninth parallel, extending from the Great Lakes to the Rockies. Although the British refused to concede the Columbia River—most of which runs south of 49°—they agreed that the Pacific Northwest country would remain "free and open" to the subjects of both countries for ten years. Meanwhile, Adams opened negotiations with the Spanish, who were preoccupied with their crumbling Latin American empire. In the midst of discussions over border disputes with Ambassador Luis de Onís, word reached the negotiating table that General Andrew Jackson had invaded Florida. To Spanish protests Adams replied that Florida had for too long been a refuge for hostile Indians, runaway slaves, and bandits and that unless Spain established order on the border, the United States would have no choice but to seize the province in self-defense. In the comprehensive Adams-Onís Treaty of 1819, beleaguered Spain agreed to cede Florida to the United States, to draw a definitive boundary between Texas and Louisiana, and to withdraw all claims in the West north of the forty-second parallel, the northern border of present-day California, Nevada, and Utah.

Finally the secretary of state turned his attention to Russia. In 1821 the tsar declared the northern coast off-limits to all but his people. Adams's response—"The American continents are no longer subjects of any new European colonial establishments"—was the first articulation of the principle he later embodied in the famous Monroe Doctrine, which President James Monroe announced in 1823. But countering the public bluster, in 1824 Adams agreed to regulate more closely the activity of American traders in exchange for a voluntary Russian limitation of their claims to latitudes north of 54°40', today's southern boundary of Alaska. When Great Britain and the United States renewed their "joint occupancy" agreement in 1827, they remained as the last of the imperial competitors for the Oregon Country. It was evident that both nations were buying time, and time for the Americans meant settlement.

Two men first brought Oregon to public attention. Hall Jackson Kelley was an eccentric Boston schoolteacher whose interest in the region was aroused by the reports of Lewis and Clark. In a flood of letters, speeches, and pamphlets during the 1820s, he echoed the words of John Winthrop two hundred years before as he established the Massachusetts Bay Colony and talked of a new "city upon a hill" in Oregon. His plans got nowhere but inspired entrepreneur Nathaniel Wyeth, who from 1832 to 1834 twice journeyed across the continent to Oregon in an attempt to lock up the trade in fur and fish. Although their schemes failed, Kelley's propaganda and Wyeth's enterprise helped make Oregon a household word.

The first actual American settlement in Oregon Country had religious under-pinnings. In 1834, in response to what was thought to be a call for missionaries by the native people of the region, the Methodists sent a small company led by the Reverend Jason Lee overland to Oregon. Once located in Oregon's Willamette valley, however, Lee seemed quickly to forget about the Indians, ministering in-stead to a community of retired trappers and their native wives. Meanwhile, the Congregationalists and Presbyterians made plans to send their own missionaries to Oregon. They selected Marcus Whitman, a young medical doctor from western New York, who yearned to combine his new medical skills with his religious zeal. The American Board of Commissioners for Foreign Missions preferred married missionaries, so when an associate told Whitman of a young woman in a nearby town whose application for missionary work had been denied because she also was unmarried, Whitman hurried there. In a quick weekend courtship Whitman and Narcissa Prentiss agreed to enter missionary work together. In 1836 the newlyweds joined Henry and Eliza Spalding, another missionary couple, in the first overland migration of American families to Oregon. Narcissa and Eliza were, famously, the first white women to cross the Rockies.

The wives quarreled and the men disagreed, and when they reached Oregon they established mission stations a hundred or so miles apart—the Whitmans at Waiilatpu near the future Walla Walla, Washington, and the Spaldings at Lapwai, near modern-day Lewiston, Idaho. The strong faith of the group persisted, but all were severely challenged by what Narcissa called "the thick darkness of heathen-ism." During their entire time in Oregon Country, they baptized no more than twenty Indians. The local Cayuse people staunchly defended their customs, and the Whitmans saw them as "insolent, proud, domineering, arrogant, and ferocious," in Narcissa's words. Meanwhile, Catholic missionaries in the region, led by the Jesuit Pierre De Smet, were enjoying a good deal of success, precisely because of their skill at crossing cultural boundaries. Gradually, the Whitmans turned their attention to groups of American settlers who began to appear in the area. Now less concerned with Indians, Whitman wrote that "our greatest work is to be to aid the white settlement of this country." He went east and promoted Oregon as a promised land for settlers. He returned triumphantly with the Great Migration of 1843, more than one thousand emigrants bound for Oregon.

The Oregon settlement that Whitman helped would indirectly bring a grim conclusion to his life's work. The colonists who marched down the upper Columbia carried diseases such as measles that were deadly to native people without immu-nity. The Cayuse were one of the tribes nearly decimated by an epidemic in 1847, and survivors turned their grief to lashing hatred. On a cold November morning in 1847, with the ghosts of their dead children behind them, Cayuse men broke into the Whitman mission and murdered the Whitmans and ten others.

How do historians explain the overland migration to the Pacific, one of the most remarkable of the many remarkable incidents in the epic of the American

West? It resulted from a convergence of circumstances. During the mid-1830s, a mania for land speculation caused the last of the public domain to disappear in the trans-Appalachian West. Soon thereafter, the Panic of 1837 inaugurated a prolonged depression. The wholesale price index of farm products fell to the lowest level in American history. Many westerners wondered whether they might not better their circumstances elsewhere. A hatred of slavery kept many from considering Texas, while others believed that the West between the Missouri and the Rockies was a desert, fit only for nomads, buffalo hunters, and Indians.

This was the moment when the missionary effort in the Far West came to wide public attention. People heard speeches by Jason Lee and Marcus Whitman or read about them in their local newspapers. In 1841 and 1842 small parties of adventurers traveled to Oregon via the trail pioneered by the fur companies. Suddenly, hundreds of people throughout the West came down with a previously undiagnosed "illness." "The Oregon fever has broke out," wrote an observer in 1843, "and is now raging like any other contagion." Oregon was a land with soil so rich a farmer could raise huge crops of wheat with little effort, declared Peter H. Burnett, an organizer of the Great Migration; with a climate so mild, livestock could forage for themselves all winter. "And they do say," he concluded with a wink, "that out in Oregon the pigs are running about under the great acorn trees, round and fat, and already cooked, with knives and forks sticking in them so that you can cut off a slice whenever you are hungry." Pioneers had told the same tall tales about Kentucky, about Missouri, about Texas.

But Oregon was farther—much farther. Emigrants counted off the two thousand miles of the Oregon Trail at the rate of just twelve to fifteen miles per day, the speed of oxen and wagons. They departed in the spring, as soon as the grass was high enough for the stock to graze, and prayed they would make it over the far western mountains before the first winter storms. They spent May and June crossing the Great Plains, following the Platte River to Fort Laramie, a lingering landmark of the fur trade. Heading up the Sweetwater River, they traveled over the broad saddle in the Rockies known as South Pass and then followed timber and water over rough terrain to Fort Hall, which they reached in early August. At that point they had traveled two-thirds of the distance, but their journey was only about half completed. It was here they began to discover the heartbreak of the Oregon Trail: the closer the destination, the tougher and slower the going. Torturous cliff ledges of the Snake River led to the dreaded Blue Mountains, surmounted only with the aid of ropes and pulleys. Finally, if all went well, they reached the Columbia River in early October and ferried the final one hundred miles to the junction with the Willamette River, their destination.

"How do the old woman and the girls like the idea of such a long journey?" one farmer asked a neighbor who had decided to move to Oregon. "They feel mighty peert about it," came the reply, "and Suke says she shan't be easy till we start." Other women were not so "peert" (an old English colloquialism meaning high-spirited or "perky"). "Oh let us not go," Mary Jones cried when her husband John told her of his decision to head west. But "it made no difference," she lamented.

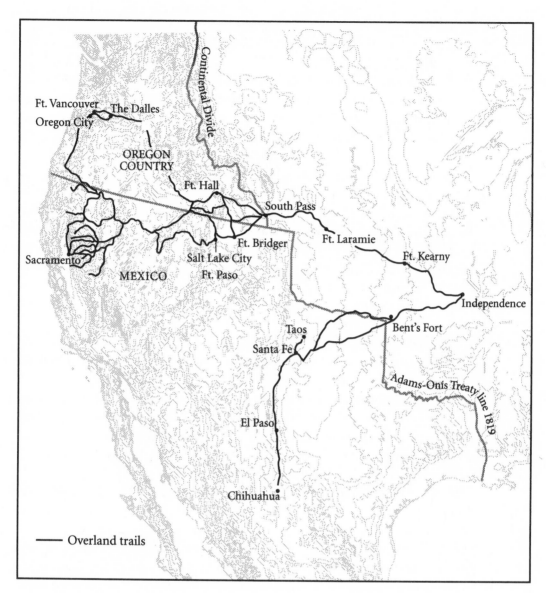

The Overland Trails

One study of women's overland trail diaries found not a single woman who initiated the idea of moving, while nearly a third actively objected. There is no way of knowing how many women successfully kept their husbands at home sweating out the "fever," but it is worth noting that only a small minority risked the overland trek. From the 1840s until the completion of the transcontinental railroad in 1869, perhaps fifty thousand emigrants traveled to Oregon, and the American population there grew from a few hundred to somewhat more than one hundred thousand. That is substantial growth, but it needs to be kept in perspective. During the same period, Iowa's population rose to 1.2 million, better than ten times that of the Pacific

Northwest. Americans were still ramblers, but most rambled to the next county or the next state, not all the way to Oregon.

During this period the federal government became increasingly involved in the emergent West. One sign of this was the growing importance of the Corps of Topographical Engineers. Printed reports of the corps' expeditions typically included expensive illustrations and appendixes detailing the botany, zoology, geology, meteorology, ethnology, and cartography of the new land. But the agenda of the corps was also practical, for its pursuit of knowledge was in the service of continental expansion.

No one better embodied this combination than John Charles Frémont, the best-known and most controversial officer of the Topographical Engineers. Frémont had an eye for opportunity. Taking advantage of a naval appointment, he mastered mathematics and engineering. Then he caught his next golden ring in the courtship and marriage of Jessie Benton, daughter of Thomas Hart Benton, senator from Missouri and a vigorous western voice in Washington. Benton became Frémont's powerful patron.

Frémont's first assignments for the corps—which Benton secured—made him into one of the great celebrities of his day. From 1843 to 1844 he surveyed the Oregon Trail with a company made up mostly of métis voyageurs. The expedition followed a carefully planned route and was to appear strictly scientific—and science did provide an important motivation. With the best European equipment, Frémont calculated innumerable latitudes, longitudes, and elevations and even observed the first satellite of Jupiter. The expedition collected fossils, new plants (such as *Fremontia*), and hundreds of birds, fish, and mammals.

But Frémont's report—skillfully revised by Jessie—was more than a scientific treatise. Attention to the availability of water and fuel, grass for pasturage, ease of the grade, all spoke directly to the needs of overland emigrants. Overnight, Frémont became known as the "Great Pathfinder." But in reality, he was guided by others. His expeditions included a number of Indian scouts and mountain men, such as Kit Carson, whose intimate knowledge of the West was a product of the nearly twenty years he spent as a fur trapper. When Jessie drafted the report, she neglected the Indians but was careful to give Carson his due, and he soon became equally famous, the mid-nineteenth-century inheritor of Daniel Boone's mantle.

Frémont's report became a best seller among easterners as well as emigrants, exciting talk in New York drawing rooms and Missouri barns. Western writer Joaquin Miller later recalled reading the report as a boy: "I fancied I could see Frémont's men, flags in the air, Frémont at the head, waving his sword, his horse neighing wildly in the mountain wind, with unknown and unnamed empires on every hand." Thousands of pioneers carried Frémont with them as they set out for the empire of the Far West.

The most impressive western migration of the era was undertaken by the Mormons, a uniquely American religious sect. In one of the greatest treks in all of American history, thousands of members of the Church of Jesus Christ of Latter-day Saints left the Mississippi valley in 1846 and 1847 headed for the isolated desert country of the Great Basin, between the Rockies and the Sierra Nevada.

The Mormon religion was founded by Joseph Smith, a visionary who translated a set of revealed golden plates into the *Book of Mormon* (1830). The text, with its references to America as the "land of promise," the "choice above all other lands," offered what historian Jan Shipps calls a "powerful and provocative synthesis of biblical experience and the American dream." Smith's followers lived in exclusively Mormon communities, pooling their labor and resources, distributing goods according to the needs of the people, and hammering out doctrines that placed the survival of the group above that of the individual. Viewing themselves as the "chosen people," the Mormons had been hounded out of New England and then Missouri, and had reassembled on the banks of the Mississippi in Illinois. With renewed vigor, they set to building once again, and the new community—which Smith christened Nauvoo—soon grew into the state's largest town, with more than fifteen thousand residents. Smith organized a large military force known as the Nauvoo Legion to protect "the Saints," as they called themselves.

But soon the Mormons were involved in more hostile relations with their neighbors. In June 1844 an enraged anti-Mormon mob murdered Joseph Smith at the age of thirty-eight along with his elder brother Hyrum. The next two years were a time of terrible struggle for the Mormons, but eventually the leadership settled on Brigham Young, one of the most talented of Smith's loyal elite. Young had a vision of a western Mormon empire, and he laid plans for an exodus that would finally remove the Saints from harm's way.

The great migration began in early 1846. The Saints first moved to temporary winter quarters near Omaha, Nebraska. Then, in the spring of 1847, several thousand set out on the Overland Trail, keeping to the north side of the Platte River to avoid conflict with other migrating Americans. Crossing the plains and the mountains, they finally arrived that fall at the Great Salt Lake, where Young determined to build a permanent refuge. By 1852 more than ten thousand people were living in the new Mormon utopia of Salt Lake City, irrigating the desert and making it bloom.

In addition to Oregon and the Great Salt Lake, the other important far western destination of the mid-1840s was the Mexican province of California, where the governor had made it clear that American settlers were welcome. Mexican independence from Spain precipitated great changes in California, most importantly the "secularization" of the mission system. The missions had always legally held title to their lands in the name of the Indians, to be divided among them once they had become "good subjects." But Mexican liberals, eager to curtail the power of the conservative Catholic Church, pointed out that the mission padres were unlikely to freely abandon their power. So in 1833 Mexico finally ordered the Franciscans to relinquish control over the neophytes. Mission resources were placed in the hands of civil administrators who were charged with distributing them to the Indians. These men, however, made sure that most of the lands and herds stayed in their own hands, or passed into the possession of friends and associates. The emerging class of *rancheros* built themselves up by plundering the missions. In 1820 there were only twenty ranchos in California; by 1840 there were more than six hundred, most carved from the mission estates.

Many former mission Indians set up their own little *ranchería* communities and found work on the ranchos as field hands or *vaqueros*. According to Salvador Vallejo, a prominent ranchero, "Indians tilled our soil, pastured our cattle, sheared our sheep, cut our lumber, built our houses, paddled our boats, made tiles for our homes, ground our grain, slaughtered our cattle, dressed their hides for market, and made our unburnt bricks; while the Indian women made excellent servants, took care of our children, made every one of our meals." Although they gained a degree of cultural independence during this transition, many Indians were bitter over what amounted to a second round of dispossessions.

The rancheros were soon enmeshed in the international Pacific market, with Americans as their principal trading partners. Americans began bartering manufactured goods and Asian luxuries for the hides and tallow of the vast cattle herds of the ranchos; these raw materials were soon supplying the shoe and soap industries of New England while Californians became dependent on American products. To increase their production, the rancheros began to mount expeditions into the great central valleys of the province in search of Indian captives to enslave, for more workers meant more cattle.

But the independent Indians of the interior had different ideas. Like the peoples of the plains a century before, they became warriors mounted on horseback, supporting themselves by raiding the herds of the rancheros. When Frémont led his expedition through California in 1844, he encountered these fierce people, who, he wrote, made "frequent descents upon the settlements west of the Coast Range, which they keep constantly swept of horses; among them are many refugees from the Spanish missions." The Indians sold horses to American traders, who herded them to eastern markets across the mountains and deserts.

By encouraging foreigners to settle the interior valleys, California officials hoped to gain control over these tribes. The most prominent settler was John A. Sutter, a Swiss emigrant, who in 1839 obtained a large tract on the interior Sacramento River where he built a large trading post. He came to California via Fort Vancouver and Honolulu, bringing with him Hawaiian workers who lived in Polynesian grass shacks until Sutter made arrangements for local Indians to construct his headquarters. Like the rancheros, Sutter was utterly dependent on Indians for labor. Sutter's Fort on the Sacramento soon became a lodestone for American settlers.

⤙ ⥶✦⥸ ⤚

Meanwhile, in 1843 settlers in the Oregon Country were setting up a framework of government. Within two years five thousand Americans lived in the Willamette valley, south of the Columbia, and their numbers grew with each annual migration. John McLoughlin, at the Hudson's Bay Company post of Fort Vancouver, graciously took an oath of allegiance to the Oregon provisional government, but he remained responsible for the 750 British subjects scattered north of the Columbia. The fur trade of the area was dwindling, and that summer the London directors of the HBC decided to move their post north to a site on Vancouver Island, which has since grown into the city of Victoria, British Columbia. McLoughlin stayed in Oregon with his métis wife until their deaths.

Once the HBC had literally given ground, the time seemed right for a final settlement of the boundary controversy between Great Britain and the United States. President James K. Polk, the Democrat who had beaten the Whigs in a campaign of spread-eagle expansionism, privately asked the British ambassador for acceptance of the forty-ninth parallel, the boundary first proposed by John Quincy Adams. When the ambassador refused, an angry Polk made a public declaration that he would accept nothing less than the whole of the disputed territory from the northern border of California to the southern boundary of Russian America at latitude 54°40'. *Fifty-four forty or fight!* became the slogan of the hour. There was bluster on both sides of the Atlantic, and newspapers printed ominous reports of preparations for war. But there were also voices of reason. A war over Oregon, declared the editor of a prominent Whig paper, would be one of "the most reckless and insane exhibitions that the civilized world has ever witnessed." Such a war soon would come, but it would not be fought over Oregon.

Chapter 7 **War and Destiny**

If he could have his way, young Stephen A. Douglas of Illinois declared on the floor of Congress in 1845, he would "blot out the lines on the map" that marked the national boundaries at the time, and "make the area of liberty as broad as the continent itself." An empire for liberty! This oxymoron was an old American ideal, but never before had Americans asserted it so boldly, or with such aggressive intent. Its watchword was coined by a prominent Democrat and editor of the *New York Morning News*, John L. O'Sullivan, who insisted on "our manifest destiny to overspread the continent."

Manifest Destiny was not, as historians so often imply, a deeply held American folk belief. Rather, it was the self-conscious creation of political propagandists like O'Sullivan, determined to uncouple the politics of expansion from the growing sectional controversy over slavery. Slavery first alarmed the country ("like a fire bell in the night," Jefferson wrote) in 1820, when Missouri applied for admission to the Union as a slave state. But Congress was able to pass the famous Missouri Compromise, agreeing that henceforth slavery would be "forever prohibited" in the territory of the Louisiana Purchase north of 36°30', the southern boundary of Missouri. The slavery controversy repeatedly blocked the admission of Texas. In 1844 James K. Polk of Tennessee, presidential candidate of the Democrats, ran on an explicitly expansionist platform that attempted to shift the focus from the expansion of slavery to expansion per se. The opposing Whigs were skeptical about expansion. The young Illinois Whig Abraham Lincoln declared his belief "in keeping our fences where they are and cultivating our present possession, making it a garden, improving the morals and education of the people." What the country needed, argued the Whigs, was *improvement*, vigorous federal support for economic development. No, countered the Democrats, what the country needed was *expansion*, vigorous federal action to acquire more land, and with it more opportunity for ordinary people and their rapidly multiplying offspring.

The election was touted as a referendum on expansion, and its outcome suggested a nation of closely divided opinions. With just 49.6 percent of the national vote, Polk became only the second president to win election without a popular majority, although he carried fifteen of twenty-six states. Had his opponent Henry Clay attracted but five thousand additional ballots in the state of New York—where a third party drained support—he would have won in the electoral college. The Democrats nevertheless insisted they had won a mandate for a program of national expansion. Presidential elections, of course, are not about gauging public opinion but capturing political power and putting it to use. A mandate is what you make of it, and the Democrats were about to make a western empire with theirs.

After the election, lame-duck president John Tyler, with his eye on history, pressed Congress to admit Texas to the Union through the device of a joint resolution, which required only a simple majority. The Democrats pushed the measure through, presenting Polk with an accomplished fact when he assumed office in March 1845. By the end of the year, the Lone Star had become one of twenty-eight on the flag of union. Flushed with success, the Democrats moved on to the Oregon question. In his first annual message to Congress, Polk had announced his intention of seizing the entire Pacific Northwest from the British. What did it matter that the United States could offer no valid precedent for a claim to the northern land of 54°40'? In public Polk blustered, but in private he arranged an amicable treaty with the British, dividing Oregon at the forty-ninth parallel. The president wanted to concentrate on the greater prize he could obtain by confronting Mexico and did not feel that he could risk armed confrontations on both the southern *and* northern borders. The Senate ratified the international agreement with Great Britain in June 1846. By that time Polk desperately needed it, for he had already provoked a full-scale war with Mexico.

For decades, American filibusters had sought to subvert the northern provinces of Mexico, while American presidents simultaneously sought to purchase them. As far as the Mexicans were concerned, it amounted to gringo imperialism either way. Mexico's president, Antonio López de Santa Anna, notified the U.S. government that the annexation of Texas would be "equivalent to a declaration of war," and as soon as the Mexicans heard of the congressional vote, they severed diplomatic relations. Soon, both nations had moved troops to the contested border region, and Polk secretly sent Democrat partisan John Slidell of Louisiana to Mexico City to negotiate a settlement. He found that while the Mexicans officially disclaimed the legitimacy of Texas independence, in private they were willing to accept annexation if the United States would agree to the traditional provincial boundary at the Nueces River. But following Polk's instructions, Slidell insisted on a boundary along the more southerly Rio Grande. The region in dispute, called the

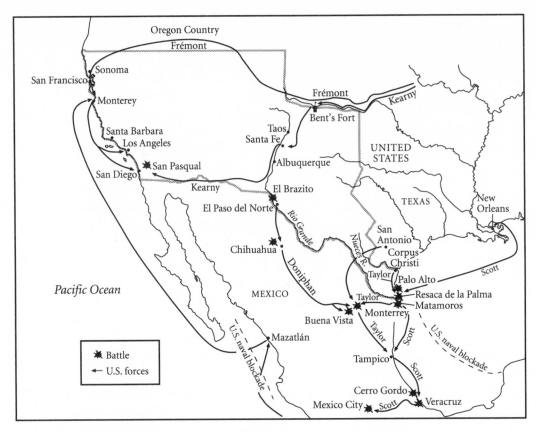

The Mexican War

Nueces Strip, was a one-hundred-mile swath along the left bank of the Rio Grande, populated almost entirely by Tejanos. Slidell also pressed the Mexicans to sell the provinces of New Mexico and California. The Mexican public was deeply hostile to the United States, and knowing that such an agreement would be the equivalent of signing their own death warrants, Mexican leaders were left with no choice but to terminate the negotiations, and Slidell returned to Washington empty-handed. "We can never get along well with them until we have given them a good drubbing," he reported to the president.

The Mexicans were angry, but they were not about to invade the United States to reclaim their lost province. Polk, however, was spoiling for a fight. He announced to his cabinet that the acquisition of California—with the fine Pacific ports of San Diego and San Francisco—was the prime goal of his presidency. To force the issue, in March 1846 he ordered General Zachary Taylor, veteran of campaigns against Tecumseh, Black Hawk, and the Seminoles, to march his "Army of Observation" into the Nueces Strip. The Mexicans warned Taylor to retire, but he refused, and on April 24 they crossed the Rio Grande, attacked a party of U.S. dragoons, and killed eleven Americans. Polk had his rationale for war. "Mexico has passed the boundary of the United States," he announced in his war message to

Congress, "has invaded our territory and shed American blood on the American soil." Congress voted for war on May 13.

"I wish now that you would judge these events with a Mexican heart," the distinguished Mexican journalist Carlos María de Bustamante appealed to the American people soon after the war began. "Ask yourself: which has been the aggressor country?" Many Americans agreed with him. "That region belonged to Mexico," argued Whig senator Charles Sumner of Massachusetts. "*Certainly* it did not belong to the United States. . . . Here was an act of aggression." The war was "one of the most unjust ever waged by a stronger nation against a weaker nation," Ulysses S. Grant wrote years later.

The Mexican War ostensibly began as a limited war for limited objectives. But it was, in fact, a war of conquest and proved far easier to start than to finish. The Mexican Army performed badly, but the Mexican people excelled at guerrilla fighting, which took a bloody toll. In the final tally it would cost the U.S. Treasury nearly $100 million to win California and the new Southwest. By official and conservative government reckoning, it was also the most destructive war in which the United States had yet engaged, claiming the lives of nearly thirteen thousand Americans and at least twenty thousand Mexicans.

Polk planned a campaign with three principal theaters of operation. In the first, the American Army under General Taylor invaded northern Mexico and destroyed the numerically superior Mexican Army of General Santa Anna at the battle of Buena Vista near Saltillo. The second, in New Mexico, was directed by General Stephen Watts Kearny, whose sixteen hundred men entered Santa Fe in August 1846 without firing a shot.

The third was in California and was Polk's main objective. Kearny set out for the Pacific coast but on the way learned that California had already fallen. On an early morning in June 1846, a small, irregular force of American settlers had ridden into the village of Sonoma in the northern part of the province, invaded the home of General Mariano Vallejo, and proclaimed the independence of the "California Republic." They were supported by Captain John Charles Frémont of the Topographical Engineers, who with forty men was there on another scientific expedition. Frémont later reported that the president had instructed him that in the case of war with Mexico, he was to act decisively to secure California for the United States. Appointing Frémont as their leader and spokesman, the American rebels raised a flag with a lone star and a crude drawing of a bear. The star signaled the intention of the Americans to "play the Texas game," and the bear indicated their intention to secure "rough justice." But to the Mexican Californians (or Californios), cattle-thieving bears, *los osos*, were symbols of piracy. The Americans played the part well, imprisoning and insulting Vallejo and other Californios, plundering homes, and killing civilians.

The "Bear Flag Republic" lasted only one month. In July, Commodore John Sloat of the U.S. Navy sailed into San Francisco Bay with the first news that the

United States and Mexico were at war. Promising guarantees of Californio lives and property, Sloat put a stop to Frémont's terror. This could have been the end of the conflict because a good number of Californios, including Vallejo himself, agreed that the province should break with Mexico. But Sloat, who was ailing, was soon relieved by Commodore Robert Stockton, a bellicose old salt with anti-Catholic and anti-Mexican views. Frémont was commissioned commander of a new fighting unit, the California Battalion of Volunteers, composed of his own sharpshooters, Bear Flaggers, and Indian mercenaries hired at Sutter's Fort. Frémont's marauders so outraged the Californios that they roused an effective guerrilla resistance that ousted the American force in Los Angeles.

Unaware that the Californios had retaken most of southern California, Kearny arrived from New Mexico with only 125 men. At San Pasqual, in the hills west of San Diego, mounted Californios inflicted heavy casualties on Kearny's unsuspecting troops. Only Stockton's rush of emergency forces saved them from destruction. The next month, Kearny and Stockton finally recaptured Los Angeles, but despite the presence of a general and a commodore, it was Frémont who loftily accepted the surrender of the city. With egotistical bravado, Captain Frémont refused orders from General Kearny, his superior, and reported instead to Commodore Stockton. This led to his court-martial on charges of mutiny, and his resignation from the army.

By early 1847, then, the Americans controlled all of northern Mexico. But there was little evidence that the Mexican government was about to give up. The United States might simply retain what it had conquered, of course, but the idea of taking territory without the benefit of legal cover did not sit well, even with an expansionist like Polk. A treaty duly ratified by both governments would be preferable. Surely the Mexicans would negotiate if the United States seized their capital. In March, General Winfield Scott, directing the first large-scale amphibious operation in U.S. military history, landed ten thousand troops at Vera Cruz and marched toward Mexico City over a route Cortés had traversed more than two centuries before. Through the spring and summer, Scott engaged the Mexican Army in a long series of battles. Mexican guerrilla action harassed supply lines and slowed progress. Americans retaliated with outrages against civilians. Even General Scott admitted that his troops had committed atrocities, including "murder, robbery and rape of mothers and daughters in the presence of tied-up males of the families." The Americans reached Mexico City in September, storming the palace of the viceroys at Chapultepec, then swiftly moving to capture the center of the capital. On September 14, 1847, Mexicans sullenly watched the supreme ignominy of U.S. Marines raising the American flag above their city. More than a century and a half later, it remains a memory that still stings.

Early in the Mexican War, Polk affirmed that the United States would never fight for conquest, but he soon began to hedge under the guise of seeking repayment for the cost of the war. California seemed a logical reparation, and geopolitical logic demanded that the territory between Texas and California be included. But grander dreams were abroad. Extreme expansionists began to argue for the complete annexation of Mexico. Secretary of the Treasury Robert J. Walker commissioned a study of the fiscal implications of total annexation, and Secretary of State James Buchanan reported to the cabinet that Mexicans dreaded the day when American troops would withdraw. "More! More! More!" shouted O'Sullivan from the pages of the *New York Morning News*. "Why not take all of Mexico?"

The attack on this "all-Mexico" position came from southerners who trembled at the thought that American institutions would be contaminated by "the colored and mixed-breed" population of Mexico. Senator John C. Calhoun of South Carolina argued on the floor of the Senate that more than half of Mexico's residents were Indians, and the rest "impure races, not as good as Cherokees or Choctaws." Were Mexico annexed and made a territory of the United States, those mongrel peoples would be placed on an equal level with the racially pure Americans. "I protest utterly against such a project," Calhoun thundered.

A third body of opinion considered the war immoral and unworthy of the nation. Abolitionists charged that the South had incited the war as a way of extending slavery into Mexican territory. The abolitionist leader Frederick Douglass, himself an escaped slave, declared that the war made him "sick at heart" and "the spirit of slavery reigns triumphant throught [*sic*] all the land." Henry David Thoreau, also believing the war was fought to extend slavery, refused to pay his taxes and went to jail for a night before his friends bailed him out. Transcendentalist writer Margaret Fuller lamented that the nation's gaze was "fixed not on the stars, but on the possessions of other men."

Yet even these opponents were little concerned for the struggles and the bravery of the Mexicans. Who credited the band of Californios who nearly turned back the Americans at San Pasqual? Who applauded the guerrillas defending their homeland along the road to Mexico City? Few Americans of the day paid attention to the Mexican side. Few do today.

President Polk sent a peace emissary, Nicholas Trist, to march with Scott and seek negotiations at the first opportunity. Trist was instructed to win Mexican acceptance of Texas annexation and acquire California and New Mexico. Negotiations went slowly. Yielding to the demands of the all-Mexico extremists in his party, the president recalled his negotiator to issue new, presumably more extensive demands. But in Mexico City, Trist stubbornly ignored Polk's message and kept negotiating. In January 1848 he won a treaty based on the earlier American aims. When news of his accomplishment arrived in Washington, it undercut the extremists. Polk felt he had no choice but submit the treaty to Congress, which ratified the agreement in March. The Treaty of Guadalupe Hidalgo confirmed the annexation of Texas and set the Rio Grande as the international boundary. As reparations for the cost of the war, Mexico ceded California and the province of New Mexico (the present-day states of New Mexico, Arizona, Utah, Nevada, and southern Colorado). The United States paid Mexico $15 million and reimbursed American citizens for claims they held against Mexico amounting to $3.75 million. In 2005 dollars the total price, including the cost of the war itself, would be in the range of $2.9 billion—real money, but still a monumental bargain.

A joint United States–Mexico commission was established with the power to draw an exact boundary from Texas westward to the Pacific. When the American commissioner, John Russell Bartlett, a New Englander, allowed the boundary to be the most northerly line of several possibilities, southerners howled. To make up for his gaff, in the Gadsden Purchase of 1853 (named for American negotiator James Gadsden), the United States acquired for $10 million the land south of the Gila River in present-day New Mexico and Arizona. The total loss to Mexico, including Texas, came to 602 million acres, a third of its national domain.

The Treaty of Guadalupe Hidalgo stipulated that "male citizens of Mexico" in the transferred territory could choose either to retain their former citizenship or to become citizens of the United States and be "maintained and protected in the free enjoyment of their liberty and property, and secured in the free exercise of religion without restriction." In the war's aftermath, however, Mexican Americans found their civil rights slipping away, their property in jeopardy, and their Catholic religion under assault. The 1850s were notable for the rise of intense nativism and anti-Catholicism in the United States, and Anglo newcomers treated the native population as "Mexicans" regardless of their formal U.S. citizenship. Anglo-Americans expected either conformity or exclusion, and the tenacious determination of Mexican Americans to hold on to their traditions provided a justification for relegating them to menial economic and social status. With the complicated inconsistencies between Mexican and U.S. law, many Mexican American landowners lost their titles or were forced to sell to cover legal costs, and the poor people who worked for them were also thrown off the land.

One consequence was the rise of social banditry, the frequent response of persecuted peoples in times of social disruption. Robbing the rich to provide for the poor, the bandit was a criminal in the eyes of the state but a hero in the eyes of the people from whom he sprang. There were numerous Mexican social bandits in the years following the conquest, but the most famous was Joaquín Murrieta, a semifictional hero in whom was combined the exploits of at least five men. Facts were less important than the legend, in which the Murrieta family was attacked on their land by a group of Yankees who tied up Joaquín, flogged him, and forced him to watch while they raped his wife. His vow of revenge echoed the frustration of California's oppressed Mexicans. Murrieta and his outlaw band so terrorized the Anglo community that the California governor placed a $1,000 bounty on his head. Although it was collected by an experienced bounty hunter, Mexican Californians refused to believe that their hero was dead, and for the next half-century his accomplishments continued to be celebrated in story and song.

In the valley of the Rio Grande in Texas, where Tejanos had long remained a majority, discontent moved beyond social banditry to guerrilla warfare. Law in south Texas was administered through the guns of the Texas Rangers, who considered Mexicans their natural enemies. "I can maintain a better stomach at the killing of a Mexican than at the crushing of a body louse," one Ranger boasted. The Rangers' arrogant bullying was deeply resented by Tejanos, including Juan Nepomuceno Cortina, son of a respected ranchero family. Roused to rebellion by the abuse of his fellow Tejanos, Cortina and his armed followers attacked the predominantly Anglo town of Brownsville. Proclaiming the "sacred right of self-preservation," Cortina issued a broadside to Tejanos. "You have been robbed of your property, incarcerated, chased, murdered, and hunted like wild beasts," he declared, and "to me is entrusted the work of breaking the chains of your slavery." During the subsequent "Cortina War," several hundred Mexican rebels destroyed the property of dozens of Anglos. Cortina was finally chased into Mexico by federal troops under the command of Colonel Robert E. Lee.

With the acquisition of Oregon, Texas, California, and the new Southwest, the United States became a transcontinental nation. The unorganized territory of the trans-Mississippi West constituted 49 percent of the country's land. In this vast region, the federal government would assume unprecedented authority over the next forty years. Federal armies would conquer the native peoples of the West, federal engineers would survey the land, and federal bureaucrats would administer the territories in a process that amounted to federal conquest and colonization.

One of the first steps in this process was the creation by Congress, in 1849, of the Department of the Interior, consolidating in one government agency the Bureau of Indian Affairs and the General Land Office, and soon the Geological Survey and the Territorial Office. The federal department charged with protecting the Indians' rights to their lands thus also became responsible for assessing the value of and dividing up the national domain, distributing it to settlers, and creating new territories and states. That this did not strike Americans as an absurd contradiction speaks volumes about the attitude of the government on the eve of the violent period of disempowerment that was beginning.

The designation of the Great Plains as Indian country in perpetuity had been essential to the logic of "Indian Removal." Both native peoples and emigrant Indians were signatories to federal treaties promising to protect their homelands "for as long as the grass grows and the waters run." But the new geopolitical reality of continentalism invalidated this premise. Already, officials were seriously discussing possible routes for a transcontinental railroad, and thousands of Americans were traveling across the plains on the overland trails to the Pacific. Although few Americans were settling the plains themselves, emigrants were consuming the timber of the river bottoms for their campfires, grazing their livestock on the crops of native farmers, and hunting buffalo and antelope by the thousands. Frequently, they blundered into conflicts with Indian hunting parties. Officials in Washington, D.C., began to call for change. "The Indian barrier must be removed," declared Senator Stephen Douglas of Illinois.

In treaties negotiated with plains peoples during the 1850s, the United States

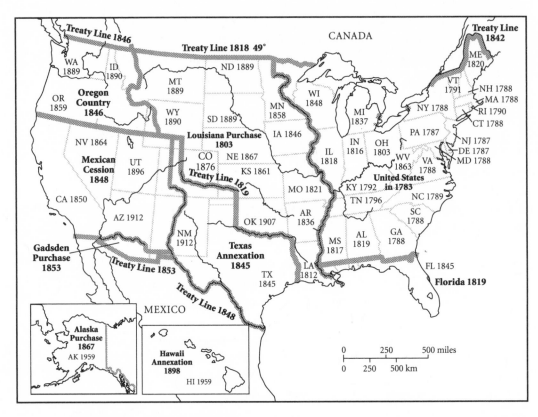

Territorial Acquisitions and Statehood

began the construction of a new order presaging the end of permanent Indian country. In 1851 at Fort Laramie on the North Platte River, more than twelve thousand Indians stood witness as the leaders of the Sioux, Northern Cheyennes, Arapahos, Crows, Assiniboines, Mandans, and Arikaras granted the United States the right to establish posts and roads across the plains in exchange for the guarantee of annuities compensating them for the loss of game. In 1853 the tribes of the southern plains, including the Southern Cheyennes, Comanches, and Kiowas, agreed to similar provisions. The Americans also pressed the plains nomads to agree to territorial boundaries, hinting at the reservation system that would become the hallmark of federal Indian policy in the years to come. But the lines on a map were practically meaningless for people whose way of life required them to circulate within huge territories in pursuit of buffalo, and Indians chaffed at the idea of territorial restriction. "You have split my land [and] I don't like it," declared Black Hawk, a spokesman for the Oglala Sioux.

If the outcome of the Mexican War exposed the sham of "permanent" Indian country, it also killed the hope that sectional differences over slavery might be subsumed in the national enthusiasm for expansion. Democrats had anticipated that a patriotic war for territory would unify the country. Instead, the Mexican War opened a divisive and violent new conflict on the question of slavery's extension that led directly to the Civil War.

That controversy began during the first months of the Mexican War when Democrat congressman David Wilmot of Pennsylvania introduced an amendment to an appropriations bill that applied the precise restriction of the Northwest Ordinance of 1787 to land acquired from Mexico: "neither slavery nor involuntary servitude shall ever exist in any part of said territory." The debate over the Wilmot Proviso shattered the expansionist coalition. The legal stipulations over slavery in the new lands now had to be determined by a sectionally divided Congress. The House passed the proviso, but southerners in the Senate blocked it. Should the magic line of the Missouri Compromise be extended indefinitely westward? To do so would mean legalizing slavery in the new Southwest and in the southern part of California. While Congress stewed, California waited for two years under military government. Finally, another "grand compromise" was patched together in a series of bills passed in 1850. California, which rejected slavery in its own state constitution in 1849, would be admitted as a free state, skipping the territorial interlude altogether. New Mexico and Utah territories would be organized without restrictions on slavery, the residents of each territory left to decide the question themselves, a solution the Democrats called "popular sovereignty."

But the peace of 1850 was short-lived, broken just four years later when Senator Douglas offered a bill to organize the old Louisiana Purchase territory beyond the Missouri River into the territories of Kansas and Nebraska. Douglas was eager to promote a transcontinental railroad that would begin in his home state of Illinois and head west across Kansas, but such a project required the formation of a territorial government. Not daring to alienate the southerners in the Democratic Party, he proposed to abandon the old Missouri Compromise line—which would have barred slavery in Kansas—invoking instead the principle of popular sovereignty.

Over the next four years the Kansas prairie became a killing field where men took sides and fought for their uncompromising beliefs. Proslavery militias from Missouri crossed the border to battle heavily armed abolitionist settlers from New England. In the spring of 1856 a mob of eight hundred proslavery men invaded the antislavery town of Lawrence, Kansas, demolishing the two newspaper offices, plundering shops and homes, and killing one man. Shortly after, the abolitionist settler John Brown of Kansas vowed to "fight fire with fire." In an act designed to "strike terror in the hearts of the proslavery people," he and four of his sons seized five peaceful proslavery settlers on Pottawatomie Creek and laid open their skulls with broadswords. Brown was enacting the traditional role of the western vigilante. But never before had white American settlers used such violence against each other. It was a dark omen of things to come.

The old politics finally expired on the plains of Kansas, and a new politics arose to take its place. In order to win a national election, the Republicans, an antislavery party of northern interests, needed western support. In 1856 they played the western card by running peripatetic John C. Frémont under the banner "Free Soil, Free

Men, Frémont." Frémont lost, but not by much. Indeed, the Republicans came very close to uniting the North and West against the South. As the transportation revolution redirected the commercial connections of the Old Northwest from New Orleans to New York, support grew for the Republican program: protective tariffs for northern industry, internal improvements and cheap public land for westerners. That sectional political bargain was finally sealed in 1860 when the Old Northwest voted as a block for Abraham Lincoln and the Republicans. When the South refused to accept the outcome of the election and seceded, the East and West ("the North" of the Civil War) joined forces to preserve the Union. The payoff came when Congress, purged of southern representation, enacted two of the West's most cherished political goals—a Homestead Act providing free land for settlers and a Pacific Railroad Bill to sew together the distant allies with steel.

Facing an accelerated pace of settlement—stimulated in part by the rising price of wheat during the Civil War—the Republican Congress carved the rest of the trans-Mississippi West into territories in preparation for their settlement. It was one thing, however, to organize a territory in Washington, D.C., and quite another to establish it on the ground. The incorporation of the trans-Mississippi West into the political structure of the nation required a generation of offensive warfare. For the several hundred thousand Indian people who called the West home, it meant thirty years of desperate resistance.

New means of violence exacerbated the situation. In 1836 Samuel Colt had patented the first modern revolver, an inexpensive weapon that had no utility as a hunting piece but was designed solely for violent human confrontations. Colt advertised his guns with heroic scenes—a man protecting his wife and child from Indians armed only with a Colt. Sales were brisk. By the 1850s the Colt factory in Hartford, Connecticut, was turning out a variety of new handguns, while the Sharps and Winchester companies perfected the manufacture of new breechloading and repeating rifles. During the Civil War hundreds of thousands of these weapons were issued to troops, and the West was soon flooded with firearms of every type and description, from tiny pocket derringers to .50-caliber buffalo guns.

The arming of western America was accompanied by a hardening and coarsening of attitudes toward the Indians. Adults instructed children with "histories of Indian lying, Indian theft, Indian double-dealing, Indian fraud and perfidy, Indian want of conscience, Indian blood-thirstiness, Indian diabolism," wrote novelist Herman Melville in 1857. New "scientific" theories of race were providing authoritative support for long-assumed beliefs in Indian inferiority. "The aboriginal barbarous tribes cannot be forced to change their habits," two distinguished American ethnologists wrote in the 1850s. "It is as clear as the sun at noon-day, that in a few generations more the last of these Red men will be numbered with the dead." They offered these words as prediction, but they could as easily be read as a death warrant. A new rhetoric of violence also appeared in the official government discourse regarding the Indians. Officials at the Bureau of Indian Affairs did not shirk from the draconian design of their new reservation policy of fixed locations for the formerly nomadic tribes. "A stern necessity is impending over them," one official warned. "There is no alternative to providing for them in this manner but to exterminate them, which the dictates of justice and humanity alike forbid." Get out of the way or be damned! Such was the thinking of Commissioner of Indian Affairs Alfred B. Greenwood as expressed in his annual report for 1859.

The West harvested the first bitter fruits of these trends among the Eastern Sioux of Minnesota in 1862. In treaties of 1851 and 1858, the United States had forced these communities to relinquish title to twenty-eight million acres in exchange for annuities and a crowded reservation on the Minnesota River. By the summer of 1862, a combination of crop failure and diminished supplies of game had reduced the Eastern Sioux to practical starvation, yet their authoritarian agent refused to issue emergency stores from the abundant supplies in the agency warehouse. "So far as I am concerned, if they are hungry let them eat grass or their own dung," he declared. When this was translated, the Sioux were thunderstruck. Two days later the reservation exploded. In an orgy of violence directed against surrounding farms, towns, and forts, the Sioux killed some five hundred settlers before the state militia crushed the rebellion. The body of the offending trader was later found, his mouth stuffed with grass. After the uprising, thirty-eight Sioux were executed before a cheering crowd of settlers; several hundred more were imprisoned, and the remaining Eastern Sioux were forcibly removed to a reservation in the Dakota Territory.

The Southwest became the focus for the next round of violence between the federal government and the Indians. Former mountain man Kit Carson was commissioned to lead a campaign to eradicate Navajo and Apache raiders. "There is to be no council held with the Indians nor any talks," his commander ordered. "The men are to be slain whenever and wherever they can be found. The women and children may be taken as prisoners." The subdued tribes were to be exiled to a desolate spot in arid east-central New Mexico called Bosque Redondo. In a brutal campaign that included the murder of two surrendering Apache chiefs and the torture and beheading of another, several hundred Indians died and several hundred more were forced onto the barren reservation and put to work digging ditches. Most of the Apaches, however, eluded the troops, fleeing into the mountains or south of the border into Mexico. Rather than pacifying the Apaches, the campaign actually marked the beginning of more than twenty years of fierce resistance to the Americans.

Carson was next turned onto the Navajos who lived in the northern border region between New Mexico and Arizona. Although the Navajos had long raided Hispano and Pueblo communities, they were a farming and pastoral people, with gardens, orchards, and large flocks of sheep and goats. Consequently, Carson ordered a scorched-earth policy for the Navajo homeland, destroying hogans and crops, burning orchards, killing livestock. By the late winter of 1864, the Navajos were desperate. Some eight thousand Indians surrendered and were forced to march four hundred miles through the desert to Bosque Redondo. The "Long Walk," as the Navajos call this brutal removal experience, was seared into their collective memory. When in 1868 they were finally allowed to return to their homeland—much constricted in size, of course—the Navajos had determined never again to go to war against the Americans.

From Minnesota to New Mexico the Americans proved themselves ruthless and effective conquerors. But in the annals of Civil War Indian fighting, few events could match the infamy of what happened in Colorado. In 1861 the Arapahos and Southern Cheyennes of the region were assigned to a barren reservation along the Arkansas River where it was nearly impossible to support themselves. A group of conciliatory chiefs appealed to territorial governor John Evans in Denver. "We must live near the buffalo or starve," explained Black Kettle of the Cheyennes. Evans offered nothing but threats in return, for he was hoping that war would give him an excuse to clear all the Indians from the territory. As the meeting was about to conclude, Colonel John Chivington, military commander of the territorial militia, directed a remark at Black Kettle: "My rule of fighting white men or Indians is to fight them until they lay down their arms and submit to military authority."

Black Kettle and the other chiefs were puzzled by what Chivington said, but to avoid any possibility of conflict, the chief asked to be placed under the protection of federal soldiers at Fort Lyon in southeastern Colorado. Following the instructions of the fort commander, he led his people to a place called Sand Creek, where they camped. The encampment was a fair representation of the inclusive world of the upper Arkansas valley frontier, including a few white men married to Indian women, and a liberal number of métis. Three of the four children of trader William Bent and his two Cheyenne wives were there. "All the Indians had the idea firmly fixed in their minds that they were here under protection and that peace was soon to be concluded," wrote his son George Bent.

But Chivington was acting under instructions received from the militia commander of the region: "I want no peace till the Indians suffer more." Chivington was the man for the job. Soon he was leading the seven hundred men of the Third Colorado Regiment toward Sand Creek. The colonel made his position very clear to his men. "I have come to kill Indians," he told them, "and believe it is right and honorable to use any means under God's heaven to kill Indians."

The Colorado volunteers surprised the Cheyenne camp at sunrise on November 29, 1864, while most of the young warriors were away hunting. No Cheyenne ever forgot that day. George Bent awoke to the sound of excited people rushing by his lodge. "From down the creek a large body of troops was advancing at a rapid trot," he later wrote. "All was confusion and noise, men, women, and children rushing out of the lodges partly dressed; women and children screaming at sight of the troops; men running back into the lodges for their arms, other men, already armed, or with lassos and bridles in their hand, running for the herds. . . . Black Kettle had a large American flag tied to the end of a long lodgepole and was standing in front of his lodge, holding the pole, with the flag fluttering in the gray light of the winter dawn. I heard him call to the people not to be afraid, that the soldiers would not hurt them; then the troops opened fire." It was a slaughter.

Many Indians ran for the high bank of the creek, where they desperately tried to bury themselves in the sand. The Coloradans followed, firing round after round. Some women exposed their bodies so they would not be mistaken for warriors, but this only inflamed the ruthless fury of the troops. As George Bent ran down the creek, he could see "men, women, and children lying thickly scattered in the sand, some dead and the rest too badly wounded to move." In the end, the bodies of some two hundred Cheyennes and Arapahos littered the cold ground, three-quarters of them women and children. Chivington, reflecting his disposition, boasted that his men killed nearly five hundred.

"Colorado soldiers have again covered themselves with glory," the *Rocky Mountain News* gloated. But there was public outrage in the East. A congressional committee investigated and issued a scathing report. Witnesses testified that the troops had carved the genitals from women's bodies, stretching them over their saddle horns or pinning them to their hats. Governor Evans was forced to resign, but Chivington had already left the state militia and was beyond the reach of military law. He became a sheriff of Denver and later served as county coroner. Hating Indians was respectable in the West. In 1869 western commander General Philip H. Sheridan reportedly put the public sentiment into a memorable phrase: "The only good Indians I ever saw were dead."

In the aftermath of the Sand Creek Massacre, the entire central plains exploded into war. Previously, the Cheyennes had been divided on the issue of war or peace, but the Colorado brutality settled the matter. In early 1865 Sioux, Cheyenne, and Arapaho bands retaliated for Chivington's attack by burning virtually all the ranches and stage stations along the South Platte, killing scores of American men, women, and children. Efforts to subdue the warriors were ineffective. "At night the whole valley was lighted up with the flames of burning ranches and stage stations," said George Bent.

Now, as the struggle for the Union concluded in the East, and war-weary soldiers clamored to be sent home to their families, it became difficult for the U.S. Army to find volunteers for the renewed Indian fighting in the West. In response to this crisis, Congress sanctioned the recruitment of soldiers from the ranks of Confederate prisoners-of-war and authorized the formation of the African American Twenty-fourth and Twenty-fifth infantries and the Ninth and Tenth cavalries, the famous "Buffalo Soldiers," as the Indians called them because of the texture of the men's hair. The black troops were segregated and paid significantly less than white soldiers, but they compiled an extraordinary record for discipline, courage, and high morale; over the next quarter-century fourteen troopers won the Congressional Medal of Honor. Thus, in 1865, regiments of Yankee veterans, "Whitewashed Rebs," and former slaves joined in the fight against the western Indians.

Chapter 8 **Mining Frontiers**

"Boys, by God I believe I have found a gold mine!" James Marshall, in charge of constructing a sawmill for John Sutter, shouted these words on January 24, 1848, and began the California gold rush. Some Americans argued that this discovery, coming just ten days before the official announcement of the treaty ending the Mexican War, was a kind of divine reparation. "God kept that coast for a people of the Pilgrim blood," preached a New England minister.

It might seem curious that the Spanish, who had previously seemed so preoccupied with precious metals, had not found gold. The Spanish economy in California, however, did not create conditions conducive to such discovery. Settlements there clustered around the harbors, and the missions were spread over the coastal valleys. Stock raising does not involve disturbing the earth, so minerals were unlikely to be revealed, even accidentally. Newly arrived Anglo-American farmers in the Sacramento valley, however, wanted wooden houses, and men such as John Sutter built sawmills among the pines in the foothills to meet the demand. Sawmills require waterpower, the diversion of water from stream to spillway, and it was at such a site that Marshall found those first bits of glittering gold. Americans discovered gold in California because of their demand for lumber, not the workings of Providence.

The California gold rush was the prelude to the exploitation of the Far West during the second half of the nineteenth century. Up to the 1840s, the United States absorbed and incorporated new territory contiguously, but the gold rush caused the sudden movement of tens of thousands across the continent to the Pacific coast. The 1850 census revealed a new pattern that would characterize this new West: clusters of settlement separated by hundreds of miles. From California, prospectors spread out across the mountains and deserts, making a series of strikes that spawned a seemingly endless round of rushes: to the Fraser River in British Columbia in 1858; to the Colorado Rockies west of the emerging city of Denver, as well as the Washoe country of Nevada in 1859; to Idaho and Montana in 1860 and 1862; to the Black Hills of the Dakotas in 1876; to Leadville, Colorado, and Tombstone, Arizona, in 1877; to the Coeur d'Alene region of Idaho in 1883; and, closing out the era, to the Yukon country of Canada and to Alaska in 1896–97. Each rush created new isolated centers of population.

Practically every rush also presented the familiar kaleidoscope of lonely prospectors with their mules and pans, crowds of jostling men of every conceivable nationality, jerry-built stores along muddy streets, mirrored saloons, prostitutes and dance hall girls, outlaws, claim jumpers, and vigilance committees—all soon supplanted by smelters and mills, slag heaps and underground burrows, company towns, and labor unions, leading finally to strikes with the fist instead of the shovel. Mining added a significant dimension to the social, economic, and imaginative development of the West.

John Sutter tried to keep the discovery of gold at his millrace quiet. A vain hope. But he succeeded in slowing the spread of the news; reports did not reach San Francisco until May. Within days, the town was emptied of able-bodied men, and the cry of gold quickly spread throughout the territory. Editors suspended publication of their newspapers, and city councils adjourned for months. Americans, Mexicans, and Indians alike poured into the foothills with picks, shovels, and pans.

For five hundred miles along the Sierra Nevada, the icy streams of the higher range had eroded the rock, washing out the gold-bearing ores and depositing them in the alluvial sands of the rivers. A person needed little knowledge and minimal skill to swish the sand in a flat pan with enough water to wash away the lightest ores, leaving the heavier gold grains in the bottom. This was *placer mining*, and during the summer of 1848 many miners struck a *bonanza*. These were Spanish words, and the fact that both were incorporated into the American argot at this moment suggests the important role of Mexican miners in educating the first rushers, called the "forty-eighters." In 1848 plenty of streams held an abundance of sand for all who came, and the lore was rich in tales of miners panning gold worth thousands of dollars in a week. A territorial report estimated that $10 million was taken out of Sierra streams that first year.

President Polk confirmed the rumors about California in his State of the Union address in early December 1848. It was the spark that ignited the frenzy of 1849. Apocryphal stories circulated through the newspapers—tales of the man who washed $16 in gold dust from his beard, of the sick miner who sweated out gold worth $49.50 in a Turkish bath. (Multiply these figures by about twenty-five to convert to 2005 values.) This "news" hit while the country was still awash with thousands of dislocated veterans of the Mexican War, not only in the United States but in Mexico. In Europe, residents of the capital cities were recovering from the revolutions of 1848 that had pushed a fearful establishment into severely repressive

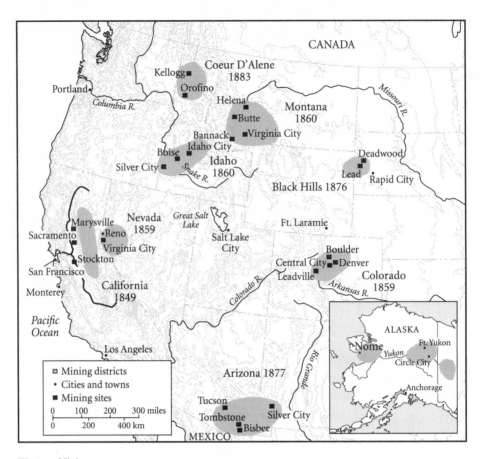

Western Mining

measures. In Ireland, rural people were suffering from a long famine resulting from a blight on potatoes. By slim clippers around the Horn; by square-rigged ships from Hawaii, Australia, and China; over the Isthmus of Panama and across the plains and mountains, Sweet Betsy from Pike and more than eighty thousand Ikes jostled into California.

But the supply of placer gold was running thin before the first of the forty-niners arrived in California. The big money-makers of the gold rush were the men who realized that fortunes could be made selling supplies—like the durable canvas and denim pants that made a fortune for Levi Strauss, a young Jewish merchant. Prices skyrocketed, and miners found that most of what they made ended in the pockets of merchants. Just procuring initial supplies—pan and pick, tent and blanket, food and incidentals—easily cost a miner more than $100.

Placer mining gave way to quartz mining, which required elaborate processes to extract the gold from the rock. In 1852, only four years after the first discovery, 108 crushing mills already pounded out the ores that time and the river had not yet reached. As early as 1853, men were using high-pressured jets of water to flush mountains of alluvial deposits into the rivers. These hydraulic operations required capital investment as well as a large labor force, so the disillusioned Ikes who had rushed across the continent to get rich quick were forced to work for wages. Mining ceased being an individual pursuit and instead became a corporate enterprise.

The amount of gold and silver dug out of California and the rest of the West over the next several decades dwarfed all previous mining, not only in the United States but worldwide. In 1848 and 1849, the federal government reported the mining of seventy-six tons of gold, more than twice the total recorded since bookkeeping had begun in 1792. The production of silver, previously calculated in thousands of ounces, surged to millions after the discovery in 1859 of the Comstock Lode in Nevada. As a result, world production of gold and silver more than doubled in the second half of the century.

Historians debate the economic effects. For most ordinary Americans of the day, the California gold rush began an economic boom that would continue until the Panic of 1873. From 1848 to 1851, the nation's gold coinage increased twentyfold, creating a unique opportunity for the expansion of the money supply with only a mild rate of inflation (the Civil War years excepted). This came while the manufacturing Northeast was moving into a phase of self-sustained industrial growth. Not only did the new supply of specie provide a medium for the greatly increased pace of investment during this critical half-century of industrialization, but much of that investment was financed by western gold and silver. Precious metals made possible the importation of capital goods, particularly iron for railroads.

Furthermore, California gold created the first of the great extractive industries that dominated the economic history of the American West for a full century. Mining, lumbering, ranching, and commercial farming were all enterprises in which western workers produced raw materials and sent them to distant markets. Each was highly susceptible to wild economic swings of boom and bust. Each was financed in large part by eastern capitalists with little regard for the balanced economic development of the West. According to American mythology, of course, a gold rush was supposed to be a golden opportunity for "the little man" to improve his social standing. But the idea of frontier social mobility best applied to earlier Wests, not to the industrial Far West born during the California gold rush. The California experience pointed the way to a new kind of economic colonialism.

Still, the gold rush jump-started the California economy. Within months of Marshall's discovery, the state had become the center of a thriving Pacific market. Western mining booms were a vivid demonstration of the growing interdependence of the world's economies. Into the port of San Francisco in 1849 came dozens of foreign ships loaded with Chilean wheat, Mexican coffee and cocoa, Australian potatoes, Chinese sugar and rice, and Alaskan coal, fish, and even ice. As soon as they docked their ships and unloaded their cargoes, the foreign crews jumped ship and rushed for the diggings. San Francisco's waterfront soon was clogged with rotting hulks from all over the world.

Gold rush society was composed of the most polyglot collection of nationalities since Babel. Mrs. Louisa Amelia Knapp Smith Clappe, who wrote literate and observant letters to eastern newspapers under the pseudonym Dame Shirley, walked through a mining camp called Indian Bar and overheard conversations in English, French, Spanish, German, Italian, and Kanakan (Hawaiian), as well as various American Indian languages. In the middle of the nineteenth century, gold rush California was perhaps the most multicultural spot on the globe.

But for the lapse of a few years, of course, American citizens would have been the foreigners. In the California mining regions, however, there had been no previously settled Mexican Californio population, and with the flood of forty-niners, Americans instantly formed the majority. But thousands of Latino miners were not far behind, including hundreds of Peruvians and Chileans. Many were experienced placer miners, in great demand as technical advisers. It was one of several glimmers of interethnic cooperation.

The California constitutional convention included eight Californios among the forty-eight elected delegates. But during a contentious debate over granting the franchise to former "male citizens of Mexico"—a provision of the Treaty of Guadalupe Hidalgo—one delegate proposed amending the phrase with the adjective "white." Californios protested, but the amendment was approved, along with another provision barring Indians and Negroes from testifying against whites in court. Several years later, one of the Californio delegates, Manuel Dominguez of Los Angeles, a wealthy landowner and elected county supervisor, was prohibited from testifying in a civil suit because the court declared that "Indian blood" ran in his veins.

As it became evident that not everyone was going to get rich in the goldfields, the tight jaw of prejudice set in. "Mexicans have no business in this country," a veteran of the late war wrote to the *Stockton Times*. "The men were made to be shot at, and the women were made for *our* purposes." Yet there is reason to suspect that the hostility toward Mexicans had less to do with their race than with their skill and success as miners. The American miner may have learned to pan gold from his Mexican neighbor, wrote an English observer, but "as soon as [he] got an inkling of the system, with peculiar bad taste and ingenious feeling he organized a crusade against these obliging strangers."

Like most crusades, however, this one had official sponsorship. In January 1849, the military governor of California issued an order warning foreigners that they were mining "in direct violation of the laws." There were, in fact, no such laws. Indeed, until the federal government formally opened the public domain to private mining in 1866, practically every miner in the West was an illegal trespasser. But the order provided official cover for groups of miners calling for the removal of foreigners from the diggings. The mass expulsions of Mexicans awaited the enactment of a Foreign Miner's Tax, a prohibitive monthly levy of twenty dollars on all "aliens," by the California legislature in the spring of 1850. Over the next several months, mobs of American miners accompanied county tax assessors on their rounds, collecting the tax from Mexican miners who could pay and driving the rest from the mines. Most of the expelled miners probably would have qualified as citizens under the terms of the Treaty of Guadalupe Hidalgo. There is no evidence, however, that any assessor bothered to distinguish Mexican American citizens from Mexican aliens, nor that foreigners from Europe were required to pay a penny.

Some Californians protested this latest version of removal. One meeting of miners resolved "that the citizens of this Bar will discountenance any act of violence committed against peaceable persons of any race." The *Daily Alta California* of San Francisco lectured its readers: "Shame! Shame! To spit on a man because he was born under a warmer sun than shone upon our birth." Unfortunately, it would not be the last time humane voices found themselves drowned out by the vulgar chorus of political pandering and popular prejudice.

The place of departing Mexicans was soon taken by another group of immigrant miners. Several hundred Chinese arrived in California in 1849, and within a year they were passing through the Golden Gate by the thousands. By 1859 an estimated twenty-four thousand Chinese were working the California diggings, and they joined in the rush to each subsequent strike in the West. The Chinese proved to be diligent and enterprising workers, often forming companies to work over the deposits that American miners had rejected. They came as temporary sojourners. Most were married, but almost none brought their wives to *Gam Saan*, or "Gold Mountain." In the cities, towns, and mining camps of the West, Chinese men clustered together in their own little "Chinatowns" that included social clubs, temples, opium dens, and brothels, most under the control of Chinese companies and "tongs" (fraternal societies). In the eyes of many white Americans, this grouping made the Chinese even more suspect than the Mexicans. The "clannishness" Americans loved to hate, however, was largely the result of discrimination and prejudice. In 1852 the California legislature passed a new Foreign Miner's Tax targeting the Chinese. Before it was voided by the Civil Rights Act of 1870, Chinese miners had contributed a total of more than $5 million, a quarter of the state's total revenue for those years, to the state's coffers.

Despite prejudice, discrimination, and attempts at removal, the Chinese, the Mexicans, and immigrants from dozens of other countries were in the West to stay. Whether narrow-minded Anglo-Americans liked it or not, a multicultural West was being born.

When California's territorial governor toured the diggings in the summer of 1848, he found four thousand miners at work, "of whom more than half were Indians." Many Indians labored for Anglo and Mexican contractors, but others in that first year mined for themselves or for their communities. Indian mining, however, ended abruptly with the arrival of the forty-niners. Suddenly, Indian homelands were overrun by tens of thousands of Americans. Violence broke out immediately. Miners drove the natives into the barren high Sierras, depriving them of their food supplies and forcing them to raid the livestock of valley ranchers in order to survive.

Ranchers retaliated with attacks on Indian retreats in the mountains. Americans, wrote one federal official, "value the life of an Indian just as they do that of a *cayota* or a wolf, and embrace every occasion to shoot [them] down."

Much of the violence was condoned, even sponsored, by government officials. In a special message to the legislature, Governor Peter Burnett made it clear, declaring, "A war of extermination will continue to be waged between the races until the Indian race becomes extinct." Over the next few years, with the encouragement and sponsorship of the state, miners, ranchers, and militia murdered thousands of Indians. It was the clearest case of genocide in the history of the American frontier.

Adding greatly to native suffering was the Act for the Government and Protection of Indians, passed by the California legislature in 1850. The pretense was that the law provided a way of disciplining dangerous Indian vagrants and caring for dependent Indian orphans; but in fact, under its cover, thousands of Indian men, women, and children were kidnapped and sold to Anglo and Mexican employers. Spanish and Mexican California had been built by forced Indian labor, and until this pernicious law was repealed in 1863, Anglo-Californians contributed their own dark pages to that history. The conclusion of anthropologists Robert Heizer and Alan Almquist is admirably candid: "This was a legalized form of slavery of California Indians. No other possible construction can be made of the facts."

As a result of the genocidal violence, the forced labor, and the inevitable epidemics of disease, the Indian population of California, estimated at 150,000 in 1848, fell to only 30,000 by 1860: 120,000 lives lost in just twelve years, a record of brutality without parallel in the history of the United States. A minority of the remaining natives lived in isolated rancheritas, others in dingy shanties on the outskirts of towns and cities, eking out a livelihood as cheap day laborers. It wasn't until the mid-twentieth century that California Indians used the courts to obtain compensation for the lands stolen from them during the gold rush, but the final awards totaled less than $1,000 per person.

The mining strikes in the West were an unmitigated disaster for the Indians. The Colorado rush of 1859 led directly to the massacre of the Cheyennes at Sand Creek. Thus when gold was discovered in the Yellowstone country in 1864, the Sioux, longtime allies of the Cheyennes, took it as an ominous sign. After three years of fighting, chief Red Cloud succeeded in 1868 in winning a treaty that "set apart for the absolute and undisturbed use and occupation of the Indians" the "Great Sioux Reservation," which stretched from the Missouri River westward through the Black Hills. Sensing that the days of Indian armed resistance were over, Red Cloud led the majority of his people onto the reservation, promising to remain there. But militant leaders like Crazy Horse and Sitting Bull opposed giving up access to the hunting grounds of Montana, and their followers totaled perhaps a third of the Western Sioux.

In 1874 an army expedition commanded by Colonel George Armstrong Custer discovered gold in the Black Hills, on the Sioux reservation. Within two years the town of Deadwood was swarming with ten thousand miners, and the nearby Homestake mine was exploiting the richest lode of ore in American history. The treaty of 1868 required the army to keep miners and settlers off the reservation, but officers deliberately looked the other way, hoping that miners on the ground would force the Sioux into agreeing to sell the Black Hills. But the militant Sioux leader Sitting Bull was contemptuous. "I want you to go and tell the Great Father that I do not want to sell any land to the government," he declared. And bending down he picked up a pinch of dust: "Not even as much as this." With gold beckoning, the federal government was in no mood to wait on stubborn Indians. Reasoning that if they smashed the rejectionist Sioux they would have an easier time negotiating a bargain price with more cooperative chiefs like Red Cloud, officials began planning for a campaign of total war.

Knowing what was coming, free bands of Sioux, Cheyenne, and Arapaho joined together for the summer buffalo hunt of 1876. In June, with leaves full in groves along the Powder River and the Little Bighorn, more than four thousand men, women, and children assembled in what was the largest encampment any of the chiefs could remember. On June 25, Colonel Custer, leading six hundred troops of the Seventh Cavalry on a reconnoiter, came upon the combined Indian camp. Custer was a cavalry hero of the Civil War who had become a leader in the army's struggle against the plains Indians. In 1868 at the Washita River in Indian Territory he had led a victorious charge through a sleeping village of Southern Cheyennes that left 103 Indians dead, including Chief Black Kettle, sad survivor of the Sand Creek Massacre. Now Custer would try to repeat the same maneuver at the Little Bighorn. "Hurrah, boys, we've got them," he called out to his men as they prepared for the engagement. All the players were in place for the most famous moment in the war for the plains.

Foolishly refusing to wait for reinforcements, Custer made a fatal decision to divide his forces; he flanked the encampment to the north with about two hundred men while Major Marcus Reno attacked the southern end. "Soldiers are here! Young men, go out and fight them," cried an old man in the camp. Wooden Leg, an eighteen-year-old Cheyenne warrior, joined the skirmish and recalled, "Many hundreds of Indians on horseback were dashing to and from in front of a body of soldiers. . . . Thousands of arrows were falling among them." Suddenly the American soldiers panicked, mounted, and raced for the river. "We gained rapidly on them," Wooden Leg said. "I saw a Sioux put an arrow into the back of a soldier's head. Another arrow went into his shoulder. He tumbled from his horse to the ground." The warriors inflicted heavy casualties on Reno's troops, but the Americans were able to regroup and hold out in an entrenched position until the Indians withdrew the next evening.

The troops under Custer's command were not so lucky. None of them would see the sun go down that day. Custer seems to have directed them in an attack on the northern fringe of the large camp. "I saw flags come up over the hill," recalled the Cheyenne chief Two Moons, "then the soldiers rose all at once." He and hundreds of other warriors met the charge head-on, and Custer's troops were quickly overwhelmed and surrounded. "The shooting was quick, quick," said Two Moons. "The smoke was like a great cloud, and everywhere the Sioux went the dust rose like smoke." The battle lasted only minutes. Afterward, Sitting Bull's nephew White Bull was walking among the dead with another Sioux who had known some of the soldiers. He pointed out a naked corpse, identified it as Custer's, and said, "He thought he was the greatest man in the world, and there he is."

Custer sought personal acclaim, the kind the nation bestowed on those who hunted down Indians and took care of them permanently. But indirectly he was also the instrument of many western interests—the men of the gold rush to the Black Hills, railroad investors who watched their tracks rusting because the Sioux would not lay down their arms, ranchers who saw the plains ready for expanded herds of cattle from Kansas and Texas, and settlers bearing seeds of wheat and hollyhocks and dreams of neat furrows across the earth. Compared with the seriousness of Sitting Bull, who believed that his people must have the buffalo country or perish, Custer with his flowing hair, his red-top boots, and his grandiose ambition may seem faintly ridiculous. But he represented historical forces of immense magnitude, and in his death he achieved an apotheosis that outranks almost any other American hero.

The famous "Last Stand" of the Seventh Cavalry turned into the last major stand of the Sioux. The U.S. Army pursued the free bands relentlessly, keeping them from hunting or gathering food. No rations were distributed on the reservation. When the war ended that winter, it was not because the Americans had beaten the Indians in battle, but because they starved them into submission. By the end of the year, the reservation chiefs agreed to cede the Black Hills.

Not until the following spring, however, did Crazy Horse surrender at the Red Cloud Agency in Nebraska. Rumors understandably flew that he would not remain on the reservation. When the army tried to arrest him in September, he offered just enough show of resistance to provide the soldiers with a pretext for bayoneting him. Crazy Horse died within hours. Sitting Bull meanwhile had escaped with his followers across the border into Canada, where he petitioned the authorities for food and land. But worried about their own Indian problems and the precedent such action might set, Canadian officials refused. Eventually, Sitting Bull was forced to return to the United States, where federal authorities imprisoned him for years. Yet to his people he remained a beloved leader to whom they listened. Sitting Bull summed up his feelings about the Americans in a phrase that more than a century later still resonates: "The love of possession is a disease with them."

In 1867 the United States purchased Russian America for the bargain-basement price of $7.2 million (the rough equivalent of $94 million in 2005 dollars). Although some Americans ridiculed the region as nothing more than an icebox, others saw it as a storehouse. To Senator Charles Sumner (who came up with the name *Alaska*, derived from an Aleutian word meaning "great land"), the region was the sum of its resources: "forests of pine and fir waiting for the ax, mineral products among which are coal and copper, if not iron, silver, lead and gold; . . . furs, including precious skins of the black fox and sea-otter; and lastly the fisheries, which in waters superabundant with animal life beyond any of the globe, seem to promise a new commerce." For most Americans, however, Alaska did not register on their mental maps until the discovery of gold there.

The Russian-America Company had not been interested in gold. Its principal concern had been furs, and it profited from the supply offered by the Tlingit Indians of the Pacific coast, who controlled much of the trade with the interior tribes. The organization of the Tlingit economy shifted from subsistence to commerce, but it only strengthened their traditional culture. Indeed, this was the golden age of Tlingit art: beautiful Chilkat blankets, fabulously painted wooden screens, and totem poles carved from monumental Sitka spruce. The Tlingits offer an instructive contrast to the general devastation of Indian peoples by colonialism.

But the Americans were little interested in continuing the operations of the Russian-America Company, and consequently, the Tlingits lost their valuable intermediary role. When the Tlingits resisted the American presence, the newcomers bombarded their coastal villages from offshore. The decline of Tlingit power and prosperity dates not from the first contact with Europeans but from the beginning of the American period. Indians found few roles to play in the mining economy that the Americans wished to establish. Thus it was ironic that the first important discovery took place in 1880 when a Tlingit chief led French-Canadian Joe Juneau to a coastal site where the miners found gold. Within a year the number of white men at the Juneau mines was greater than the population of all the rest of Alaska combined. The Juneau miners produced more than $170 million over the next sixty years. Tlingits worked alongside East European immigrants in the mills and mines, but they were prevented from sharing in the prosperity. A number of Indians tried to file mining claims, but because they were not citizens, the federal government rejected their applications.

Soon, Tlingit guides were leading prospectors over the coastal mountains to explore the rivers of the interior. Gold was discovered on a feeder stream of the Yukon River in the mid-1880s, and within a few years as many as a thousand Americans, Canadians, and Indians were working the interior valley. At first, yields were low. But in 1896 George Carmack and his Indian partners Dawson Charley and Skookum Jim struck a bonanza, and by the next year a full-scale rush to the Yukon was on. Over the next several years, some one hundred thousand miners steamed north from Seattle through the Inside Passage. Dawson Charley, Skookum Jim, and a few other Indians made fortunes, but for most natives the effects of the gold rush were disastrous. The miners disrupted the pattern of native hunting and fishing, and in order to support themselves, Indians were forced to work as laborers and packers. Following a familiar story, many communities were devastated by disease and alcoholism. Gold again proved to be a plague for Indians.

Luckily for the Indians, most of the miners soon moved on. Western miners had the highest rates of mobility of any group in American history. In two California mining communities, for example, of every one hundred people there in 1850, only five remained in 1856. When rumors swept through California in 1858 of rich pay dirt in British Columbia, some thirty thousand men left for the Fraser River. The following year there was a similar rush to Colorado. From there, many hurried on to the great Comstock Lode in Nevada, where a series of independent finds had been made by such prospectors as James "Old Virginny" Fenimore and Henry "Old Pancake" Comstock. In their heyday, more than $300 million was taken from those mines, but that money would feed the fortunes of only a small group of "Silver Kings" in San Francisco. Henry Comstock sold one of his claims for $11,000, the other for two mules, and then rambled on to Oregon, Idaho, and Montana.

Comstock's mobility was typical. "I've dug in Alaska and made a bit," says Howard, the old prospector in B. Traven's classic novel of gold fever, *The Treasure of the Sierra Madre*. "I've been in the crowd in British Columbia and made there at least my fair wages. I was down in Australia, where I made my fare back home, with a few hundred left over to cure me of the stomach trouble I caught down there. I've dug in Montana and in Colorado and I don't know where else." This rushing between dozens of gold, silver, and hardrock mining regions for seventy years created in the West a sense of obsessive restlessness. Gold rushing was a kind of nineteenth-century rite of passage for American men, an opportunity, as contemporaries put it, "to see the elephant." The gold might be elusive—but oh, the thrill of the rush!

Gold rush camps were predominantly male. The California census of 1850 reported that women made up less than 8 percent of the state's population, and in the diggings their numbers were even lower. Countless numbers of "gold rush widows" were left behind, tending the children, running the farm or the business, waiting for the mail, worrying through the days and nights. Women responded in a variety of ways. Some took their husband's absence as an opportunity to claim new rights. From the Colorado mines James Fergus wrote his wife Pamelia that his sojourn would "be a great benefit to you, by throwing you on your own resources and learning you to do business for yourself." He got more than he bargained for. When they finally reunited after four years, she was no longer the acquiescent wife. They disagreed, sometimes in public, and frequently quarreled. But eventually they adjusted, and many years after his dear wife had died, James confessed that he and Pamelia had never really understood each other "until she had her own way."

The few wives who accompanied their husbands to the camps immediately found themselves in demand. Upon her arrival at the diggings near Nevada City, California, Luzena Wilson was interrupted at her campfire by a miner gazing longingly at her simple cooking. He "said he would give ten dollars for bread made by a woman, and laid a shiney gold piece in my hand." Knowing a good thing when she saw it, Wilson determined to set up her own makeshift boarding house. "With

GEORGE WASHINGTON
PRESIDENT.
1792.

Peace medal struck by the federal government and presented to the Iroquois leader Red Jacket by President Washington in 1792. Using peace medals as a visual symbol of good relations was a practice begun by British, French, and Spanish colonial powers and continued by the United States. From the Buffalo Historical Society, *Publications* 3 (1884).

Indian Record of a Battle between the Pawnees and Konzas, being a Fac Simile of a delineation upon a Bison Robe

American Indians had their own traditions of visual art. This copy of a Pawnee rendering of a battle with Kansa (or Kaw) warriors was produced by Samuel Seymour, an artist attached to the Stephen Long expedition to the Great Plains in 1819–20. From "The original views drawn by the artist S. Seymour during the expedition from Pittsburgh to the Rocky Mountains under the command of Major Stephen A. Long" (c. 1820).

Gallery of important Indian leaders of the early nineteenth century. *Clockwise from top left:* Red Jacket (Seneca, Iroquois Confederacy), from Thomas McKenney and James Hall, *History of the Indian Tribes of North America* (1836–44); Tenskatawa (the "Shawnee Prophet"), from James Otto Lewis, *The Aboriginal Port-Folio* (1835); Major Ridge (Cherokee), from McKenney and Hall; and Black Hawk (Sauk), from Lewis.

Gallery of American frontier leaders. *Clockwise from top left:* David Crockett, Tennessee politician and Alamo martyr, from *Col. Crockett's Exploits and Adventures in Texas* (1836); Sam Houston, leader of Texas independence, from a lithograph copy of a daguerreotype by Matthew Brady (c. 1860); Jim Bridger, famous mountain man, copy of a photograph taken in Saint Louis (1857); Brigham Young, leader of the Mormon migration to Utah, from Frederick Hawkins Piercy, *Route from Liverpool to Great Salt Lake Valley* (1855).

Captain Lewis & Clark holding a Council with the Indians.

First visual depiction of the negotiations between western Indian tribes and captains Meriwether Lewis and William Clark during their exploration in 1804–6. From Patrick Gass, *A Journal of the Voyages and Travels of a Corps of Discovery* (1812).

Meeting between the Stephen Long expedition of 1819–20 and the Pawnees. Such negotiations were a regular part of the explorations sponsored by the federal government. Samuel Seymour, from "The original views drawn by the artist S. Seymour during the expedition from Pittsburgh to the Rocky Mountains under the command of Major Stephen A. Long" (c. 1820).

The 1845 published report by John Charles Frémont *(left)* of his expedition to the Rocky Mountains was a best seller, largely owing to the literary skill of his wife, Jessie Benton Frémont *(right)*, the daughter of a powerful senator from Missouri. Engraving by J. C. Buttre (c. 1845); photograph by Carleton E. Watkins (c. 1860).

Frémont's report publicized the overland route to Oregon and California. This romantic engraving, with its fantasy landscape, was one of the first published views of the overland migration. From *California: Its Past History, Its Present Position, Its Future Prospects* (1850).

YOUNG TEXAS IN REPOSE.

Left: Many northerners opposed the admission to the Union of Texas, a slave state. Propaganda could be vicious, as shown in this lithograph (1845) depicting Texas as a monstrous slave driver atop a whipped and prostate slave. *Right:* While there was considerable opposition to the subsequent war with Mexico, there was also considerable popular support, as suggested by this sheet music cover (c. 1846) celebrating the first victories of General Zachary Taylor.

BATTLE OF CERRO GORDO.
APRIL 18 1847.

Hundreds of popular prints, both Mexican and American, chronicled the progress of the Mexican War, but this lithograph (1847) is one of the few that presented both sides with equal respect. Cerro Gordo was a small village where the Mexican army tried but failed to turn back the American drive toward Mexico City.

The conquest of the Far West was accomplished with a great deal of lethal violence. In 1868 at the Washita River in Indian Territory, Lieutenant Colonel George Armstrong Custer led a vicious charge through a sleeping village of Cheyennes that left 103 dead. From Custer, *My Life on the Plains* (1874).

Ralph Morrison, a buffalo hunter, was murdered and scalped near Fort Dodge, Kansas, in the immediate aftermath of the Washita attack. Photograph by William Soule (1868).

The cast of characters in the drama of the American West was always diverse. *Clockwise from top left:* Unidentified African American Buffalo Soldier poses with his Colt revolver (tintype, c. 1870). George Bent, son of trader William Bent, and his wife Magpie, daughter of Black Kettle, chief of the Southern Cheyennes (photograph, c. 1867). American soldier with Mexican children during the Mexican War (daguerreotype, c. 1846).

my own hands I chopped stakes, drove them into the ground, and set up my table. I bought provisions at a neighboring store, and when my husband came back at night he found, mid the weird light of the pine torches, twenty miners eating at my table. Each man as he rose put a dollar in my hand and said I might count him as a permanent customer." Mrs. Wilson's boarding produced far more income than Mr. Wilson's mining. The census of 1850 recorded only twenty-three women in Nevada City, but fifteen of them were running boarding houses or taverns.

At the end of the century, a number of single women joined the rushes precisely to take advantage of such entrepreneurial opportunities. "Yes, there are women going into the mines alone," one returned Klondiker declared, "widows and lone women to do whatever they could for the miners, with the hope of getting big pay." Belinda Mulrooney was one of those who set out on her own. By the time she was twenty-six, she had become one of the wealthiest residents of the Klondike, holding a number of claims and managing several businesses.

It was inevitable, given their overwhelming male character, that the camps attracted prostitutes by the dozens, many from outside the state, and even the country. Crowded into one small house in the camp of Coloma, California, a census enumerator found six prostitutes ranging in age from seventeen to thirty and hailing from Canada, Ireland, Chile, Mexico, and New York. Prostitution could be a profitable business, according to historian Paula Petrik. A "fancy lady" in late-nineteenth-century Helena, Montana, could expect a monthly income of $233, compared with less than $100 a month for a miner. A small group of "dowager queens of the *demimonde*" became prominent landladies in Helena's tenderloin. But as Anne Butler demonstrates in her careful study of western prostitutes, most came from the poorest and most exploited groups on the frontier and were often the victims of violence, disease, and drug abuse, which could result in suicide.

Miners had to create a corpus of mining law, for which they had almost no usable precedent. Practical questions arose immediately. Who owned what? How could a man stake out land on which to dig or pan for gold? How much could he claim—a mountain ridge or a whole valley? Where would the deed be recorded? Could a man own land and leave it to be worked later? Who would protect the weak from the strong, the unarmed from the armed?

In California, in a process that was repeated hundreds of times, a group of miners came together in a mass meeting, elected officers, and drafted a few rules. No one has estimated how often this occurred throughout the West. Similarities among rules from place to place emerged, partly because the problems were predictable and partly because of the movement of men from one place to another. Models worked out in California were often adopted elsewhere. In general, the laws allowed a man to stake out any "reasonable" amount of land, by which was meant an amount he could work in a season. He had to mark it clearly and file a claim with the local recorder. Most important, he had to actually work the land. If he left it, he lost it. There would be no absentee owners in the mines. The Spanish-Mexican influence was evident in the attachment of water rights to all land. Thus, even if a man claimed a parcel far back from the banks of a stream, he still had the right to divert a reasonable amount of water to wash his dry gravels. Conflicting claims were arbitrated by committees, panels, and juries, or sometimes by entire town meetings. In some respects, these miners' codes appear highly idealistic, weighted in favor of the small miner. Large mining companies amassing extensive holdings found them quaint and irrelevant and lacking uniformity. As individualism in the mines gave way to corporatism, local codes gave way to state law. By then, the first comers, like Henry Comstock, were long gone.

Yet many westerners looked back fondly on the days of the miners' meetings. They admired the idea of men applying common sense together to their immediate problems. But when life and civil liberties are challenged, the lack of humbug and the disregard for due process appear far less attractive. Legal complexity is what protects people from harm until they are proven guilty. In truth, the miners' meetings were a principal agency of violence against Indians, Latinos, and Chinese, and miners were quick to resort to lynchings and vigilante action, with or without the approval of courts and legal systems. The spirit of the Regulators and the Paxton Boys was alive and well in the Far West.

The social ramifications of gold rushes spread widely. Storekeepers had to be supplied with goods, of course. Urban centers, merchandising, freighting, shipbuilding, and the merchant marine felt the boom. One dramatic effect was seen in the clipper ship, designed to bring cargoes as quickly as possible from the East to San Francisco. In their high noon during the 1850s, the ships placed America in the forefront of the world's maritime powers. In California, fortunes were made by men who could corner markets in crucial items. Merchant Collis P. Huntington would row out in a dinghy to meet incoming ships with so many gold bags around his belt that capsizing would have sent him straight to the bottom. With gold on the barrel head, he would buy every shovel on board.

The effects were not simply felt in trading and transportation but in local farming as well. The cattle ranches of southern California supplied meat for the northern mines, and Yankees like the elder James Irvine acquired the vast acreage that would later become the Irvine Ranch (and still later the planned city of Irvine) in order to participate in the boom. In the San Joaquin valley, the increase in wheat farming was even more dramatic. Production there in the decade after 1850 grew annually, from seventeen thousand bushels to nearly six million. This initial expansion was underwritten by eastern capital.

By the 1870s the mining industry throughout the Far West was concentrated in the hands of a wealthy elite. Some of these "bonanza kings" had clawed their way up from the diggings. George Hearst, father of the newspaper baron William Randolph Hearst, crossed the plains on foot in 1850 and within a few years had made a pile in placer and quartz mining. In 1859 he invested in the Comstock Lode and laid the foundation for a great fortune. "If you're ever inclined to think that there's no such thing as luck," Hearst once remarked, "just think of me." In 1877 Hearst and his partners purchased the Homestake mine in the Black Hills, the most fabulous of all western gold mines. More frequently, capital came from investors who had never lifted a spade. Eastern and British capitalists loaned huge sums to western bankers who in turn invested in western mining.

Although individual prospecting and mining continued, by the 1860s the majority of western miners were laboring for corporations. Within a few decades, the most fabulous profits were in the mining of base rather than precious metals. After a brief moment as a gold and silver mining center, the Montana town of Butte became the mother of all western copper mining. At the turn of the century, there were copper strikes at places such as Globe and Bisbee in southern Arizona, and at the Bingham open-pit mine near Salt Lake City. These operations were in the hands of large mining corporations with names like Kennecott, Phelps-Dodge, and Anaconda. By the eve of World War I, the West was producing 90 percent of the nation's copper, as well as most of its lead and other heavy metals. Work in these hardrock mines was extremely dangerous. One investigation of Butte's deepest shaft measured the air temperature at 107°F, the water and rock temperatures at 113°F, and the relative humidity at 100 percent. The heat and humidity magnified the overwhelming odor of human excrement, sweat, blasting powder, rotting food, and tobacco. Men sometimes dropped dead from such conditions. The accident rate was incredibly high. Western mining had become the most hazardous industry in the country.

As early as the 1860s, miners began organizing unions. One of the biggest challenges confronting organizers was the ethnic diversity of the workers. The Americans fought the Irish, the Irish fought the English, the English fought the Germans, and all in turn fought the Mexicans and especially the Chinese. Unions tried to bring together groups of Americans and Europeans, although for the most part they excluded African Americans, Latinos, and Asians. The first successful labor organizing began at the Comstock Lode of Nevada, where miners in 1864 successfully conducted a strike to maintain the four-dollar daily wage. The struggle to maintain wage rates became the hallmark of western miners' unionism. But miners' unions were equally committed to mutual aid. In response to the dangers that beset miners on the job, unions created trust funds that paid benefits to sick and injured workers and provided assistance to miners' widows and orphans. This dual strategy characterized all the miners' unions of the West.

Miners remained relatively moderate in their demands until the strike for union recognition at the mines in the Coeur d'Alene region of Idaho in 1892. Seven miners died in a confrontation between strikers and troops. The next year, at a meeting in Butte, organizers formed the Western Federation of Miners (WFM). The federation called for a prohibition of the use of armed force against workers, a direct reference to the wounds of Coeur d'Alene. From the start, the WFM took a radical position, arguing for fundamental change in the economic and social systems of the country. Soon, organizers for the union were in nearly every mining town and camp in the West. As a young miner in Silver City, Idaho, Bill Haywood was approached by an organizer. "I had never heard of the need of workingmen organizing for mutual protection," Haywood later wrote in his colorful autobiography. Converted to the cause, Haywood soon rose to WFM leadership. Within a few years, the union enrolled more than fifty thousand members and became the strongest workers' organization in the American West.

The WFM was one of the unions that helped found the Industrial Workers of the World (IWW) in 1905. Not only miners but all kinds of migratory workers were attracted in large numbers to the IWW. This umbrella organization made it easy for itinerant workers to transfer from one local union to another as they moved from place to place. Members of the IWW, nicknamed Wobblies, also specialized in organizing among the unskilled, including African Americans, Mexicans, and Chinese. IWW leaders, Haywood included, were implacable foes of industrial capitalism, and over the next ten years they battled the captains of the West's great extractive industries in the name of revolution. In 1917, after the United States had entered World War I, they led strikes in the great copper mines of Montana and Arizona. Soon thereafter, President Woodrow Wilson's Department of Justice raided IWW offices throughout the West, arresting leaders on charges of obstructing the war effort. Local, state, and federal authorities combined to crush the movement.

But the IWW's success in organizing among miners, lumberjacks, longshoremen, and migrant harvest workers was an indication of the way in which the West had changed from the early days of the California rush. "Working men who travel westward are for the most part imbued with the restless spirit of enterprise, born of the desire for improved conditions," wrote one IWW organizer. "But unlike the old pioneer seeking a homestead and finding it, the modern wage worker who 'goes West' finds no alternative except to hunt for a master." The Wobblies were an ironic outcome, perhaps, of the great rush for gold and riches in the West. But they succeeded because they understood something essential about the restless way of life on the wageworkers' frontier.

Chapter 9 **The Power of the Road**

Bret Harte, western writer and editor of the *Overland Monthly*, was among the crowd at Promontory, Utah, in 1869, that witnessed the driving of the Golden Spike joining the tracks of the first transcontinental railroad. He watched as the steam engines, with overblown smokestacks and ox-sized cowcatchers, faced off for one of the most iconic photographs in American history. Harte wondered:

What was it the Engines said,
Pilots touching—head to head,
Facing on the single track,
Half a world behind each back?

No one could doubt the power of the railroad to transform. Over the previous quarter-century, railroads had reshaped the landscape of the eastern half of the continent, propelled the country into sustained industrial growth, and made possible the victory of the Union over the Confederacy. What miracles would they work for the West?

Once in place, the national railroad system would undergird a fabulously valuable exchange of people and products between East and West. Thousands of settlers would steam onto the plains and over the mountains to the Pacific coast, settling on farms and ranches and in dozens of rapidly growing cities and towns. The late-nineteenth-century West was inconceivable without the railroad. Back-country folks may have been isolated during an earlier era, but the railroad would provide the people of the West with easy access to eastern goods. In turn, the West would become a vast resource windfall for industrial America, supplying bread and meat, lumber and minerals. Wealth and power would ride the rails, but they would be ticketed eastbound, always moving from the West toward the metropolitan centers of the Atlantic coast and Europe. Consider what the railroad would bring to Montana: the copper boom at Butte, which attracted thousands of people, made enormous fortunes and turned that town into what one historian describes as "possibly the most miserable city in the Western world." The railroads would bring to the West the best and the worst of Gilded Age America. "What was it the Engines said?" Too often, they spoke with forked tongue.

The golden spike made earlier methods of transportation seem antiquated and primitive. But before 1869, people, mail, and freight had moved rather efficiently through the West by horse and mule. There had been unique regional variations: the two-wheeled, ox-drawn carts of the métis communities along the Missouri and Red rivers; the big, heavy Conestoga wagons, drawn by large teams of mules on the Santa Fe Trail. After the Mexican War the military became the biggest customer on the plains. In 1854 the army awarded a huge contract for supplying all its western posts to the company of Russell, Majors, and Waddell, which turned that firm into the largest freighting business in the country.

Federal subsidies were also critical to the development of western stage lines. The first large-scale federal contract for overland mail service went to John Butterfield of New York. The government provided grading, bridges, and 141 station stops along the "Ox Bow Route"—so-called because it avoided the Rockies in a great loop through the Southwest—2,795 miles from Saint Louis to Fort Yuma to Los Angeles, then up the inland valleys of California to San Francisco. These improvements, in addition to the annual federal subsidy of $600,000, allowed Butterfield and his partners to build the Overland Mail into a stage-coaching business of imperial design, employing eight hundred men to operate 250 leather-braced Concord coaches. With luck, passengers embarking in Saint Louis on the twice-weekly "jackass mail" could arrive in San Francisco twenty-five days later.

The Civil War forced Butterfield to abandon the Ox Bow Route, and for a brief period the focus shifted to the Pony Express, a mail service between Missouri and California organized by Russell, Majors, and Waddell. The Pony Express was speed incarnate. The jockey-sized riders covered 1,966 miles in an average of ten days, less than half the time of the Overland Mail. One hundred fifteen stations provided for the change of horses, and 120 men mounted the relays. In an effort to conserve weight, horsemen carried no guns; speed was their only protection. The mail pouches were kept slim by the prohibitive cost of the letters—$10 an ounce, the equivalent of $220 in 2005 dollars! The Express lasted for less than two years. Even as the first riders galloped over their route, they saw workers stringing telegraph wires westward from Kansas City and eastward from Sacramento. The lines were joined on October 24, 1861, killing the Pony Express. Russell, Majors, and Waddell went bankrupt the next year.

The firm was taken over by Ben Holladay, a boisterous westerner who won a series of million-dollar federal western mail and freighting contracts during the

Civil War and soon had twenty thousand wagons and coaches and more than 150,000 animals on the trails. Mark Twain delighted in the story of a boy who belittled Moses for the forty years he took to get the people of Israel across the desert: "Ben Holladay would have fetched them through in thirty-six hours." The finale in this series of mergers and takeovers occurred in 1866 when the American Express Company bought out Holladay, consolidated his lines with Butterfield's, and turned the entire operation over to the Wells Fargo division. But its coaching days were numbered. The stagecoach age had created comfortable fortunes, but these would be small potatoes compared with the fortunes ahead for the builders of the Pacific railroads. After leaving the stagecoach business, Ben Holladay wisely invested his capital in Pacific railroad stock.

By the 1850s there was no doubt that the transcontinental railroad would be built. The only questions were where, when, and how. Since it was assumed that the nation could initially afford only a single main line, the issue quickly became enmeshed in sectional antagonism. New Orleans, Saint Louis, and Chicago all competed to be the eastern terminus of the transcontinental trunk line. In 1853, hoping that scientists and engineers might undo this political knot, Congress passed the Pacific Railroad Survey Act to ascertain the "most practical and economical route for a railroad from the Mississippi River to the Pacific Ocean." Four western expeditions surveyed potential routes along the forty-seventh, thirty-eighth, thirty-fifth, and thirty-second parallels. The results were published by the federal government in fourteen magnificent volumes. But the survey teams concluded that good routes to the Pacific were possible at each of the four parallels, thus failing to transcend sectional politics.

The where, when, and how were settled only after the South seceded from the Union in 1861, leaving Washington to Lincoln and the Republicans. During this time, power shifted from agrarian to industrial and financial interests—what Charles and Mary Beard, in their classic history of the United States, called the "Second American Revolution." In the words of financial historian Robert Sharkey, the Republican program left "the developed East holding the whip over the undeveloped West and South." There would be plenty of complaints about "colonialism" from westerners in the future. But in 1862 their attention was transfixed by congressional action on two programs uppermost on the wish list of the West: the Homestead Act, which provided free land for settlers, and the Pacific Railroad Bill, which cleared the way for a transcontinental rail line.

The railroad legislation empowered two corporations, the Union Pacific Railroad and the Central Pacific Railroad, to construct (westward and eastward, respectively) "a continuous railroad" along the forty-second parallel, the Platte River route of the Overland Trail. The companies secured a four-hundred-foot right-of-way and were granted alternate sections of the public domain within ten miles of each side of the line, amounting to ten sections (ten square miles) for each linear mile of track. To prime the pump of private capital, the legislation authorized the federal government to loan the companies construction money in amounts ranging from $16,000 per mile of level ground to $48,000 per mountainous mile, all in the form of thirty-year bonds at 6 percent interest.

Congress assumed that if society at large wished to bind together the coasts, society would have to pay a good deal of the cost. Some politicians—old Thomas Hart Benton among them—argued that the government should build the road itself and rent the line to private carriers, but such notions ran against the scruples of constitutional strict constructionists and capitalists alike. Much better, from a business point of view, were government guarantees that removed much of the risk but allowed ample room for profits. The trinitarian formula of right-of-way, land grant, and loan, however, proved insufficient to produce the additional private investment required to get the corporations moving. By holding out for two years, the companies got the federal government to up the ante by a factor of two. In 1864 Congress passed a new bill, increasing the land grants to twenty sections per mile instead of ten and reconfiguring the bonds as a second mortgage, which allowed the companies to issue their own bonds and reduce their risk to nil.

These lavish federal subsidies were controversial at the time and remain controversial today. There has been little argument over the bond issue, which cost the taxpayers nothing; here, the federal government was advancing credit, not cash, and the bonds were eventually repaid in full with interest, although not before both the corporate descendants of the Union Pacific and Central Pacific tried to renege on their obligations. The controversy has always focused on the grant of public lands. To be sure, this was a time-honored American method of financing "internal improvements," and the first grant for a railroad came in 1850 when Congress voted a generous donation to the Illinois Central Railroad. Over the next quarter-century, the federal government gave away more than 131 million acres to support the construction of transcontinental trunk routes and numerous feeder lines.

Federal beneficences turned the railroad companies into "empire builders," landlords on a par with the federal land office itself. Unlike the government, however, the companies could charge whatever they liked for land made valuable by the access to transportation that the railroad provided. Sometimes, the companies waited to select their sections until they could see more clearly how settlement was proceeding. In the meantime, no one else could take up claims. Even after it had made a choice, the company might lease the land, refusing to sell until prices had risen. And since unsold railroad land was exempt from taxation, the burden of paying for local government shifted from giant corporations to middling farmers and ranchers. Later in the century, Grangers and Populists would argue that society as a whole had a right to expect some return from the rising value of the land. But during the 1860s, the government's concerns were short range—the immediate transportation of people and supplies—and land grants did the trick. In the long run, society paid heavily, and a few men reaped rich rewards.

Prominent among the railroad millionaires were the "Big Four"—Collis P. Huntington, Mark Hopkins, Leland Stanford, and Charles Crocker—the founders of the Central Pacific Railroad. As the principal stockholders of this, the first of California's giant corporations, they grew fabulously wealthy, but their collective nickname came not from their wealth and power, but from their collective bulk, weighing in at some 860 pounds. Each man hailed from modest roots in the Northeast, and each would later loudly proclaim the importance of Puritan virtues like diligence and thrift. But, as Crocker once admitted, "luck had a hell of a lot to do with it," as did their willingness to play hard and fast with the rules when necessary.

All four were forty-niners. When Huntington and Crocker arrived in the goldfields, they immediately grasped the fact that fortune lay not in the gravel at the bottom of a pan, but in the sale of the pan itself. Hopkins and Stanford—the first an accountant with an unsurpassed talent for juggling numbers and the second a glad-handing lobbyist—had learned the same lesson before their overland treks, and both went west intending to become prosperous merchants in the gold region.

In 1861, in an upstairs room of the Sacramento store that Huntington and Hopkins jointly owned, this group was called together by a zealot of a railroad builder, Theodore Judah, who spread before them his plans, surveys, and dreams for a Pacific railroad. Each of the four pledged to buy $15,000 of stock in the company that Judah proposed to incorporate. But Judah unexpectedly died, and operations fell directly to the Big Four. Although they barely knew each other—and would never become personal friends—they quickly developed a most effective division of labor. Hard-headed Crocker supervised construction, inscrutable Hopkins kept the books, Huntington bid for supplies in the East, and Stanford worked the state legislature and the halls of Congress, an assignment immeasurably advanced when he won election as California governor. The Big Four were about to undertake one of the most spectacular construction projects of the age, yet as Crocker remembered, "none of us knew anything about railroad building."

Not so the leader of the Union Pacific, Thomas C. Durant, who had won his spurs building eastern railroads before the war. Durant's invention of a way of making fabulous profits for the Union Pacific on the construction of the road itself marked the highpoint of his financial "evil genius." Instead of paying outside contractors to build the railroad, the company's biggest stockholders would pay themselves. Durant set up a subsidiary corporation, Crédit Mobilier, wholly owned by Union Pacific insiders. Through dummy third parties, he channeled all construction contracts to Crédit Mobilier, which in turn exaggerated expenses by two or three times. Though Union Pacific accounts showed little profit, Crédit Mobilier paid handsome dividends to the conspirators. It was precisely the kind of "self-dealing" that would, in our own time, characterize the great Enron financial scam. The con game was plain enough to see, but Durant and his cronies also devised a scheme to keep official Washington from noticing. Republican congressman Oakes Ames, appointed head of Crédit Mobilier, distributed Union Pacific stock certificates, as he put it, "where they will do the most good for us." When the scandal broke into the open—with the publication in 1869 of an exposé by Charles Francis Adams, grandson of the nation's sixth president—the subsequent congressional investigation revealed that the entire Republican leadership, including the vice president and the chairmen of some of the most important House and Senate committees, had accepted Ames's bribes. Massachusetts senator George Hoar, one of the few Republicans untouched by the scandal, denounced the Union Pacific: "Every step of that mighty enterprise had been taken in fraud."

The Crédit Mobilier scandal was only one piece of a scandalous period. The Central Pacific had its own version of the same idea, the Credit and Finance Corporation, which charged $90 million for work worth only a third of that, but the Big Four avoided public exposure because their records just "happened" to be destroyed in a fire. In his day, Huntington corrupted officeholders, officers of the law, and regulatory commissioners, just as he pressured and blackmailed news reporters in order to manipulate public opinion. An acquaintance captured Huntington's spirit: "If the Great Wall of China were put in his path, he would attack it with his nails."

With financing in place, in 1865 the Union Pacific and Central Pacific began a frantic race to see which could build the fastest, get the largest subsidy, and engross most of the future commerce. At least twenty thousand men were working almost constantly to build what Oakes Ames, without exaggeration, called "the greatest public work of this century." Supervisors of the Union Pacific drove the workers demonically. American legend has it that the majority of those workers were Irish, and for the most part they were, although there were also ex-Confederate and Union soldiers, Mexicans, and former African American slaves.

The Central Pacific at first had a harder time finding workers. The gold-rush hordes had rushed elsewhere, and labor in California was dear. Charles Crocker considered importing Mexicans but instead decided to give the abundant Chinese population a try. The Chinese workers soon impressed everyone with their persistence, diligence, and courage and became the workers of choice. Along some of the nearly impassable gorges of the Sierras, Chinese workers chipped away at solid granite walls with claw hammers, carrying off the rock by basket loads—a job so difficult that despite their numbers, they were able to average only eight inches of laid rails per day. They became expert in handling the nitroglycerin used to blast through the mountains, although many died in the inevitable accidents. By 1867 Crocker was employing twelve thousand Chinese, 90 percent of his workforce. The Chinese were paid the same wages as white workers, but they shunned the board supplied by the company and ate their own food—dried bamboo sprouts, mushrooms, cuttlefish, salted cabbage, rice, and peanut oil. Chinese workers drank tepid green tea, while white workers washed down their heavy meals with strong coffee or raw whiskey. Chinese workers might use opium on their days off, but they rarely drank booze. "You do not see them intoxicated with it," wrote one observer, "rolling in gutters like swine."

Such debauchery was common in the Union Pacific camps, which swarmed with whiskey vendors, gamblers, and prostitutes. The most notorious end-of-track village of vice was Julesburg in northeastern Colorado, the temporary home for thousands. By a ratio of four to one, more Union Pacific workers died from exposure, violence, and disease in these "Hell-on-Wheels" tent towns than in the many industrial accidents. It was a brawling, whoring, drunken civilization that the railroad brought West.

The workers may have been left to their own pleasures after hours, but the supervisors drove them furiously during the days. At the peak of construction in 1868 and 1869, the workers were whipped into a frenzy of six to seven miles of track per day. The Central Pacific, too, once it had blasted through the Sierras and reached the Nevada deserts, began to calculate its daily distance in multiple miles. Indeed, on one remarkable day in early 1869, the Chinese workers established an unbeatable world record by laying ten miles and fifty-six feet of track in a single twelve-hour period, winning Crocker a $10,000 wager with Durant. But desperate for the extra miles, the two companies refused to agree on a meeting point for their lines. Advance parties of surveyors and graders actually passed each other in the Utah desert and were working on parallel routes when President Ulysses S. Grant demanded a halt to the foolishness, summoning company representatives to a White House summit and negotiating all night until at last the two companies picked a place of junction—at Promontory, near Ogden, Utah.

There, the symbolic joining of the rails was enacted on May 10, 1869. Railroad workers gathered with dignitaries from both coasts. A gang of Chinese workers laid the last few rails and drove all but the last spike, then were hustled off so as not to dominate the official photographs. As the band played and the crowd cheered, Leland Stanford came forward and set in place an eighteen-ounce Golden Spike, crowned with a large gold nugget. A telegraph wire was attached to the spike and another to the hammer in Stanford's hand, so that on impact the news would flash to a waiting world. Stanford took a weak little swing . . . and missed his mark. He shrugged in embarrassment and handed the hammer to Durant, who took his shot. He, too, missed. Realizing the signal had not been sent, a telegrapher tapped out "DONE."

But the work was *not* done. The race between the companies had taken precedence over careful construction, resulting in shoddy work. Ballast had been improperly laid and roadbeds collapsed; curves had been engineered too sharply and trains derailed. Government specifications called for twenty-four hundred hardwood ties per mile, but Union Pacific records indicated that in some locations the contractor got by with fewer than half that number, all of them fabricated of soft cottonwood that rotted quickly. In 1869, while Crédit Mobilier reported profits of $16 million, a government inspection of the line indicated that it would cost nearly $10 million to correct faulty construction.

Regular transcontinental service began immediately anyway. First-class travelers paid $100 for the trip from Omaha to Sacramento, coach passengers $75. It is hardly surprising that service was intermittent and amenities few. The English

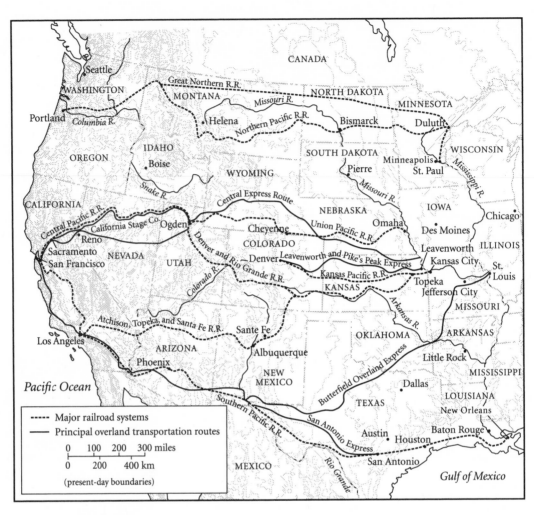

Western Railroads

writer Oscar Wilde complained of his six-day trip from Omaha to Sacramento, confined to "an ugly tin-kettle of a steam engine." Other travelers lambasted cramped
quarters, stifling heat alternating with freezing cold, and insufferable food at the
station stops, including in the words of one traveler, "muddy water out of dirty
glasses." But the inevitable complaints were less remarkable than the effusive
praise. "The crossing of the Sierra Nevada Mountains is the greatest achievement
yet accomplished in civil engineering," concluded Henry Varnum Poor, publisher of
Poor's Manual of Railroads. Americans had fashioned the proverbial Northwest
Passage.

In the thrall of railroad fever, Congress offered huge donations of public land
to three more companies. But the Atchison, Topeka, and Santa Fe Railway (often
called the Santa Fe), the Southern Pacific Railroad, and the Northern Pacific Railway would make little headway through the Panic of 1873. Late in the decade, they
began a second round of construction. Finally reaching New Mexico, the Santa

Fe constructed a line down the Rio Grande valley where it linked up with the eastward-building Southern Pacific, opening the nation's second transcontinental route in 1881. The Big Four (actually the Big Three, Hopkins having died) were determined to keep California for themselves, but after armed confrontations with agents of the Santa Fe, they finally allowed the line to build across northern New Mexico and Arizona into Los Angeles, while the Southern Pacific ran its track to El Paso, across Texas to San Antonio and Houston, finally terminating in New Orleans. Meanwhile, the Northern Pacific reached Portland in 1883. The last of the great transcontinental railroads was James J. Hill's Great Northern Railway, from Lake Superior to Puget Sound on a route paralleling the Canadian border. When Hill reached Seattle in 1893, five transcontinental lines linked the West with the rest of the country.

To the Indian people of the West, the railroad was a dagger penetrating their heartlands. The transcontinental lines made it possible for the army to rush troops and supplies to endangered areas. Native peoples understood this potential full well. Spotted Eagle, chief of the Sans Arcs Sioux, vowed that "he would fight the rail road people as long as he lived." But it was too late. More to the point was Chief Red Cloud's lament upon the completion of the Union Pacific through the former hunting grounds of the Sioux: "The white children have surrounded me and have left me nothing but an island."

In the Southwest, the Santa Fe and Southern Pacific lines encircled the territory of the troublesome Apaches. The Apaches were perhaps the most brilliant guerrilla fighters in the history of mounted warfare, but with dogged determination, General George Crook defeated the Western Apaches, the largest of the six Apache tribes, and in 1875 moved them onto a reservation at San Carlos in southeastern Arizona. Crook recruited reservation Apaches to assist in tracking down and defeating the "hostiles" from the other tribes. They were led by Geronimo of the Chiricahuas, famed among his people as a spiritual leader and a healer as well as a war chief. As a young man, Geronimo had a vision in which a spirit told him that "no gun can ever kill you." From that moment he was fearless. But pursued relentlessly by Crook's scouts, he finally laid down his arms and brought his people into the San Carlos reservation in the late 1870s.

They found it hard to live in that desolate and confining place, and in 1885 Geronimo and his Chiricahuas escaped. For more than a year, these last unconfined Apaches eluded the army. Seventeen settlers died in Chiricahua attacks. There was panic in Arizona and alarm throughout the nation. Newspapers proclaimed Geronimo as the "wickedest Indian that ever lived." Finally, after months of being hounded, he accepted an American promise of a new reservation for his people. But once they had surrendered, all five hundred Chiricahuas were hustled into sealed railroad cars and shipped along the new rails eastward to an army prison in Florida. Without sanitation facilities or ventilation, their transcontinental journey was hellish. The Chiricahuas would never return to their native land.

The same railroads that removed Apaches brought mining engineers and investment bankers to the new Southwest. Large-scale copper mining began in southern Arizona, and within a decade the copper companies were the largest employers in the Southwest. As historian William Robbins writes, "the railroad was the key instrument in transforming the area from preindustrial forms of economic activity to modern industrial technology." Railroad and mining companies—based in New York, Philadelphia, San Francisco, or other distant cities—exercised outside control over the Arizona economy and long dominated local and territorial politics. The railroad was a capitalist connection, and it introduced a new version of colonialism.

Locomotives now hauled the products of western mines, farms, ranches, and forests directly to highly developed markets in the East, providing westerners with access to the latest eastern goods. Railroads encouraged specialization. Unlike the trans-Appalachian West, which had been occupied first by farmers producing almost exclusively for themselves or for local markets, the settlement of the Far West would proceed on a fully "business basis." Every farmer and rancher would be a competitor in a rapidly expanding world market. But this meant competing against giants, like the railroad companies, that conspired with each other to divide territories and set shipping rates to the disadvantage of the small producer.

"The locomotive is a great centralizer," wrote San Francisco journalist Henry George. "It kills little towns and builds up great cities, and in the same way kills little businesses and builds up great ones." No railroad company dominated more completely than the corporate spawn of the Big Four. Combined, their network was known as the "Octopus," with tentacles reaching into every niche and corner of California. By the 1870s the Southern Pacific controlled more than 80 percent of the state's rail traffic. George raised the fundamental question of why railroads and other corporations should reap the benefit of the rising value of the land while society at large received so little. "Just think of it!" he wrote, "25,600 acres of land for the building of one mile of railroad. And this given to a corporation, not for building a railroad for the Government or the people, but for building a railroad for themselves."

In the dusk of a July evening in 1873, a small band of men loosened a rail at a blind curve on the tracks of the railroad near Council Bluffs, Iowa. Within minutes, an eastbound train hit the curve and derailed, killing the engineer. The masked men clamored aboard the cars, guns drawn, and while some of them collected money and valuables from the passengers, others blew the express company safe and took $2,000. Then mounting their horses and waving their hats, they rode off into the night. The brothers Jesse and Frank James and their gang of outlaws—former Confederate guerrillas—had been robbing banks in western Missouri and Iowa since the end of the Civil War, but this was their first train robbery. For the next few years, their holdups continued while detectives hired by the banks and the railroads pursued them fruitlessly. The end did not come until a member of the James gang, bribed by government authorities, shot Jesse in the back at his home in Saint Joseph, Missouri, in 1882. To the western Missouri farmers who decried the monopoly of the railroad, the James brothers only preyed on the institutions that were preying on them. Their legend grew out of the passions people felt about the railroad and its capitalist conquest of the West. Two currents were flowing together here: the western antilaw tradition and newer protests against corporate industrial power.

A greater challenge to the power of the road took place in 1877 when railroad workers staged a nationwide strike, shutting down the entire rail system. During the depression of the 1870s, workers suffered a series of crippling wage cuts; by the middle of the decade, for example, for a grueling twelve-hour day brakemen were being paid only $1.75 (about $30 in 2005 values), down from $2.50 ten years before. When, in the summer of 1877, the nation's four largest railroad companies adopted yet another 10 percent wage cut, eastern workers spontaneously left their jobs and seized control of switching yards and depots. President Rutherford B. Hayes sent in federal troops; there were armed confrontations, and during the two weeks of the strike, more than one hundred people died. The strike spread westward, first to Saint Louis and Kansas City, then to the Union Pacific yards at Omaha, across the plains to the Central Pacific facilities at Ogden, Utah, and finally to the Pacific coast.

But old ethnic antagonisms would distract and dilute the protest. In San Francisco, Dennis Kearney of the Workingman's Party harangued the Big Four and at the same time called for discharging all Chinese workers. Three days of anti-Chinese rioting followed. Taking note, Congress soon passed the Chinese Exclusion Act of 1882, suspending further immigration of "all persons of the Chinese race" for ten years. Yet exclusion did not prevent racist populism from rearing its head in dozens of western places in the coming decades. Perhaps the most barbaric incident happened in 1885 in the railroad town of Rock Springs, Wyoming, when the Union Pacific tried to replace white workers with lower-paid Chinese. In a coordinated attack, workers invaded the Chinese section of town, shooting, burning, and looting, while a group of their wives and mothers stood to the side, laughing, cheering, and firing gunshots at fleeing Chinese. Chinatown was burned to the ground, and twenty-eight Chinese died in the flames. In the aftermath of this massacre, there were attacks on Chinatowns all over the West. The Knights of Labor, the premier national labor organization of the 1880s, were implicated in this campaign of ethnic violence. The inability to close ranks with workers of color would prove to be their greatest weakness. In 1886 workers on Jay Gould's southwestern system struck the line. Gould hired hundreds of Mexicans to run the trains and armed hundreds of deputies to clear the tracks. In Fort Worth, Texas, a gun-slinging marshal engaged in a shoot-out with strikers in which several men were killed.

With this defeat the Knights of Labor faded in the West. But they were replaced by a new militant organization, the American Railway Union (ARU), founded by Eugene Debs. In one of its first actions, the ARU successfully struck the newly completed Great Northern when that line attempted to put in place a lower wage scale. The new union soon had 150,000 members nationwide, with its strength in the West. In 1894, in support of striking workers at the Pullman Sleeping Car Company, the union called on its members to refuse to handle trains running Pullman cars. In a reprise of the events of 1877, President Grover Cleveland called out federal troops, and an armed confrontation in Chicago left thirteen strikers dead and fifty wounded. In the aftermath of this violence, ARU members brought the nation's rail traffic to a halt.

The Pullman strike proved to be the high point of western protests against the railroads. Strikers occupied and held the rail yards in Omaha, Ogden, Oakland, and Los Angeles, where the militia was called out. "If we had to fight Indians or a common enemy there would be some fun and excitement," one soldier exclaimed to a reporter. "But this idea of shooting down American citizens simply because they are on a strike for what they consider their rights is a horse of another color."

The national strike was finally broken, but it demonstrated the depth of western feeling about the railroad. To some, the iron rails that stretched across the continent were the achievement of the age. Robert Louis Stevenson, an early passenger, likened the mythic qualities of the railroad to those of ancient Troy. It was a monument to the perseverance and power of a people, and the people who built that monument were only a little lower than the gods. To others, the railroad was not a monument but a monster, and the Frankensteins who created it were, in the words of the *Sacramento Union*, "cold-hearted, selfish, sordid men." To opponents of the railroad, the brave hearts were the wild boys who struck the lines, burned the bridges, and robbed the eastbound train, loaded with western plunder.

Chapter 10 **Open Range**

One hot summer day in 1883, Teddy Blue Abbott, trailing a herd of cattle from Texas to Montana, surmounted a hill, stretched tall in his saddle, and surveyed the Platte River country spreading before him. "I could see seven herds behind us," he remembered. "I knew there were eight herds ahead of us, and I could see the dust from thirteen more of them on the other side of the river." To Abbott, "all the cattle in the world seemed to be coming up out of Texas." With the new western railroads providing access to eastern markets, the cattle kingdom had expanded until it stretched high, wide, and handsome from Texas north to the Canadian prairies. Within a few years, however, the harshest winters in living memory would sweep down upon the plains, bringing a sudden end to the world in which Teddy Blue came of age. "Just when everything was going fine, and a cowpuncher's life was a pleasant dream," he later reminisced, "the whole thing went Ker Plunk, and we are now a prehistoric race."

What Abbott lamented was the end of the open-range cattle industry and the extinction of the rambling cowboy, the most renowned of all America's folk heroes. This colorful character whoopee-ti-yi-yo'd his way onto the American scene in the aftermath of the Civil War. Abbott was assuming that the cowboy's heyday lasted less than twenty years. Yet despite the end of the big trail drives, cowboying continued on countless ranches throughout the West, and more than a century later, the Great Plains states remain the largest producers of beef in the nation. Nor was the cowboy's appearance as sudden and abrupt as legend would have it. He was, in fact, the offspring of a history of frontier mixing and mingling as old as the European invasion of the Americas itself.

The Spanish brought the first cattle to the New World, along with a tradition of open-range herding by horse-mounted drovers. As early as 1500, Spanish cowboys called *vaqueros* were raising cattle commercially in the Caribbean, where their techniques mingled with those of slaves who had herded cattle in their African homelands. Indeed, linguists believe that the word *dogie*—a term for the motherless calves that lingered in the drag of the herd—came from the Bambara language of West African slaves. Spanish stock from the Caribbean first crossed to the North American mainland with Cortés and the conquistadors. Herding soon became an important part of the Mexican colonial economy, and later in the sixteenth century, when silver mines opened in the northern country, vaqueros followed with herds of cattle to supply the demand for beef.

Juan de Oñate's men trailed more than one thousand head into the Rio Grande valley in 1598. Mission friars later built up large cattle herds in California and Texas, and by the end of the eighteenth century, several million cattle grazed on the thousand hills of the California coastal range and on the grasslands of Texas. Where the stock ran wild for most of the year, nature selected for the hardy. The evolutionary result was the Texas longhorn, with horns that could span six feet, a wild glint in its eye, and a racy flavor to its meat. Vaqueros learned to manage them with a combination of superb horsemanship and skillful roping, and by the 1760s Tejanos were driving their cattle to market in New Orleans.

Anglo-Americans first encountered Hispanic traditions of cattle raising in Louisiana. Herding had long been an occupation in the backcountry of the colonial South. Herders known as "cow-boys," either slaves or indentured servants, pressed into the Appalachian foothills in pursuit of fresh grazing land. About the time of the Louisiana Purchase, backcountry cowboys and Indian drovers leapfrogged the Mississippi floodplain and soon were learning and adapting the vaquero traditions of horsemanship and roping. The large number of Spanish loan words in the lingo of western cattle raising—*lariat, lasso, rodeo, rancho*—testify to this process of cultural fusion.

Southwestern Louisiana was the proving ground for a composite backcountry-vaquero herding culture that became indelibly associated with Texas once Americans began filtering into the province in the 1820s. Herding rivaled cotton as the most important economic pursuit in the region. After the Texas Revolution, rancher violently replaced *ranchero* across the savannas of south Texas. Cattlemen typically drove their cattle to Shreveport or New Orleans and eventually farther north. By the 1850s a sizable market for Texas beef had developed in Kansas City, but the Civil War brought an end to these early northern drives.

After the Civil War, with New Orleans a commercial wreck, cattle drovers turned their attention north again. Enterprising Texans soon discovered a northern market in Abilene, Kansas, where the Kansas Pacific Railway established a stockyard and depot in 1867. That year 35,000 head of cattle arrived at the railhead, but over the next half-decade, Abilene shipped out more than 1.5 million Texas longhorns. The new western railroads badly needed this traffic, and cattle quickly became one of their most important cargoes. The Santa Fe line established

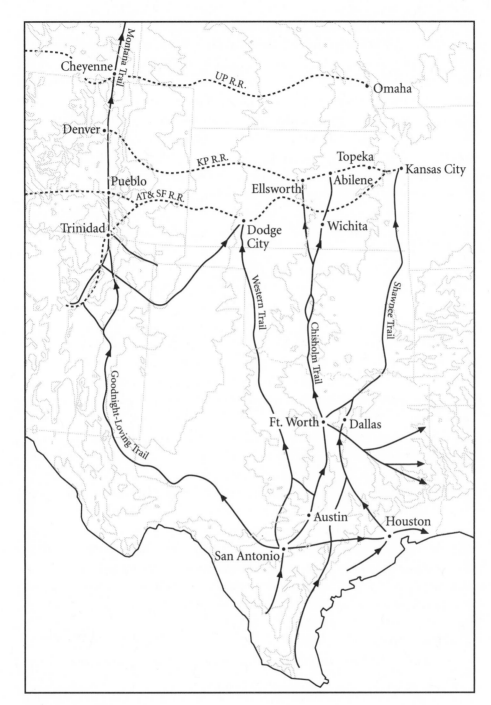

Texas Cattle Trails

competing market towns at Wichita and Dodge City, Kansas, and soon thousands
of western cattle were arriving by rail at distribution points in Kansas City, Saint
Louis, and Chicago, where the huge Union Stockyard was capable of handling up
to 21,000 cattle each day.

Traditionally, pork had been the most common meat on the American table, but faced with this new and abundant supply of beef, Chicago meat packers Philip Armour and Gustavus Swift quickly transformed the national diet. Rather than follow the standard practice of sending live cattle east to local slaughterhouses, they pioneered the practice of killing and butchering the animals on "disassembly" lines, then using refrigerated railroad cars to ship great quantities of dressed beef to eastern markets. Since salable meat constituted only about half of a steer's total body weight, this method produced dramatic savings in shipping costs and allowed the packers to undercut the price of locally butchered beef. Packers made their biggest profits, however, on the "waste": dried blood packaged as fertilizer, hooves and feet boiled into glue, bone carved for knife handles, and fat converted into margarine. Nearly everything else was ground up for sausage and stuffed into casings. What finally remained was dumped into the Chicago River, producing a fetid, overpowering stench. Not until Upton Sinclair's 1906 muckraking novel *The Jungle* would the unsanitary and corrupt practices of the meat packers be exposed, resulting in the passage of federal inspection programs.

With the increased demand for beef, cattlemen found that a steer selling for ten dollars or less on the overstocked Texas range could bring twenty-five dollars or more at one of the Kansas railheads. With prices climbing to forty dollars a head and more in Chicago, stockdealers further up the food chain also made substantial profits. What the market created, of course, it could as easily destroy. When the bottom dropped out of the American economy in 1873, for example, hopeful drovers arrived in Kansas to find that prices had fallen below costs. But until the 1880s, prices generally favored the producer. The accountant's bottom line created the conditions for the great long cattle drives of American legend.

Driving a herd of some two thousand three-year-old steers several hundred miles north required the labor of ten or fifteen drovers with 100 to 150 horses, as well as a trail boss and a cook equipped with a chuckwagon stocked with flour, salt, sugar, and canned goods. Teddy Blue Abbott remembered the dust, thick as fur, on the eyebrows of the drag men, and the black phlegm they coughed up for weeks after the drive. Days of deadly dull work were punctuated by moments of high drama: sudden stampedes of hundreds of steers, dry runs with animals bellowing from thirst, and infernal weather.

If headed for the stockyards at Wichita or Abilene, drovers took the Chisholm Trail, a path blazed before the Civil War by an old métis trader named Jesse Chisholm. Later drives shifted to the Western Trail leading to Dodge City, or the Goodnight-Loving Trail—named for gruff old Texas rancher Charlie Goodnight and his partner Oliver Loving. Where the trail connected with the railroad, there was the cattle town, a bustling commercial center set down in the middle of nowhere. The town's business centered on the stockyards and the hotel, the bank, and the mercantile establishments, like Mayer Goldsoll's Texas Store in Abilene, or Jacob Karatofsky's Great Western Store in Wichita, where wranglers replaced their worn-out clothes for brand-new denim pants made by Levi Strauss of San

Francisco, broad-brimmed hats by the John B. Stetson Company of Philadelphia, and hand-tooled boots by Joe Justin of Texas. After his first trail drive, Teddy Blue Abbott bought such an outfit and traveled home to Nebraska just to show it off. But his sister took one look at him and declared: "Take your pants out of your boots and put your coat on. You look like an outlaw."

The reputation for cowboy outlawry came largely from the wild doings in the cattle town demimonde, brawling, hard-fisted meccas of vice and vulgarity, cousins to the end-of-track Sodoms and the mining camp Gomorrahs. In 1870 Abilene counted thirty-two saloons, more than a sufficient number for a town that had a permanent population of just five hundred but that was consistently crowded with hundreds of drovers, gamblers, and prostitutes all through the shipping season.

The volatile mix of unattached young men, alcohol, and firearms made cattle towns violent places. Firearms were the principal cause of death, but less than a third of the victims died in exchanges of gunfire. Most were gunned down unarmed. Even the mythic lawmen like Wyatt Earp rarely fired their guns with mortal results. Despite the thousands of "high-noon" walkdowns of movie and television Westerns, cattle town newspapers made almost no mention of gun duels fought in dusty streets. Few wranglers went looking for trouble, and in fact few were even proficient with their six-shooters. Most gunshot wounds, it turns out, were accidental. Men shot themselves while working, while removing their guns from wagons or packs, and even while undressing.

Cowhands may not have been the gunslingers legend makes them out to be, but violence was built into the everyday life of handling cattle. They drove herds cruelly to the limits of the animals' endurance. At trail's end, they forced steers into cramped railroad cars, prodding them forward with steel rods (hence the name *cowpuncher*). During the roundup, ropers snagged calves by their hind feet as they nursed from their mother's udders, then dragged them kicking and bellowing to the branding fire. It took two men to hold the animal down so that the hot iron could be pressed to its side, creating smoke and stink. Meanwhile, another man was at work with his knife, dehorning the animal, cropping its ears, bobbing its tail, and, if the poor thing was male, carving out its testicles. That these things were necessary did not make them any less brutal. Such hard and callous experiences can breed hard and callous men.

Most cowhands were white southwestern boys from Texas or Louisiana, but African Americans, Mexicans, and even Indians participated in the drives. George Saunders, president of the Old Time Trail Drivers' Association, in 1925 estimated that those groups made up one-third of all trail cowboys. In southeastern Texas, at least one in four cowboys was black. Indian cowboys were common on herds driven up from the Cherokee or Creek nations. One cattleman judged Indian wranglers "the best in the world." Mexican vaqueros were often hired because they were so familiar with the tools and techniques of the trade. The Indians and vaqueros remain mostly anonymous, but the names of a few African American cowboys found their way into the record. Former slave Bose Ikard helped Goodnight and Loving blaze their famous trail and then worked for years on Goodnight's JA Ranch. Perhaps best known was Nat Love, who trailed cattle for a time and later published a popular autobiography that included more than the usual portion of western braggadocio.

The motley groups of men on the trail enjoyed an earthy and ribald humor that early folklorists and historians unfortunately bowdlerized. "In the singing around camp," one old hand remembered, "a cowboy would often cut loose with a song too vile to repeat; great cheers and hurrays would usually follow and there would be calls for more." Such songs were often sung at stag dances, an important aspect of this lonely, all-male culture. A cattleman remembered a drunken ball at which two of his drovers danced together happily all night. "She ain't much for pritty," one of the hard-bitten hands exclaimed about the other, "but she's hell for active on the floor."

Yet after the ribaldry, men were likely to strike up some old-time hymn, or sing movingly of homesickness, lost love, or death. In his memoir of a boyhood spent among the wranglers on the northern plains, western novelist Wallace Stegner captured both sides: "Many things that those cowboys represented I would have done well to get over quickly, or never catch: the prejudice, the callousness, the destructive practical joking, the tendency to judge everyone by the same raw standard. Nevertheless, what they themselves most respected, and what as a boy I most yearned to grow up to, was as noble as it was limited. They honored courage, competence, self-reliance, and they honored them tacitly. . . . Practicing comradeship in a rough and dangerous job, they lived a life calculated to make a man careless of everything except the few things he really valued."

In April 1871 Mrs. A. Burks, riding in a little buggy, accompanied her rancher husband and his Mexican vaqueros on the drive from Texas to Kansas. They experienced frightening thunderstorms and tough river crossings because of high water. They lost cattle to stampedes and to rustlers. Then they found disappointingly low prices at the railhead. But despite these difficulties, she found the trip invigorating, and her account suggests that she enjoyed the attention that came with being the only woman in camp. One day the foreman told her: "In the heat of the day when I am riding behind my cattle, I think of you and am sorry for you. But when I see your smile of happiness and contentment I know all my sympathy is wasted." His comment tickled her. "For what woman," she wrote, "youthful and full of spirit and the love of living, needs sympathy because of availing herself of the opportunity of being with her husband while at his chosen work in the great out-of-door world?" Most women remained back at the ranch, but they could display the same spunky spirit as Burks, taking over day-to-day management of the operation in their husbands' absence. Cora Slaughter, who ran the home place during the annual cattle drives, found "real pleasure" in ranch work. "I loved to work with cattle," she wrote, "and spent a good deal of my time on the range."

Often, women took over the ranch after their husbands became incapacitated or died. One of the most famous of these "cattle queens" was Elizabeth Collins, who assumed the operation of a large ranch when her husband fell ill, made a fortune as a shipper, and published her recollections under the title *The Cattle Queen of Montana.* But other women were ranchwomen in their own right. Long before she married, Ann Bassett, according to the recollection of a friend, "could fit right in the toughest cow camp, [and] take her place in the saddle with the rest." She is even said to have rustled cattle—like her mother before her—from a large cattle company that was encroaching on her ranch in Utah. Girls who grew up on western ranches, as Bassett did, often worked outside with their fathers. In her memoir of growing up on a ranch in Lincoln County, New Mexico, Lily Casey wrote of learning "to ride, rope, brand, and perform the various functions of a cowboy." There seems little doubt that growing up on a ranch helped to develop women of strong and independent character.

In his memoirs, William Tecumseh Sherman, commanding general of the army, pointed to the expansion of the open-range cattle industry as a decisive factor in the conquest of the Far West. It was a "potent agency," he wrote, "in having in so short a time replaced the wild buffaloes by more numerous herds of tame cattle, and by substituting for the useless Indians the intelligent owners of productive farms and cattle-ranches." Sherman was right about the succession on the range—cattle replaced buffalo and cowboys replaced Indians—but wrong about the agency, for while cattlemen profited from the elimination of the great buffalo herds, they had little to do with the work of destruction. That was something accomplished by buffalo hide hunters, aided and abetted by the frontier army and Sherman himself.

Plains Indians greatly increased their buffalo hunting with the development of the equestrian tradition in the eighteenth century. From a peak of perhaps thirty million, the number of buffalo declined to perhaps ten million by the mid-nineteenth century, partly as a result of commercial overhunting by Indians, but also because of environmental competition from growing herds of wild horses and the spread of bovine diseases introduced by cattle crossing with settlers on the Overland Trail. By overgrazing, cutting timber, and fouling water sources, overland migrants also contributed significantly to the degeneration of habitats crucial for the health and survival of the buffalo. The confluence of these factors produced a crisis situation for buffalo-hunting Indians by the 1860s. Tribal spokesmen protested the practice of hunters who killed merely for hides to make robes, leaving the meat to rot on the plains. It was a practice that cynical officials encouraged. "Kill every buffalo you can!" Colonel Richard Dodge urged a sport hunter in 1867. "Every buffalo dead is an Indian gone."

The extension of railroad lines onto the Great Plains, and the development in 1870 of a technique for converting buffalo hide into commercial leather, sealed the buffalo's fate. Lured by the profits to be made in hides, swarms of hunters invaded the plains. Using a high-powered rifle, a skilled hunter could kill dozens of animals in a single afternoon. General Philip Sheridan applauded their work. "They are destroying the Indians' commissary," he declared. As the hunters did their work, Indians, too, accelerated their kills, trying to capture their share of the market. At the Santa Fe depot in Dodge City, mountainous stacks of buffalo hides awaited shipment to eastern tanneries. Historians estimate that between 1870 and 1875, five or six million buffalo died on the southern plains alone. The Sioux holy man Black Elk later testified that "the last of the bison herds was slaughtered by the Wasichus," the Lakota term for white men, in the summer of 1883, when he was twenty years old. With the exception of a small wild herd in northern Alberta, Canada, and a few remnant individuals preserved by sentimental ranchers, the North American buffalo had been destroyed. This campaign of extinction remains one of the most shameful in the American annals of nature's conquest.

To most westerners, the disastrous effect on the Indians was a prime justification for and a happy result of the buffalo's slaughter. Missionaries and other humanitarians, who perhaps wished only to salve their consciences, argued that now Indians would have to cease their nomadic hunting and become Christians and farmers. Reservation Indians became dependent on deliveries of government beef. A great deal of the cattle driven north from Texas fed reservation Indians. The cattlemen hardly objected, for they got good prices from the government and sent the worst of their animals to the reservations. Who would care? Certainly the Indians were in no position to object.

Soon the range where the buffalo had roamed was being stocked with Texas longhorns. Cattlemen bought heifers and bulls in Texas and drove them north where they opened new ranches along the watercourses. In 1880, buffalo in Montana far outnumbered the 250,000 cattle; three years later, the buffalo had disappeared and the number of range stock had increased to 600,000. It was, in the words of cultural geographer Terry Jordan, "one of the most rapid episodes of frontier advance in the Euroamerican occupation of the continent." Not surprisingly, the transition had an unfortunate ecological effect, though it was not immediately apparent. In the natural cycle, the buffalo ate the grasses, produced manure for new plant life, and in death returned nutrients to the earth. The cattle, however, after fattening on the plants of the plains, were transported long distances for slaughter at maturity. Their blood and unused remains were dumped in rivers, and their flesh went even farther afield. The natural cycle of life on the plains was thus broken, with negative consequences that would unfold in time.

During the 1880s, plenty of outside investors expected to get rich from the cattle business. Profits were high and well publicized. Capital poured in from New York, London, and Edinburgh. In 1883 Scots investors dumped $2.5 million (about $48 million in 2005 values) into the huge Swan Land and Cattle Company, which controlled more than six hundred thousand acres of range in Nebraska and Wyoming. Another Scots firm, the Espuela Cattle Company, opened a half-million-acre spread in Texas called the Spur Ranch. A movement of consolidation swept over cattle country, inaugurating the brief ascendancy of what historian J. C. Mutchler calls the "super ranch." Richard King, owner of the enormous King Ranch of south Texas, employed three hundred vaqueros to work his sixty-five thousand cattle. On John Chisum's Rancho Grande, a massive spread straddling the Texas–New Mexico border that covered a territory the size of southern New England, wranglers in 1884 branded eighteen thousand calves in a single season.

Cowhands increasingly found themselves working in what was truly a cattle *industry*. An experienced wrangler of the late nineteenth century could expect to earn about $30 or $40 a month (about $600 to $800 in 2005 dollars—just about what ranch hands are paid today). The poor pay and the seasonal nature of the work made it unlikely that many cow*boys* could ever rise into the ranks of cattle*men*. Some cowboys tried to organize. At the same time that the Knights of Labor were signing up railroad workers, they were also active among cowhands; there were cowboy locals and strikes for higher pay and better working conditions throughout the cattle kingdom just as elsewhere in industrializing America. In the spring of 1883, the *Denver Republican* reported that a demand for a wage increase to $50 per month had resulted in "an extensive strike among the cowboys" on the largest outfits in the Texas panhandle. Three hundred men held out for more than a year against paid gunmen and Texas Rangers, but lost in the end when cattlemen replaced them with scabs. Cowhands organized the Northern New Mexico Small Cattlemen and Cowboys' Union in the mid-1880s. But cattlemen broke this and all other unionization efforts by organizing powerful stockmen's associations.

The expansion of the cattle industry also brought ranchers into conflict with sheepmen, a struggle that had ethnic dimensions. Hispanos and Navajos had been herding sheep in New Mexico since the seventeenth century, but in the 1870s ranchers began to compete with them for access to grass and water. Violence was the predictable result of the ranchers' belief that, as one Texan put it, "cattle cannot thrive on the same range with sheep." The enduring conflict most often pitted Anglo cattlemen against Hispano or Basque sheepmen. At least thirteen men died in the ethnic fighting among these adversaries in Lincoln County, in the southeastern portion of the New Mexico Territory. New Mexico's territorial governor Edmund Ross wrote that he understood "very well . . . what a cow-boy or cattle herder with a brace of pistols at his belt and a Winchester in his hands, means when he 'asks' a sheepherder to leave a given range." From 1860 to 1890, as the population of Lincoln County grew from eighteen hundred to more than seven thousand, the proportion of Hispanos dropped from more than 80 percent to less than 50 percent, and cattle ranchers prevailed over sheepherders. Lincoln County became known as "Little Texas."

Hispano sheepherders were more successful in defending against the invasion of cattle in San Miguel County in northeastern New Mexico. In the early 1880s, ranchers began to fence off large tracts of grassland that Hispano communities had traditionally considered part of their common pasture. The vigilante group *Las Gorras Blancas* rode out at night to cut the fences and torch the haystacks of offending ranchers. Authorities condemned these nightriders as "lawless mobs," but as one federal judge wrote, their actions were, in fact, "the protests of a simple, pastoral people against the establishment of large landed estates, or baronial feudalism, in their native territory." Las Gorras Blancas fought the ranchers to a stalemate.

Even bigger troubles were ahead for ranchers. During the 1870s and 1880s, American farmers began to colonize the eastern fringes of the Great Plains, leading to the legendary confrontation between cowpunchers and sodbusters. In Abilene in 1871 thousands of longhorns awaiting shipment overran dozens of newly settled farms on the town's outskirts. In an attempt to avoid further trouble, most cattlemen trailed their herds farther west in subsequent years, but the same conflict eventually recurred in Wichita, Dodge City, and elsewhere. Farmers grew increasingly aggressive, using barbed wire—patented in 1874—not only to protect their fields but also to block trails and fence off watering holes. Also at issue was splenic or Texas fever, a tick-borne parasitic disease that longhorns carried; the tough Texas breed was immune, but the disease wiped out domestic shorthorn stock. Pressured by farmers, the Kansas state legislature created quarantine districts and later rigorous inspection regulations. In 1885 state inspectors along the Kansas border were so thorough that the resulting traffic jam backed up more than one hundred thousand head on the Western Trail.

The destruction of the buffalo along with the abundance of investment capital gave cattlemen the incentive to expand into the arid western plains where they did not have to compete with hostile farmers. But ranchers stocked the western range with far too many cattle, inevitably driving prices down by the mid-1880s. Determined to wait out the market slump, stockmen's associations kept tens of thousands of steers off the market. Soon, the grasslands were overgrazed. Everyone knew that this would mean weak cattle and a die-off in the winter, but the expansion of open-range herding had occurred during an extended period of unusually wet and mild conditions on the Great Plains, and based on the expectations, cattlemen believed they could take the loss. That's when nature returned to the more typical pattern of arid summers and frigid, stormy winters. First, drought struck the overstocked ranges. Fearing their herds would starve, many cattlemen drove their stock north to the still lush meadows of Montana. But this exposed even more cattle to the harshest of the winter blizzards. It was a vicious cycle. Losses from the one-two punch of drought and freeze already had many ranchers on the ropes when they were clobbered by the brutal winter of 1886–87, the worst on record. On the northern plains, cattle losses reached as high as 90 percent. The *Rocky Mountain Husbandman* observed that cattlemen had to face the fact that "range husbandry is over, is ruined, destroyed, and it may have been by the insatiable greed of its followers."

The "great die up," as the winter of 1886–87 became known, made large cattlemen aware of just how precarious their business was. Eastern and foreign investors bailed out, cutting their losses. Some ranchers moved toward smaller, fenced spreads on which they could confine their cattle, improve their stock through selective breeding, and make a profit by selling high-quality beef. These ranchers planted fields of hay for winter feeding. Many big ranchers resisted these innovations, trying to hold on to their crumbling open-range empire. The old system would make its last stand in a conflict between big and small ranchers known as the Johnson County War.

In Wyoming, many start-up ranches were concentrated in isolated Johnson County, where the grassy valleys of the Powder River meet the Bighorn Mountains. The Wyoming Stock Growers' Association—representing the established cattlemen—thought of these newcomers as interlopers and accused them of building their herds by rustling "mavericks," calves and yearlings that had missed being marked during the roundups. The politically powerful association got the territorial legislature to pass the Maverick Law of 1884, which declared every unbranded calf on the open range to be the property of the association. There is little doubt that many small ranchers were engaged in rustling. Cowboys believed this was only fair play. In the words of an old cowboy adage: "If you stole a few cattle you were a rustler. If you stole a few thousand you were a cattleman." When the association's "stock detectives" brought accused rustlers to court, juries of local citizens refused to convict them.

Failing in the courts, the cattlemen turned to violence. Their first blow came against James Averell and his lover Ella Watson, who were living on homestead claims that the association considered part of the "open range." The cattle barons spread rumors that Averell was the leader of a rustler band, and Watson, known as "Cattle Kate," was a notorious prostitute who had built her fine herd by accepting steers for sexual services. Historians still dispute the truth of the charges. The pair refused to be intimidated, however, and finally in 1889 a group of vigilante cattlemen invaded their ranch and murdered the couple. Although the murderers were well known, they walked free after the witnesses to the crime mysteriously "disappeared."

The lynching stirred the small ranchers to organize a competing organization, the Northern Wyoming Farmers and Stockgrowers Association, and in 1892 they arranged to drive—rather than ship—their cattle east, avoiding the big interests and their railroad connections. Nathan Champion, a trail boss with a tough reputation, was to lead the drive. The big interests responded by sending fifty gunmen into Johnson County, where they killed three men and besieged Champion in a cabin along the Powder River. He held them off for twelve hours before the invaders succeeded in burning him out and murdering him. Outraged Johnson County citizens organized into a vigilante mob of their own and surrounded the invaders, determined to hang them all. But the screams of the cattle magnates were heard as far away as Washington, D.C., and President William Henry Harrison sent in U.S. troops to restore order. It is debatable whether federal intervention brought law and justice, for the cases against those who killed Champion were quietly dropped when the witnesses once again disappeared. In the Johnson County War, the most powerful political forces in Wyoming stood in opposition not only to the rustler but to any cowboy individualistic enough to remain on his own.

With this fiasco, the days of the western open range came to an end, just twenty-five years after the first trail drives to Abilene. Even big ranchers began to adopt newer methods. Production and capital costs mounted, but the price for beef remained low. Prices rose during World War I, but with the inevitable postwar bust, thousands of small producers were forced out of business. Perhaps the most telling sign of change was the introduction of blooded Angus Hereford and Brahman bulls. Soon, the ubiquitous longhorns became something of an endangered species—another character in the myth of the frontier. According to Teddy Blue Abbott, most of the "prehistoric" trail hands shared the same fate as the longhorn and the buffalo. But he was one of the minority who successfully made the transition from cowboying to ranching. He and his wife homesteaded a small ranch in Montana. "We got a little better off year by year," he recalled. They made a bundle during World War I, but hard times followed. "I lost most everything. Such is life in the Far West."

Chapter 11 **The Safety Valve**

Most mid-nineteenth-century Americans believed in the Jeffersonian promise that ordinary citizens—armed only with courage, stamina, and self-reliance—could move west, stake modest claims to the land, and make a success of it. The promise depended on the availability of boundless, fertile, and cheap western land—and in post–Civil War America, this land was underwritten by the Homestead Act. Congress passed this historic legislation during the Civil War in the spring of 1862. "We doubt whether any endowment on so magnificent a scale has ever been conferred on the moneyless sons of labor," read one rhapsodic editorial.

Before the Homestead Act, American land policy opened the western public domain to settlers—but at a price. In response to citizen complaints that the original Land Ordinance of 1785 favored capitalists and speculators over actual settlers, Congress had gradually lowered the price of land to $1.25 per acre and reduced the size of the minimum purchase from 640 to 40 acres. But what settlers most wanted was the legalization of *squatting:* the right to select and improve lands anywhere on the public domain—even before they were surveyed—with the guarantee that when the land was officially "opened," the squatters would be granted the opportunity to buy at the minimum price. In the American vernacular, this right became known as *preemption.* In 1841, soon after the election of William Henry Harrison ("Old Tippecanoe") to the presidency, Congress passed what was known as the Log Cabin Bill, which granted preemption rights to all Americans. The land was still not free, however, for sooner or later squatters, like everyone else, had to pay for the acres they tilled.

Soon, Americans were arguing over whether the time had come for dropping the revenue principle altogether and providing *free* land for settler families. Labor leader George Henry Evans of New York proposed a federal program to grant 160 acres in the West to any citizen willing to improve it. Free land, he believed, like the safety valve on a steam boiler, would "carry off the superabundant labor [of eastern cities] to the salubrious and fertile West." Like many other nineteenth-century reformers, Evans was disturbed by the increasing concentration of land in the hands of wealthy Americans—what his contemporaries called the "land monopoly." Evans urged that strict legal limits be placed on the quantity of public land an individual could acquire.

Powerful support was offered by Horace Greeley, editor of the nationally distributed New York *Weekly Tribune.* "Every smoke that rises in the Great West," he reminded the merchants and manufacturers among his readers, "marks a new customer to the counting rooms and warehouses of New York." Western expansion was good for eastern business. Greeley, too, was an avid believer in the notion of a western safety valve, emphasizing the benefits that free land would have for employers: strikes, he argued, "will be glaringly absurd when every citizen is offered the alternative to work for others or for himself." Greeley's editorials kept the homestead issue at the top of the political agenda, and in the minds of millions of Americans, his name became indelibly linked with the phrase "Go West, young man."

In the mid-1850s the new Republican Party embraced the homestead program as part of its effort to build an alliance between northeastern and western politicians. In exchange for eastern votes for homestead legislation, westerners would support higher tariffs to protect "infant industries" like textiles and iron. Southern legislators, fearing that the agitation for free land inevitably would lead to "Free Soil"—the political movement to bar slavery from the territories—became implacable opponents of the homestead bill.

The secession of the southern states and the mass departure of southern members of Congress after the Republican electoral triumph of 1860 removed the final obstacle to the passage of the "Act to Secure Homesteads to Actual Settlers on the Public Domain." It took effect on January 1, 1863. People over the age of twenty-one—both men and women, both citizens and immigrants who had declared their intention to become citizens—were eligible to file for up to 160 acres of surveyed land on the public domain. Homesteaders had to cultivate the land, improve it by constructing a house or barn, and live on the claim for five years, after which they would receive full title, paying only a ten-dollar fee. The dream of free land had become law.

The Homestead Act created farms for more than four hundred thousand families. Altogether, these homesteaders received 285 million acres, an achievement of historic proportions, but one that needs to be put in perspective. Over the same seventy-year period, more than 700 million acres passed from the public domain to private hands through *purchase* rather than grant. In other words, for every 160 acres of western land given away, another 400 were sold. Most western settlers, it turns out, were not homesteaders. A large proportion took up public land under the terms of the Log Cabin Bill. Because only surveyed land was open to homesteading, and government surveys of the vast West proceeded at a snail's pace, the odds were great that to get the land they wanted settlers had to "squat," that is, establish a preemption claim, and buy the land later. Furthermore, homesteading was not permitted on lands taken from the western Indian nations (approximately 100 million acres after 1862), lands given to the states to support "land-grant colleges" (140 million acres), and lands in the alternating sections the government retained along the routes laid out by the railroads (183 million acres). Most lands in these categories were available by cash purchase only. Lands along the rail lines, of course, were the most attractive of all and were sold at top dollar, since by definition they offered access to transportation, without which western farming was not feasible.

On the tenth anniversary of the Homestead Act in 1873, the federal government circulated a pamphlet boasting that the law had "prevented large capitalists from absorbing great tracts of the public domain." This was a barefaced lie. The Republican Congress had refused to enact limitations on the amount of public land that individuals could acquire, so the Homestead Act failed to realize reformers' hopes of forestalling the land monopoly in the West. Speculators were able to amass large holdings by purchase from railroads or states, both only too happy to lower prices for big buyers. As a result, speculators grabbed the best farming land in the West before any of it was available to homesteaders. Almost all the land remaining was far from rail lines, putting homesteaders at a distinct disadvantage.

Then there were the notorious strategies that unscrupulous men devised to defraud the government and frustrate the intentions of the legislation. "Dummy" homestead entries became so common they were standing jokes in late-nineteenth-century America. Working at the bidding of speculators, hired men set up tiny, prefabricated, movable shacks on 160-acre quarter-sections to satisfy the minimum legal requirements of "improvement," then signed over the deed to their employers. Cattlemen and lumbermen were able to acquire tens of thousands of acres by using such methods. In one shocking episode, uncovered by federal investigators at the turn of the century, the California Redwood Company rounded up foreign sailors in San Francisco, marched them to the courthouse to file citizenship papers, then to the land office to take out timber claims, then to a notary public to sign blank deeds transferring title to the company, and finally to paymasters who gave them each fifty dollars. The fact was, the engrossment of land was more prevalent after the Homestead Act than before.

Meanwhile, 49 percent of all genuine homesteaders failed to patent or "prove up" their claims. While the land may have been free, the cost of equipment, seed, and supplies for the first year or two was often more than families could manage. Others found themselves unable to stick it out in isolated locations for the required residency period. Still others failed to make their acres pay commercially because of the poor quality of their land and its distance from the railroad. Thus small western farmers still became, as often as not, tenants on land owned by others. The homestead program, politician George Washington Julian lamented in 1879, had become "a cruel mockery."

Although railroads and land developers continued to promote the post–Civil War West as a haven for the working man, the whole idea of the safety valve was a farce. At a time when the cost of a railroad ticket for a family of five was the equivalent of half a year's wages, few "young men" could afford to take the advice to "go West." Without farming skills, most of the urban easterners who headed west settled not in the country but in western towns and cities, trading industrial work in places like Buffalo, New York, for industrial work in places like Butte, Montana. Indeed, the dominant population trend in the late nineteenth century was the movement from farm to city, not from city to farm. It is far more accurate, historian Fred Shannon concluded, to say that the city "was a safety valve for *rural* discontent."

Nevertheless, by purchase and through grant from the public domain, Americans opened more farmland during the last third of the nineteenth century than during all of the nation's previous history. The most productive of these were the prairie lands of Minnesota, Iowa, and eastern Nebraska and Kansas, where adequate rainfall nourished tall and luxuriant grasses and loamy topsoil that was several feet deep. Here, settlers found it possible to transplant the "corn and hog" farm economy of the Mississippi valley.

Farther west, beyond the ninety-eighth meridian, erratic rainfall totaled less than twenty inches per year, and the undulating prairie grasses gave way to a short, tough cover of bluestem and buffalo grass. Rivers ran across the high plains from the Rockies to the Mississippi but were separated by hundreds of miles of arid land. The high mountains squeezed most of the moisture from the clouds and left the winds dry and pitiless. This was the "Great American Desert" noted by Stephen Long's expedition of 1820.

In *The Great Plains* (1931)—one of the most influential books ever written about the American West—Texas historian Walter Prescott Webb argued that before Americans could successfully settle the plains, they had to find a means to adapt to its environment. Settlers built shelters of sod and burned buffalo dung or "chips" for heat and cooking. Improved drilling equipment made it possible to sink wells hundreds of feet deep, drawing water up from underground aquifers through the use of prefabricated windmills powered by the prevailing winds that reliably swept across the plains. The American settlement of the arid plains also required a shift of attitude. In the post–Civil War West, respected scientific authorities proposed that the very act of farming arid land would transform the climate. The connection between science and speculation was most blatant in the case of amateur climatologist and Nebraska town-site developer Charles Dana Wilbur, who in 1881 coined the inspired slogan of a practiced pitchman: "Rain follows the plough."

Wilbur had the good fortune to write near the beginning of one of the periodic wet cycles that punctuate the climate history of the Great Plains. From the late 1870s to the mid-1880s, rainfall was relatively abundant, creating conditions for one of the greatest land booms in American history. Thousands of farmers pushed out onto the arid country of West Texas and the high plains of western Kansas and Nebraska. Then in 1886, as surely as night follows day, the wet years gave way to a drought that continued until the mid-1890s. "The farmers [were] helpless, with no weapon against this terrible and inscrutable wrath of nature," wrote novelist Stephen Crane. "The country died." Between 1888 and 1892, half the population of western Kansas and Nebraska pulled up stakes and moved back east to Iowa and Illinois. People told of two farmers meeting on a dusty trail, one headed east, the other west. "This would be a fine country if we just had water," said Mr. Westbound with a touch of hope in his voice. "Yes," Mr. Eastbound replied wearily, "and so would hell."

The drought finally ended in 1896 and ushered in another wet cycle, and with it yet another mass migration to the plains. The single biggest land boom in North American history took place from 1900 to 1909. Thousands of families purchased railroad land and took up homestead claims in the western Dakotas and eastern Montana as well as the prairie provinces of Canada. Most came determined to practice the techniques of "dry farming" with drought-tolerant crops such as "Turkey Red" wheat or durum wheat, imported from Asia. They adopted the methods of deep plowing, soil packing to conserve moisture, and surface harrowing to create a "dry mulch" that prevented evaporation. These techniques worked well enough during the wet years, but when drought inevitably returned to the high plains in 1910, crops again withered and died. The soil dried out to the depth it had been plowed and then was picked up by the hot winds and blown away. Settlers once again migrated eastward by the thousands. Yet a return to adequate rainfall on the plains, combined with the enormous demand for farm products during World War I, provided all the incentive needed for farmers to plow up millions of additional acres of the Great Plains before the end of the 1920s.

Farm mechanization was the most powerful adaptation of all. In the years following the Civil War, a long line of improvements appeared one after the other. Steel replaced wood and iron in the manufacture of plows. Soon, horses were pulling "gang plows" that turned over several rows simultaneously. Horsepower was also put to use with new machines that mowed, raked, and loaded hay and made it possible to load a ton of hay from a field in just five minutes. The "McCormick 'Old Reliable' Automatic Self-Rake Reaper" of 1867 cut wheat and swept it aside for binding. It was not long before an inventive westerner perfected an automatic binder that gathered the shocks together, tied them with a length of twine, and kicked them free. Power threshers appeared, the early ones using horsepower and the later models driven by coal-fired steam boilers. In 1880 harvesting and threshing were joined in the "combine" machine for the first time, and within a few years giant steam combines were producing up to eighteen hundred sacks of grain each day. By the end of the century, wheat farming was eighteen times more productive than it had been before the Civil War.

Mechanization made possible the giant "bonanza farms" of the northern plains and the great central valley of California. The most famous was the thirty-four thousand acres a few miles west of Fargo, North Dakota, managed by Oliver Dalrymple. One of Dalrymple's rippling wheat fields stretched for thirteen thousand unbroken acres. Separate gangs working on distant corners of the farm might not see each other for the entire season. According to one tall tale, a plowman would set to work in the spring and cut a straight slice across the farm until fall; then he would turn around and harvest his way back. In California, huge estates were carved from the land grants of the Central Pacific Railroad, with the largest farms stretching more than sixty-six thousand acres and producing more than one million bushels annually. By 1880 California had become the biggest wheat-producing state in the nation. Whether in the Dakotas or the San Joaquin valley, these farms embodied the vital components of industrial capitalism: the application of machinery to mass production, absentee ownership, professional management, specialization, and proletarian labor.

Those bonanza operations were a striking contrast with the farms of the thousands of emigrants who found their way to the Great Plains during the late nineteenth century. The Department of Agriculture recommended that settlers have at least $1,000 in capital; for even assuming free homestead land, the costs of moving, putting up fences, and buying seed, livestock, and equipment could be daunting. Most newly arriving families, however, probably had less than this. They were poor and probably undersupplied. Poor tenant farmers and hired hands came from the Old Northwest and Old Southwest. Thousands of former slaves came from the cotton lands of the Black Belt of Alabama and other southern states, intending to take up homesteads in Oklahoma and Kansas. Millions of immigrants came from Europe, toting a few treasured heirlooms but relatively little capital. By the end of the century, Germans made up a third of the population of Texas, and the numbers of Swedes, Norwegians, and Russians were so large in the northern plains states that according to the census of 1890 the region had the highest proportion of foreign-born residents in the country.

Many of these settler families built their houses from the very earth itself. Arriving at their claims, families worked together slicing the tough, grassbound sod into bricks about one foot wide and three feet long. Then they placed them end to end to form walls three feet thick and make an enclosure about eighteen by twenty-four feet. Two forked tree trunks held the ridgepole. Over the rafters went tar paper—if the builder was lucky enough to afford it—then a layer of sod bricks, from which grass and sunflowers eventually would flourish. Because of its insulation, the room was cool in summer and warm in winter—warmer, that is, than the blizzards raging outside. This "soddy" offered cheap accommodations, but it often sheltered hardship as well. With only one window and one door, it had little light and little ventilation. Dirt showered down from the ceiling, and the soggy roof was in constant danger of caving in.

Soddies were common during the 1880s, but in later decades the tar-paper shack, made of third-rate lumber and insulation paper, was more typical. Edith Ammons, homesteader of South Dakota, described her house as a "none too substantial packing-box tossed haphazardly on the prairie, which crept in at its very door." In a blizzard, "cowering in that tiny shack, where thin building paper took the place of plaster, the wind screaming across the Plains, hurling the snow against that frail protection, defenseless against the elemental fury of the storm, was like drifting in a small boat at sea, tossed and buffeted by waves, each one threatening to engulf you."

The ability of farm families to hunker down to bare subsistence gave them an advantage over the bonanza farms, whose managers always had the bottom line to face. Corporate agriculture on the Great Plains was eventually driven out of business by pestilence and drought. Absentee owners reinvented themselves as land speculators and tried to recoup their capital on the increased value of the land itself. But despite slim pickings, there would always be sod-house or tar-paper farmers persisting on the land.

The Homestead Act allowed women to apply for land under the same conditions as men, requiring only that they be at least twenty-one years old and unmarried (single, divorced, widowed, or head of a household). Case studies of various western locales demonstrate that single women made up from 5 to 15 percent of all homestead entries before 1900, with the proportion rising to 20 percent in the early twentieth century. Women proved their claims at a similar or better rate than men. Thirty to forty thousand is a reasonable estimate of the number of homesteading women who gained title to western land in their own names.

The most famous of them was Wyoming ranchwoman Elinore Pruitt Stewart, whose *Letters of a Woman Homesteader* was greeted with considerable acclaim when it was published in 1914, then revived as a classic of western women's history in the 1970s. (It also inspired the beautiful film *Heartland* [1979].) Stewart's charming account detailed her efforts to homestead an arid quarter-section in Wyoming. Homesteading, she argued, offered an important means by which single women could achieve economic independence. What got obscured in Stewart's telling was that she married only a week after she applied for her homestead. But this background actually strengthens the interest and importance of the story. Many (if not most) of the single women who filed claims did so as part of a strategy to enlarge an existing family ranch. Homesteading was not something easily accomplished by lone individuals—whether men or women—but required the cooperative work of the whole family. The stories of women homesteaders may be seen as feminine versions of achievement similar to those that men had told for so long.

Western farmers might have practiced subsistence living during the pioneer days or to survive the pinch of hard times, but ultimately they had to find their place in the market economy. Success had to be measured in dollars, and the disturbing truth was that from the end of the Civil War to the end of the nineteenth century, the prices for farm commodities did nothing but fall. The wholesale price index of farm products (for which the 1910–14 average is arbitrarily assigned the value of 100) fell steadily from a century high of 162 in 1864 to a low of 56 in 1896. Wheat that sold for a dollar a bushel in 1870 was down to eighty cents by 1885 and only fifty cents ten years later. These are government figures; the prices grain dealers offered at the railhead were even lower. Dakota farmers of the 1890s, for example, were getting only thirty-five cents a bushel for wheat that cost them at least fifty cents to produce.

Individual farmers responded in the only way they could, by trying to produce more and to produce it more efficiently. It was a loser's strategy. The steadily increasing flow of farm commodities into the market simply accelerated the downward pressure on prices. Thousands of farmers borrowed heavily to buy more land or mechanized equipment, mortgaging their farms, their livestock, even their personal belongings. Without adequate returns, farm indebtedness led inevitably to foreclosure. As a result of falling prices and massive indebtedness, approximately 45 percent of Kansas farmers defaulted by the early 1890s.

Western farmers tended to identify the East as the source of their problems. The two most important symbols of eastern colonialism were the railroads and the banks. Freight rates in the West (and the impoverished South as well) were frequently two or three times those for comparable distances in the East. Railroad companies, it is true, encountered special problems in the West, a region that exported far more than it imported. During peak harvest times, railroad executives complained that they were forced to send empty cars westward to handle the huge grain shipments. But the main reason for the high rates was an absence of western competition and the drive to maximize profits where possible. When farmers groaned that they were paying the value of one whole bushel of corn or wheat in order to get a second bushel to market, they were not exaggerating.

Another cause of western suffering was the country's banking and monetary system. Congress had helped finance the Civil War by authorizing the issue of $432 million in paper notes. These "greenbacks"—so-called because of the color of the ink on their reverse side—were declared "legal tender" for all public and private transactions, but they could not be redeemed at the federal treasury for gold or silver. This was the first issue of "fiat money," that is, federal currency backed only by the authority of the federal government, not by precious metals. By the war's end the circulation of greenbacks had resulted in inflation that cut the value of the dollar in half, and the Republican congressional majority ordered that the country gradually retire most of the greenbacks and return to a metallic standard. The resulting contraction in the money supply was great news for capitalists and creditors, whose investments increased with every uptick in the dollar's value, but awful news for farmers and debtors, who not only received less for their products because of deflation, but also had to repay their loans with dollars worth a good deal more than the dollars they had borrowed. Combine depressed prices with annual rates of interest that often climbed as high as 25 percent in the West, and it is easy to understand the growing hostility of westerners to banks and bankers. Many were attracted to the political argument of the Greenback Party—that a growing industrial economy needed an expanding money supply.

The image of westerners besieged by economic forces beyond their control became a cultural commonplace of the late century. Hamlin Garland, raised in rural Wisconsin and Iowa, recounted some of the sad details in "Under the Lion's Paw," one of the short stories in *Main-Traveled Roads* (1891). Farmer Haskins rents a place he could have bought for $3,000, had he the money. Husband, wife, and son work for two long, dreary years, and by scraping and saving build the place up and succeed in saving the original purchase price. But when the owner sees the improvements, he jumps the price of the farm to $5,000. Haskins must go into debt to purchase the value that the family's own sweat has added to the land. Ready to kill the owner, he swallows his anger. Western farmers could not escape from the grip of the capitalist paw.

Developing a powerful collective consciousness, farmers started their own organizations. The first one of national importance was the National Grange of the Patrons of Husbandry, founded shortly after the Civil War. By 1875 it counted 850,000 members in hundreds of local chapters or Granges (an old word for a farmer's house). At meetings and picnics, men swapped yarns and women exchanged recipes, but mostly Grangers talked politics. Together, they exerted sufficient pressure on state legislatures to win regulations governing railroads and grain elevators. Not surprisingly, the railroads and the wholesalers challenged these laws, but the Supreme Court finally upheld them in the landmark case of *Munn v. Illinois* (1876), which declared that such facilities were "clothed with a public interest." The principle of government commercial regulation—the Grangers' legacy—eventually led to the passage of the Interstate Commerce Act of 1887, the first federal attempt to regulate the railroads.

Another organization, the Farmers' Alliance, first took shape during the mid-1870s and within a decade mushroomed into hundreds of local groups spread throughout the rural South, the Great Plains, and the Rocky Mountain states with a membership of several million. Like the Grange, which was centered in the Midwest, the Alliance responded to the social needs of farm families, organizing picnics, camp meetings, and educational institutes. But the Alliance also moved directly into politics. In the early 1890s, it helped found the People's (or Populist) Party, aligning the farmers' movement with the western Knights of Labor and the Greenbackers, as well as the "silverites," who advocated the unlimited coinage of silver, representing the interests of western mining. The party platform, largely written by Ignatius Donnelly of Minnesota, was a remarkable document, calling for government ownership of the nation's transportation and communications systems; expansion of the homestead program by returning to the public domain all unsold lands granted to the railroads; creation of a national system of warehouses (called the "sub-treasury") where farmers could store their crops in exchange for government loans; commitment to a flexible national currency based not only on gold but on silver and fiat money as well; establishment of a graduated income tax; and institution of the eight-hour workday. James B. Weaver, the party's candidate for president, was the child of a settler family who worried about the widening chasm between the haves and the have-nots. Initially hoping only to make a showing, the Populists were thrilled when Weaver polled more than one million votes in the 1892 election. The Populists elected three governors and sent ten representatives and five senators to Congress. The Populist revolt had begun.

In addition to Donnelly and Weaver, the Populists brought a colorful crew of western activists to national attention. They included Kansas cattleman Jeremiah Simpson, who became known as "Sockless Jerry" to his supporters by turning to his advantage an opponent's sarcastic comment that Simpson was so "country" he wore no socks. But no one better represented the Populists than Mary Elizabeth Lease, a former homesteader and one of the first women to practice law in Kansas. She became famous for a speaking style that combined biblical imagery, frontier wit, and agrarian radicalism. What the country needed, she declared, was "the enactment into law of the truths taught by Jesus." Attempting to discredit Lease, a hostile reporter once attributed to her the comment that farmers should "raise less corn and more hell," but the phrase endeared her all the more to her supporters and it became the slogan of the day. Lease was but one of a number of remarkable women who helped to lead the Farmers' Alliance and the Populist Party.

To conservatives, the Populist platform seemed salted with radicalism, especially in its call for the nationalization of the railroads and a progressive income tax. The Populists were eager for electoral victory, however, and in 1896 they rejected these more radical ideas for "fusion" with the Democratic presidential candidacy of William Jennings Bryan of Nebraska. Bryan's most radical proposal was his opposition to the monetary gold standard and his support for the free coinage of silver, a measure designed to break the deflationary back of the depression. "You shall not press down upon the brow of labor this crown of thorns, you shall not crucify mankind upon a cross of gold," he thundered in his acceptance speech. This position ensured Bryan's popularity in western mining communities. "Silver" was more symbol than substance, standing for federal intervention in the economy and the quest for greater reforms. But Bryan's rhetoric also underlined the fact that, in the end, the Populists spoke for rural America. "Burn down your cities and leave our farms, and your cities will spring up again as if by magic," he orated; "but destroy our farms and the grass will grow in the streets of every city in the country."

Bryan waged a fighting campaign and captured the states of the South and interior West, but failed to carry the critical states of the Pacific coast and the Midwest, thus losing to Republican William McKinley. The Populist challenge faded with the decline of the Democrats into the status of a regional party based in the South, a pattern that would prevail for the next thirty years. In the end, western farmers and miners had been unable to convince industrial workers of the merits of their cause. The interests of workers and farmers sometimes clashed. Low prices for wheat translated into cheap flour used to bake cheap bread for hungry workers in hundreds of new industrial bakeries, and urban workers feared that inflation would raise the price of basic commodities.

Many of the Populist proposals would be taken up by the Progressives of the early twentieth century, although in a distinctly more urban style, with little of the rural flair of a Sockless Jerry Simpson or Mary Elizabeth Lease. Later, they would inspire the New Deal, many of whose programs, wrote westerner Thurman Arnold in 1942, could be traced directly back to "the general philosophy and specific ideas" of the Grangers, the Greenbackers, and the Populists of the late-nineteenth-century West.

The western agrarian movement also had important consequences for the development of American foreign relations. One response to the crisis of overproduction was a western push to expand overseas markets. When European governments raised tariff barriers in an attempt to protect their own farmers, western congressional representatives were prominent among those demanding that the United States pry those markets open again. There was also the lure of Asian commerce, an old dream of American expansionists. Broad western support for commercial expansion in the Pacific was premised on the hopes of opening huge new markets. Western representatives argued for a form of overseas expansion that contrasted with old-style European colonialism. What they wanted was to see freedom—American freedom of trade anyway—extended everywhere on the globe. This was the formula invoked during the Spanish-American War of 1898: America would expel the Spanish imperialists from Cuba and guarantee the political independence of the island in exchange for economic privileges that would expand the marketplace for American farmers. Historian William Appleman Williams has argued that "the roots of the modern American empire" grew out of an agreement on expansion proposed by the agrarian West and accepted by the industrial East.

In 1896 depression began to loosen its grip on the nation's economy. The same year saw the end of the long drought on the plains. Leaving the previous quarter-century of hard times behind in the dust, the American farm economy took off in a sustained boom that would carry it through World War I. For the first time in more than a generation, farmers were able to secure credit at reasonable rates and make a decent profit on their products. By 1910 the price of a bushel of wheat had risen to nearly one dollar, and the demand associated with the European war that began in 1914 drove farm prices to unprecedented heights. This would long be remembered as the "golden age" of American agriculture, when the prices for farm and industrial goods were in a good balance.

But by 1910 the best homestead land had been taken up, and authorities advised potential settlers that the costs of starting a farm now required a minimum of $1,500, the equivalent of more than $30,000. Accordingly, there was a disturbing increase in the number of farm tenants in the West. In Texas the proportion of tenants in the agricultural workforce grew from 38 percent in 1880 to more than 60 percent in 1920. Many of these encumbered farmers were African American sharecroppers, forced back into quasi-slavery. Perhaps more shocking was the increase in tenantry among the white farmers of the northern Great Plains states, where the proportion of tenants in the agricultural workforce rose from 20 percent to more than 40 percent from 1880 to 1920. People had long worried that the agricultural ladder was rickety, but now the consensus was growing that the rungs were broken.

Another sign of transformation in western agriculture was the enormous increase in the number of wageworkers in the countryside. By the late nineteenth century, an estimated two hundred thousand migrant farmworkers were harvesting wheat on the plains, moving from Texas in late May or early June to western Kansas and Nebraska in mid-summer, and finally to the prairie provinces of the Canadian West in the fall. Western farming was now tied to the restless wageworkers' frontier, a labor system with its roots in the California gold rush. There was little opportunity for harvest workers to settle down on western homesteads.

As hopes of farm ownership evaporated with the rising price of land and equipment, migrants turned toward unionization. Bill Haywood, the former western miner who now led the Industrial Workers of the World, announced a campaign to organize harvesters into a new Agricultural Workers Organization, a union affiliated with the Wobblies. Farm income had increased, Haywood argued, but farm wages remained stagnant. Farmers were improving their homes as well as their farms, adding indoor plumbing and steam heat, but hired workers continued to sleep in damp old soddies or filthy chicken coops. IWW organizers rode the rails with harvesters and camped with them in the "hobo jungles" on the outskirts of prairie towns. They argued for adequate board, good places to sleep, and a minimum daily wage of three dollars. Most farm owners reacted in fear and anger, and in many communities migrant workers and labor organizers were harassed, jailed, and in some cases murdered.

But there were also structural reasons for the failure of unionism in the western countryside. New forms of mechanization—the most important of which was the gasoline-powered tractor—aimed at making the farmer self-sufficient in labor. Assisted by the smaller combines marketed after World War I, a farmer with large acreage needed only two or three workers to help with the harvest rather than the eighteen or twenty that had been common before. It all pointed to the end of the wageworkers' frontier in the West.

Migrant labor was also an essential feature of the intensive agricultural districts—specializing in the production of vegetables and fruit—that were cropping up throughout the Far West, including the "Winter Garden" area along the lower

Rio Grande in Texas, the Gila and Salt river valleys in southern Arizona, and the Yakima valley in Washington. Most important were the fertile valleys of California, which by the turn of the century were producing most of the fruits and vegetables being canned, dried, and shipped fresh to markets around the country. Chinese immigrant farmers had been the first to introduce intensive methods of cultivation during the mid-nineteenth century. They were the first farmers in the West to produce and market commercial crops of potatoes, asparagus, strawberries, and sugar beets, leading the way to the transformation of California's wheat fields and cattle ranges into orchards, vineyards, and spreading acres of row crops.

Harvesting these diverse crops demanded an army of nearly two hundred thousand migrant workers. Thousands of people tramped from place to place, following routes determined by the pattern of ripening crops. They began, perhaps, by picking winter lettuce in the irrigated fields of the Imperial Valley near the Mexican border, moved to the navel orange groves of the southern California citrus belt, then to the pea fields of the Bay Area in the spring, the berry and fruit orchards of the Salinas valley in summer, the vineyards of the humid Sacramento valley in September, and finally ended the year picking cotton in the arid fields of the San Joaquin valley. Chinese men originally made up about half of this migrant army, but the radical decline in immigration from China after the passage of the Exclusion Act forced growers to search elsewhere for workers. After the Spanish-American War of 1898 thousands of immigrant farmworkers began to arrive from the Philippines, the Hawaiian Islands, and especially from Japan and Mexico. By the eve of World War I, Asian and Latino workers made up about half of the migrant farmworkers in California.

The IWW sought to organize the migrant workers of California just as they did the harvesters of the Great Plains. In 1913, in the Sacramento valley town of Wheatland, striking hops pickers and IWW leaders were attacked by an armed posse of growers and sheriff's deputies; in the resulting melee four men were killed—two strikers, a sheriff, and the county attorney. In a climate of fear and repression, growers reported numerous incidents of "labor sabotage," and convinced that the most radical of the farmworkers were native-born Americans, California growers determined to increase the proportion of immigrant workers, especially Mexicans, in their fields. One San Joaquin valley employer candidly explained his preference for Mexican hands: "We want Mexicans because we can treat them as we cannot treat any other living men." In 1917 the administration of President Woodrow Wilson agreed to suspend the head tax and literacy test for Mexicans crossing into the United States and, at the urging of western growers, added provisions for Mexican contract labor to the Immigration Act of the same year. Already, thousands of Mexicans were fleeing the revolutionary violence that had been tearing their country apart since 1910. During the years of World War I alone, more than one hundred thousand Mexicans entered the United States.

One of them was nine-year-old Francisco Chico, who crossed at El Paso, Texas, with his refugee family in 1918. During the next few years, his mother died and his father was killed in an industrial accident, leaving Francisco at the age of twelve thrust into the role of breadwinner for his grandparents and three younger siblings. Together they hitched a ride across the desert to southern California, where the boy found work picking oranges for one dollar a day. For immigrants like the Chicos, the American West was once again operating as a safety valve—but in ways that George Henry Evans and Horace Greeley could scarcely have imagined.

Chapter 12 A Search for Community

Americans have always had itchy feet. The movement of people from one place to another is one of the most important factors in our history. By the time of the Revolution the pressing desire for "elbow room" was so strong that in typical American communities in all regions of the country, at least four of every ten households packed up and left every ten years. In Sugar Creek, a pioneer community in central Illinois founded in the 1820s, 80 percent of arriving families had made at least one previous move across state lines, and 35 percent, two or more. Similarly, eight in ten of the families who traveled the Overland Trail to Oregon and California had already made at least one interstate move, many had made several, and a substantial minority had been almost continuously in motion. High rates of geographic mobility have continued to characterize our national life.

But there was considerably more social continuity than suggested by the raw mobility statistics. In the Sugar Creek community, for example, a quarter of the early settlers were what western writer Wallace Stegner calls "stickers," laying down roots and living out their lives in the area. Three-quarters of the children and grandchildren also made permanent homes in the community, most marrying the descendants of other sticker families. Quietly, people were weaving kinship connections and consolidating their lands. By 1860, four decades after the founding of Sugar Creek, community life there was dominated by an interconnected group of sticker families. The riddle of community in the American West is solved by recognizing the coexistence of both movers, a transient majority, and stickers, a persistent minority who passed farmland down to their descendants. Posterity and landed possessions—family and land—played a role equal to migration in shaping western communities.

Rural life in the great open spaces of the trans-Mississippi West was filled with hard work, monotony, and often stultifying isolation. What romantic travelers might describe as boundless skies, billowing grain, and the soft warmth of a kitchen fire could appear quite different to men and women laboring under the hot sun, battling to save their crops from drought and pests, or toiling long hours over a hot wood-burning stove. Nowhere were the physical hardships more starkly revealed than in the lives of pioneer women. Hamlin Garland looked upon his graying, wrinkled mother, old long before her time, and thought back over her frontier life: "My heart filled with bitterness and rebellion, bitterness against the pioneering madness which had scattered our family, and rebellion toward my father who had kept my mother always on the border, working like a slave."

It was social isolation, not movement per se, that took the greatest toll on women. On earlier frontiers, the distance between farms had been an obstacle to community, but on the Great Plains it became an overwhelming problem. Farm or ranch wives might be surrounded by husbands, children, and hired hands, but the companionship of other women was hard to come by. One woman recalled of her early years in west Texas, "it would be two or three months at a time that Mother and I would not see another white woman." And another confided in her diary: "I feel quite lonesome and solitary. My spirits are depressed. I have very little female society." The struggle to make and sustain connections between isolated western households—the work of constructing a community—was perhaps the most difficult of all pioneer tasks. Communities drew energy from numerous connections. Neighbors exchanged work and participated in barn raisings or harvesting; women sewed and quilted together; while men worked on road crews, played on local baseball teams, or joined voluntary organizations—all face-to-face ties that bind. One of the first tasks, strikingly consistent, was organizing a school. Teachers were most frequently young women, one of the few occupations open to them. Schoolmarms not only instructed the children, but played a role as community organizers. The one-room schoolhouse often did joint duty as a community center.

Groups of like-minded families might also use the schoolhouse as a meeting place for religious services. Small ecumenical congregations formed, bringing together people of various Protestant views and sometimes even including Catholics. Eventually, the most popular denominations founded churches of their own. Building and running churches brought experience in getting things done, and common beliefs and rituals helped to build sustaining bonds of affection. Religion was the greatest ally of the pioneers in the formation of western communities.

American denominations turned their attention to the frontier in the first years of the new nation. The Presbyterians and the Congregationalists, the two largest organizations of the Revolutionary era, joined forces to coordinate the western expansion of their churches. But their seminaries were never able to supply the demand for ministers to the rapidly growing West, and their missionaries were easily scandalized at unsettled frontier violence, drinking, and gambling. Other sects proved more adaptable. The Baptists authorized the use of untrained and unsalaried lay preachers, and an army of organizers founded hundreds of congregations throughout the West. The Methodists were also particularly effective. Francis Asbury, the first Methodist bishop in the United States, developed the institution of the "circuit rider," a preacher who sallied forth with his Bible, and usually on his horse, moving from community to community to battle frontier irreligion and isolation. As a result, the Methodists became the fastest-growing denomination of the early republic, expanding to more than a quarter-million members before the Civil War.

The conversion of the West depended on the work of itinerant preachers, men who understood and sympathized with pioneer conditions. The archetypal western circuit rider was Peter Cartwright, who rode throughout the Old Northwest until his death in 1872. "The great mass of our Western people," he wrote, "wanted a preacher who could mount a stump, a block, or old log, or stand in the bed of a wagon, and without note or manuscript, quote, expound, and apply the word of God to the hearts and consciences of the people." In Cartwright's mind, religious and civic responsibility were indistinguishable. "Yes my friends," he declared near the end of his long life, "I have waged an incessant warfare against the world, the flesh, and the devil and all other enemies of the Democratic party."

The fire of religious enthusiasm in men like Cartwright was first sparked in 1801 at a place called Cane Ridge in central Kentucky. At this "Great Revival" a crowd of some twenty thousand country folk came together to pray, sing, and get saved in the open air. It was the prototype for thousands of "camp meetings," ubiquitous in the nineteenth-century West. In late summer—after the crops had been "laid by," and before the intense activity of the harvest—dozens of families converged on some shady grove, many prepared to stay for several days, or even several weeks. The milling crowds, the campfires casting an eerie light through the grove at evening, the preaching, the singing, the enthusiastic reaction of those being saved—all heightened the sense of the extraordinary that suffused the successful camp meeting. It was an occasion for binding groups of people, a sacred process of community organizing.

As churches formed, the founding members often signed covenants that formally bound them together. The covenant of the Buck Run Church in Kentucky solemnly required its members to "watch over each other in brotherly tenderness," to edify one another, to succor the weak, to bear each other's burdens, and to hold in common all "hands and hearts." These were the strongest bonds a community could claim. The ideal of the small, close-knit community was carried deep in the minds of most settlers, and a covenanted community was a sacred enterprise, reaching down to the smallest detail of helping one's neighbor when in trouble or astray.

The strongest example of a covenanted community in the trans-Mississippi West was the Church of Jesus Christ of Latter-day Saints, or Mormons. Their epic exodus of the late 1840s took them from Illinois to the shores of the Great Salt Lake, where they established several dozen communities. They were strongly driven by a theological principle they knew as "the Gathering," the imperative to build a new Zion, a communal utopia, in the American wilderness. In order to build the largest possible gathering, Mormon leader Brigham Young dispatched missionaries to the East and across the Atlantic to the industrial towns of England and the farms of Scandinavia. Their preaching was spectacularly successful, and communal dreams were soon pulling thousands of converts to Salt Lake. So heavy was the migration, and so short the supply of mules and wagons, that Young even organized a series of "handcart brigades," with emigrants themselves pulling inexpensive carts loaded with their possessions. In 1856 two of these brigades were caught in early winter blizzards and at least two hundred people froze to death. But the migration continued. By 1880 some one hundred thousand Mormons were living in more than 350 communities scattered across the inland desert. Young envisioned the creation of a Mormon empire called Deseret, stretching from Idaho to Arizona, from Utah to the California coast.

The Mormons were not only communal but strongly practical. Most of Young's divine revelations concerned economic matters. The Mormons' economic system was in fact a bootstrap operation. There was no foreign or eastern capital available for development, but the church devoted its own resources to setting up sugar beet factories and mining smelters, assigning new recruits to work in those industries. The church became the owner of mercantile outlets, sugar and woolen factories, a bank, and a life insurance company as well as a major stockholder of railroads. The Mormons succeeded spectacularly, proof to them of God's blessings. Communitarian theology was happily wedded with economic development.

The federal government created the territory of Utah and appointed Brigham Young governor. But federal officials sent to administer the territory found to their chagrin that the Mormon leaders retained the real power and that non-believers ("gentiles" in Mormon parlance) were excluded. They accused the Mormons of running a "theocracy," and they were partly right. Before his murder in Illinois, Joseph Smith himself had termed the Mormon system a "theo-democracy."

The conflict between Mormons and gentiles increased greatly in 1852 when the church announced that one of its fundamental tenants was "plural marriage," producing a firestorm of controversy that would burn for half a century. Americans focused on the extraordinary cases—such as Brigham Young's marriage to twenty-seven women and his paternity of fifty-six children. But he was hardly a typical Mormon. In its heyday, no more than 15 percent of Mormon families practiced polygamy, and two-thirds of these plural marriages involved just two wives. The extent of polygamy among the Mormons has been greatly exaggerated. Still, plural marriage was woven into the fabric of the Mormon community, part of the Saints' conception of their distinctive way of life.

In 1856 polygamy went onto the nation's political agenda when the newly formed Republican Party included in its platform a condemnation of "those twin relics of barbarism—polygamy and slavery." The next year, concluding that the federal territorial government of Utah was a sham—that real power was located within the Mormon hierarchy—President James Buchanan, a Democrat, ordered a federal military expedition to the state to bring the Saints into line. The Mormons prepared to burn Salt Lake City and flee into the desert. At the last minute, armed conflict was narrowly averted by negotiators for both sides, but not before an agitated group of Mormon militia attacked a gentile wagon train at a spot in Utah called Mountain Meadows, killing 120 men, women, and children.

The controversy over polygamy continued, however. After the Civil War, feminist advocates of woman suffrage argued that the Mormons presented a case study in the consequences of women's disenfranchisement. If only Mormon women had the vote, they argued, surely they would "do away with the horrible institution of polygamy." Catching wind of this, Brigham Young sensed immediately that he could turn it to Mormon advantage. In 1870 the Utah territorial legislature passed the first universal woman suffrage bill in the nation. Feminists were overjoyed, and Susan B. Anthony and Elizabeth Cady Stanton traveled to Utah to congratulate Mormon women. But the mood shifted as Mormon women, in election after election, voted exactly as Mormon men did. Gradually, plural wives stopped being seen as victims and began being portrayed as dupes. The opponents of votes for women seized the issue as a cautionary tale—married women were incapable of being independent. It was years before the woman suffrage movement recovered from this public relations disaster.

Although federal laws proscribing polygamy were passed in 1862 and 1874, the Edmunds Act of 1882 was the first legislation to stipulate severe penalties for polygamists themselves. Armed with this statute, federal authorities began arresting Mormon men for "unlawful cohabitation," imprisoning more than one thousand of them over the next decade. But the Mormon hierarchy, aware that early Mormon settlements were accustomed to observing their own laws, refused to relent. In 1887 Congress turned up the heat yet again by passing legislation disincorporating the Mormon Church, confiscating its real estate, and abolishing woman suffrage in Utah. The struggle widened into a war against theo-democracy. Facing institutional collapse, in 1890 the Mormon hierarchy agreed to the abolition of polygamy in practice (though not in theory), and in 1896 Congress finally voted to admit Utah to the union of states.

In 1879 yet another mass exodus to the western promised land took place, this one by thousands of African Americans from the Old Southwest. The background of this episode lay in the failure of southern land reform after the Civil War, which would have required the confiscation of large plantations and the redistribution of land to the men and women who had worked it for years without compensation. Neither Congress nor the southern reconstruction governments were willing to commit themselves to such a radical violation of private property. Thus many African Americans in the Old Southwest began to look West for a better future.

Benjamin Singleton, a former Tennessee slave, led a group of African Americans to an agrarian colony in western Kansas in 1875, and three years later he

circulated broadsides throughout the Old Southwest calling for the orderly migration of several hundred black families. But the word of mouth soon grew into wild
rumors—that there was free land for ex-slaves in Kansas, and that the federal
government was going to provide free transportation and free supplies. Suddenly,
in the spring of 1879, thousands of African Americans throughout the Old Southwest
packed up and headed for the fabled land of John Brown—by steamboat, by wagon,
and by foot. Within a few short weeks, more than twenty thousand "Exodusters,"
as they called themselves, flooded into Kansas. "Kansas has a history devoted to
liberty," proclaimed Governor John Pierce St. John, and its citizens would not deny
the freedmen and women in their hour of need. A hurriedly organized state relief
association helped them settle a dozen communities in western Kansas and several
more in Indian Territory (what would later become the state of Oklahoma).

Eventually, some forty black towns were established on the southern plains.
One of the best known was Nicodemus, on the upper Solomon River, where some
150 black families had built a community by the mid-1880s. Like most settlers, the
people of Nicodemus found themselves poorly prepared for the arid conditions of
the western plains, and many moved on during the drought and economic hard times
at the century's end. Most Exodusters elected to remain in one of the previously
settled Kansas towns, where they found work as laborers or domestics. By the
mid-1880s, for example, more than three hundred African Americans were living
"across the tracks" in the town of Manhattan. But despite their historic "devotion
to liberty," turn-of-the-century Kansas joined the rest of the country in establishing
separate and unequal institutions for minorities.

Although persecution drove the flight of the Mormons and the Exodusters,
they were both migrations of hope. But the West was also the site of forced removals
and relocations—migrations of terror. The Cherokees' Trail of Tears was repeated
many times, not only for eastern Indians like the Seminoles or the Sauks, but for
the native peoples of the plains and mountains, who were forced to relocate to
God-forsaken corners of Indian Territory, or were squeezed onto small "reserved"
portions of their former homelands. One memorable migration of terror took place
in the Pacific Northwest in the fall of 1877, when the federal government insisted
that all the Nez Percé Indians move to a confined reservation. About a quarter of
them refused, a group of young warriors led a bloody raid on nearby settlers, and
the U.S. Army attacked. At that point the Nez Percé chiefs decided that their only
alternative to destruction was flight. They led fifty fighting men and three hundred
women and children over a desperate trail of more than thirteen hundred miles in
the hope of reaching Canada. They successfully beat back three full-scale attacks
by the army. Just fifty miles from freedom, they were finally surrounded. After
five days of watching his people freeze and starve, Chief Joseph, the only surviving
leader, surrendered. From a depth of feeling, he offered a moving eulogy to three
centuries of warfare: "Hear me, my chiefs. I am tired; my heart is sick and sad.
From where the sun now stands, I will fight no more forever."

The California gold rush was the prelude to the intensive exploitation of the Far West during the second half of the nineteenth century. This lithograph (c. 1849) shows the diversity of the "forty-eighters," the first miners on the scene, including Latinos and Indians, all busily engaged in washing gold from the alluvial sands of the Sierras.

As the supply of easily available gold diminished, mining became a capital-intensive operation. Hydraulic techniques used high-pressure jets of water to flush whole mountainsides into the streams, causing enormous environmental damage. Photograph by Andrew J. Russell (1869).

The construction of the transcontinental railroad was the key to the industrial development of the American West. *Top:* "Temporary and Permanent Bridges and Citadel Rock, Green River" (Wyoming); *bottom:* "East and West Shaking Hands at the Laying of the Last Rail" (Utah). Photographs by Andrew J. Russell (1869).

The railroad made cattle grazing possible throughout the West. In "Waiting for a Chinook" (c. 1888), cowboy artist Charles Russell depicted the consequences of the devastating winter of 1886–87, which marked the end of open-range cattle operations.

Cowhands found themselves working in what were truly industrial operations. The classic cowboy costume was designed to fit the nature of the work. Some hands tried to organize cowboy unions, but this became far less possible after the 1880s, when the cattle business reorganized into smaller operations with fenced spreads. From "Photographic Album of West Texas Ranch Life" (c. 1900).

Images of western manhood. *Clockwise from top left:* Nat Love, perhaps the best known of numerous African American cowboys, published a popular autobiography that included more than the usual portion of western braggadocio; from *The Life and Adventures of Nat Love* (1907). Jesse James, a former guerilla fighter for the Confederacy who with his brother Frank turned to robbing banks and became legendary as the "Robin Hood" of the West; from James W. Buell, *The Border Bandits* (c. 1883). Hardrock miners of Virginia City, Nevada, who often worked half clad. (photograph, c. 1890).

Women, particularly minority women, are underrepresented in the graphic images of the American West, making these beautiful photographs by California photographer Carleton E. Watkins all the more notable. *Top:* Chinese women of San Francisco; *bottom:* Latinas of Santa Barbara (both c. 1875).

Gallery of Indians depicted in cartes de visite of the late nineteenth century. *Clockwise from top left:* Red Cloud, chief of the Sioux, photograph by Charles Milton Bell (c. 1880); Sitting Bull, Sioux opponent of Custer, photograph by Zalmon Gilbert (c. 1880); Geronimo, war leader of the Apaches, photograph by Reed and Wallace (c. 1889); Apache mother and child, photograph by Reed and Wallace (c. 1889)

Two views of the battle of the Little Big Horn. *Top:* Sioux painting, from Hartley Burr Alexander, *Sioux Indian Painting* (1938); *bottom:* engraving by A. R. Waud, from Frederick Whittaker, *A Popular Life of Gen. George A. Custer* (1876).

The official goal of the acculturation of native people and their assimilation into the nation as citizens is showcased in these photographs of the Kiowa Delos Lonewolf on his admission to Carlisle Indian School in 1892 and his graduation four years later. From the Richard Henry Pratt Papers.

The results of Indian policy were often lethal, and there was no worse horror than the slaughter of Sioux men, women, and children at Wounded Knee on the Pine Ridge Reservation in 1890. "Bureal [sic] of the Dead at the Battle Field of Wounded Knee S.D.," photograph by L. T. Butterfield (1890).

The end of three centuries of warfare found western Indians confined to a series of reservations. Reservations were thought to be temporary expedients, not permanent institutions. Late-nineteenth-century Indian policy was premised on the assumption that Indians would become farmers, Christians, and citizens. Sioux agent Thomas J. Galbraith provided a succinct summary of federal aims during the era that stretched from the 1870s to the 1930s: "weaken and destroy their tribal relations and individualize them by giving each a separate home and having them subsist by industry." The goal, Galbraith wrote, was "to break up the community system." At the same time that western pioneers were building new communities in the West, the federal government was using its power to destroy ancient ones.

The first step was the elimination of all vestiges of Indian sovereignty. In 1870 the Supreme Court ruled that Congress had the power to supersede or even to annul treaties with Indian tribes. With this green light from the Court, the next year Congress passed a resolution putting an end to the system of treaty-making with Indians. "No Indian nation or tribe within the territory of the United States," read the text, "shall [henceforth] be acknowledged or recognized as an independent nation, tribe, or power with whom the United States may contract by treaty." In 1885 Congress passed legislation taking away the right of tribal governments to operate under their own customary law and extended federal jurisdiction over serious crimes committed on reservations.

The legal niceties arranged, an unprecedented federal assault on Indian autonomy followed. Federal Indian agents were directed to undertake a sustained campaign of forced cultural modification—outlawing Indian customs they considered "savage and barbarous," like the Sun Dance of the Plains Indians or the "pagan, horrible, sadistic, and obscene" rituals of the Pueblos. The United States was doing precisely what other imperial powers had done to their colonial subjects. We are "a great colonial power," wrote Harvard professor Albert Bushnell Hart, and "our Indian agents have a status very like that of British in the native states of India."

Cultural imperialism was notable in the curriculum of reservation schools. "If Indian children are to be civilized they must learn the language of civilization," ruled the secretary of the interior, which meant that "no books in the vernacular [the local native language] will be allowed in any school." Even more severe were practices in the Indian boarding schools, most famously Carlisle Indian School in Pennsylvania. The girls were given Euro-American names, dressed as Victorian ladies, and taught to play the piano. The boys were organized into military companies and drilled in uniforms.

On the reservation itself, said one federal official, Indians were to be placed "in positions where they can be controlled and finally compelled by sheer necessity to resort to agricultural labor *or starve*." Hunger and poverty became constant facts of reservation life. But necessity did not transform Indians into farmers, for most reservation land was too barren or too arid to support agriculture. Ironically, the most destructive blow to Indian communities was administered by reformers who thought of themselves as "Friends of the Indians." Their solution to "the

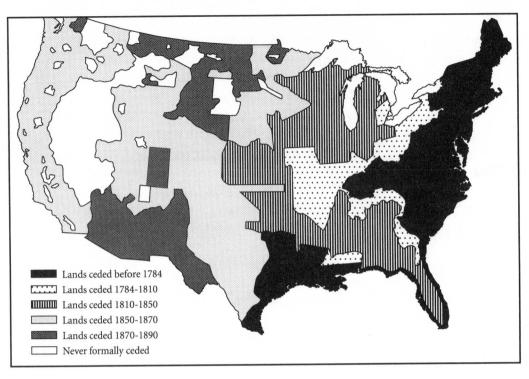

Indian Land Cessions

Indian problem" was a program called *allotment in severalty*. Collective ownership of land—the material base of Indian communities—would give way to individual ownership, emphasizing white individualistic premises over Indian collectivist sensibilities. Reservations would be divided up and "allotted" in small parcels to each Indian head of household. Once the family had demonstrated its responsibility by improving its property, they would become naturalized American citizens. After allotment, reformers believed, tribes would wither away and Indians would be absorbed into the nation as individuals. Congress passed the Allotment Act in 1888.

A majority of Indian tribes opposed allotment, but a majority of western members of Congress were enthusiastic supporters of the legislation. The reason was simple. After reservations had been allotted in parcels of 160 acres to Indian families, the tens of thousands of acres of "surplus lands" would be opened to white settlers. It was a corrupt bargain, and the results were devastating for Indians. In 1888 Indian tribes held 138 million acres; by 1934 this domain had been reduced to only 47 million.

With armed resistance impossible and their cultures and communities under attack, the Indian people of the West responded with an outburst of visionary religious energy. The Ghost Dance movement was the final flame of hope before a long period of resignation. It recalled the religious revitalization movements of earlier Indian holy men—the Delaware Prophet Neolin, who inspired Pontiac's Rebellion, and Tenskwatawa, the Shawnee Prophet, brother of Tecumseh. The Ghost Dance emerged from the vision of Wovoka, a shaman among the Paiutes of Nevada, who felt himself inspired by the Great Spirit to speak to all Indians. Wovoka foresaw a day when the white man would disappear, along with his implements—guns, whiskey, and manufactured goods. Indians would then live together in a world "free from misery, death, and disease." Wovoka's followers developed a ritual that included five days of worship by slow dancing and meditation. Impractical and illusory, yet beautiful in its simple pathos, rich in spirituality, and empowered by ethnic memory, Wovoka's message was one of community flowering from the depths of despair. It spread rapidly among the tribes throughout the Far West, suggesting yet again the power of religion as a sustaining bond of community.

Traditional Sioux people and their chiefs—men like Sitting Bull at the Standing Rock Reservation and Big Foot at Cheyenne River—transformed Wovoka's pacifist message into something far more militant and confrontational. Sioux men, women, and children came together for rituals lasting for several days and nights, singing and dancing themselves into trances. To Indian agents who had been working hard for years to suppress all traces of "pagan" ritual among the Sioux, the Ghost Dance movement was terrifying. "Indians are dancing in the snow and are wild and crazy," one agent telegraphed his superiors. *"We need protection and we need it now."*

In response, the Seventh Cavalry—Custer's old regiment, which was eager for vengeance—hurried to the Pine Ridge Reservation, but Sioux Ghost Dancers, led by Chief Big Foot, took refuge in an unmapped region in the northwest corner of the reservation. Frustrated, federal officials ordered the arrest of the traditional chiefs. Sitting Bull's friends and family tried to protect him, but in the subsequent skirmish eight men were shot, and afterward Sitting Bull and his seventeen-year-old son lay dead on the cold ground.

A few days later, in December 1890, the Seventh Cavalry caught up with Big Foot and his band of Ghost Dancers at an encampment on Wounded Knee Creek. A few miles away, in the main Sioux settlement on the Pine Ridge Reservation, a young man named Black Elk awoke to the sound of gunfire, and he and several friends jumped on their horses and galloped toward Wounded Knee. Reaching a ridge, Black Elk looked down and saw an unforgettable sight—one that will forever haunt American western history. "What we saw was terrible," he remembered. "Dead and wounded women and children and little babies were scattered all along there where they had been trying to run away. The soldiers had followed along the gulch, as they ran, and murdered them in there." The soldiers had been disarming the Sioux when a gun accidentally went off. Trigger-happy troops raked the Indian camp with the murderous fire of four machine guns. The fire left 146 Indians, including 44 women and 18 children, dead on the field. The Seventh Cavalry lost 25 soldiers, most probably killed by the crossfire of their own guns. After the battle a blizzard swept down upon the scene, covering the bodies and freezing their macabre death gestures.

At Wounded Knee the work of community destruction was revealed in all its ghastly horror. "Here in ten minutes an entire community was as the buffalo that bleached on the plains," wrote the western writer Mari Sandoz. "There was something loose in the world that hated joy and happiness as it hated brightness and color, reducing everything to drab agony and gray." In 1903 the Pine Ridge Sioux erected a monument over the mass burial of the Wounded Knee martyrs, a site that for them—indeed for many Americans—has become a shrine to the Indian victims of colonization.

After the Civil War each of the states and territories of the upper Midwest and northern plains pursued active immigrant recruitment policies, publishing guides in the languages of target groups and sending agents across the Atlantic to pitch the advantages of their lands. They were remarkably successful, for in much of rural Europe a process of agricultural consolidation was throwing tens of thousands of families off their farms. During the last quarter of the nineteenth century, from one-third to one-half of the population of the northern plains was foreign born, the highest proportion of any region in the nation. The countryside was a patchwork of culturally homogeneous communities of Germans, Czechs, Poles, Russians, Hungarians, and especially Scandinavians. Church affiliation among these groups was very high, and the role of the church as a conservative force—helping to perpetuate the old customs of the homeland, presiding over a pattern of in-marriage, and encouraging the continued use of homeland languages—should not be underestimated.

Cultural homogeneity characterized these communities until the early twentieth century, when the third generation began to move more decisively in the direction of assimilation. Swedish congregations in rural Minnesota engaged in a prolonged and divisive debate over whether God could hear prayers in English. During the "Americanization" frenzy of World War I—when a number of midwestern governors issued proclamations forbidding the public use of any language but English (even on the telephone!)—Swedish churches finally began holding their worship services in English. The declining use of homeland languages was a symbol of other assimilative trends, including increased rates of out-migration and intermarriage. One of the most voluble critics of assimilation was Ole Rölvaag, who immigrated from Norway as a young man in 1896. He became a professor of literature and then a famous novelist with the publication of *Giants in the Earth* (1927). Rölvaag, who believed American culture had little to offer except a preoccupation with material success, foresaw a bleak future: "Out of our highly praised melting pot will come a dull, smug complacency, barren of all creative thought and effort. Soon we will have reached the perfect democracy of barrenness."

The barren sameness of western community life was most famously critiqued in novelist Sinclair Lewis's *Main Street* (1920). When Carol Kennicott, Lewis's main character, arrives at Gopher Prairie, Minnesota, it seems scarcely more impressive than a hazel thicket: "There was no dignity in it, nor any hope of greatness. . . . It was not a place to live in, not possibly, not conceivably." Carol walks the length and

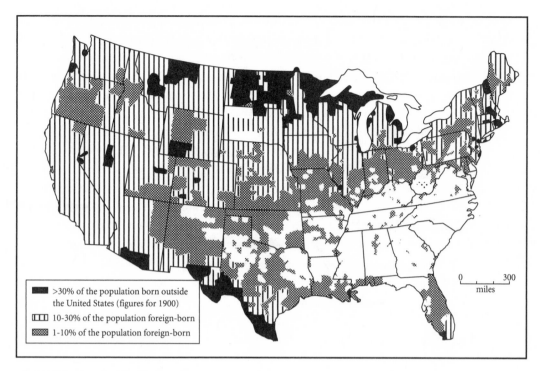

>30% of the population born outside
the United States (figures for 1900)

10-30% of the population foreign-born

1-10% of the population foreign-born

0   300
miles

The Foreign-Born Population in 1900

breadth of the town in just thirty-six minutes. The residents, she concludes, were as
"drab as their houses, as flat as their fields." Lewis had grown up in a small prairie
town. "*Main Street*," he wrote, "is the culmination of Main Street everywhere."
From the Mississippi valley to the Pacific coast, these towns were like little corn
hills—some tall, some short, some with more ears and kernels than others, but from
a distance, indistinguishable.

For decades Americans had professed that small towns were the best the nation had to offer. But that view began to seem terribly old-fashioned in the aftermath
of World War I. Lewis's *Main Street*—published the same year the Census Bureau
announced that the population of urban America for the first time outnumbered that
of rural America—conveniently marks an attitudinal sea change. Not that Lewis
was the first. Preceding him had been Hamlin Garland's realist stories of hard-bitten
western farm families in *Main-Traveled Roads* (1891) and Edgar Lee Masters's
Spoon River Anthology (1914), verses depicting the crimped lives of small-town
residents. But with *Main Street*, the cynical view became mainstream.

The myth of small-town life had pictured a homogeneous, classless society in
which anyone with ambition, thrift, and diligence could easily move upward. But in
fact, class was everything in the small town. It was true that during their earliest
years, class lines were indefinite and social mobility noticeable. The initial surge of
economic expansion into Trempealeau County, Wisconsin, in the 1850s, for example,
opened opportunities on every side. By the end of the Civil War, however, those

doors had nearly closed. Rigid class lines appeared early nearly everywhere, even in the supposedly wide-open cattle towns of the Great Plains, where within a few years of their founding, the richest 20 percent of the population controlled more than 80 percent of the real estate. The working classes were divided between craftsmen, transients, and drifters. African Americans, Mexicans, Asians, and occasionally a few Indians were isolated at the bottom of the social ladder.

Toward the end of the nineteenth century, the atmosphere in small western towns seemed increasingly uneasy. The industrial promise of links between farm and market had not been fulfilled; clearly, the railroads served eastern capital. Conflicts within communities grew more overt, especially as the quarter-century of depression from 1873 to 1898 exposed the vulnerability of the poor. The hardening of class lines bred dissatisfaction, and small-town newspaper editors had to admit the existence of discord. Social conflict became the rule rather than the exception, and cohesiveness degenerated into narrow morality. Frederick Russell Burnham, who lived in a midwestern small town in the 1870s, thought most people spent half of their time trying to reform someone else in a quiet fervor of "intolerant religiosity." This was why so many intellectuals fled to the cities and began to describe their former environments as smug, prejudiced, sterile, and joyless.

Much of the trouble stemmed from small-town America's resistance to change. Dedicated to prudential virtues and "the good old days," townspeople saw corruption in industrial values and, in the words of poet Vachel Lindsay, sighed "for the sweet life wrenched and torn / By thundering commerce, fierce and bare." True, towns often courted small-scale industry in the hope of creating more jobs and revenue in their own precincts. But monopolies beyond their control, large-scale corporations, and intervention by the federal government corroded community autonomy. Turning inward, the residents of small western towns developed intense localism as a shield against unwelcome change. Confronting fears that the "end of the frontier" would bring an end to the assimilation of foreigners, the white middle class of the small town lashed out against "un-American" immigrants. Fear and loathing marked the end of one West and the creation of another.

In the American West of the late nineteenth and early twentieth centuries, no immigrants faced more prejudice and hostility than the Chinese and the Japanese. In 1878 a federal judge in California ruled that Chinese immigrants could not become naturalized citizens because they were not "white persons" within the meaning of the Naturalization Act of 1790, a decision extended to the Japanese by the Supreme Court in 1922 and not repealed until after World War II by legislation. Throughout the West, states and localities passed legislation denying Asians the right to vote, forbidding public agencies to employ them, and restricting them to residential ghettos. But with the same dream of land ownership and prosperity that motivated other settlers, many Asian stickers raised their families and built communities. At least their children became citizens by birth.

Permanent Chinese communities began to appear in the California countryside in the 1860s wherever Chinese workers toiled in the fields and orchards. "They form little communities among themselves, do their own cooking, live in little camps together" wrote one landlord. Similarly, in the 1870s growers in the citrus belt of southern California began employing Chinese men in their groves and packing houses. Citrus growers came to depend on the industry and careful work of the Chinese, and soon every town in the citrus belt had its own Chinatown, usually on the poor side of the tracks. By the 1870s Chinese workers made up half of California's agricultural workforce. Although the growers appreciated them, there were waves of anti-Chinese violence during periods of economic depression. In countless farming communities, vigilantes and armed mobs forced the Chinese to move out—"the driving out," as Chinese Americans remember this period. By the turn of the century, most had relocated to the Chinatowns of the largest western cities where they found an uncertain refuge.

"Now that the Chinese have been excluded," Methodist missionary Merriman Harris wrote from California in 1888, "there is a demand for cheap labor and it is probable that Japanese laborers will be brought over to supply the demand." He was right. The Japanese government did not allow emigration until the end of the century, so it was not until the 1890s that Japanese men began arriving to seek work on the railroads and especially on the commercial farms of the West. By 1910 more than thirty thousand Japanese farmworkers lived in California, the single largest ethnic group toiling in what journalist Carey McWilliams would later call the "factories in the field."

Westerners often saw the Japanese as an even greater threat than the Chinese because many of them leased or purchased land of their own. Japanese growers were soon supplying most of the vegetables and much of the fruit sold in the urban markets of California. Reacting to pressures from exclusionists, in 1908 President Theodore Roosevelt negotiated the so-called Gentleman's Agreement with the Japanese government that ended the immigration of Japanese men to the United States. And in 1913 the California legislature made it illegal for aliens of Asian descent to own or lease lands for the long term, legislation that several other western states imitated. But first-generation Japanese immigrants (the *Issei*) were soon shifting the title of their farms to their second-generation American-born children (the *Nisei*) who were citizens, not aliens. By 1920 Japanese farmers, who controlled only 1 percent of California's agricultural land, were raising and marketing crops equal to 10 percent of the total value of the state's production.

The Gentleman's Agreement had permitted the continued immigration of wives of Japanese men already living in the Pacific states, and during the years between 1908 and 1924, when all other Japanese immigration was ended, approximately sixty thousand Japanese women entered the country. Perhaps half that number were known as "picture brides," women whose families arranged for their marriage-by-proxy to immigrant Japanese men in America. Women meant families, a point not lost on California's Senator James Phelan. "The rats are in the granary," he declared when asked about the immigration of Japanese women. "They have gotten in under the door and they are breeding with alarming rapidity. . . . If this is not checked now it means the end of the white race in California." In 1919, when Phelan issued his warning, the Japanese made up less than 3 percent of the state's population.

In the early twentieth century, there was an explosive increase in Mexican immigration to the western United States. Official government statistics record the entry of 728,171 Mexicans between the turn of the century and 1930, but historians who have studied this migration estimate that many more crossed the border illegally, which would place the total immigration at about 10 percent of the entire population of Mexico. This was yet another of the mass migrations that characterized the history of the American West.

Many of these immigrants were refugees of the revolution in Mexico that followed the overthrow of the dictator Porfirio Díaz in 1911 and engulfed the country for nearly ten years. Some of the bloodiest fighting occurred in Mexico's northern states, and thousands of war-torn civilians looked toward the United States for their safety. During one week in 1916, U.S. immigration agents counted nearly five thousand Mexicans trying to cross the Rio Grande at El Paso. Unable to cope with such numbers, officials closed the border crossing, but refugees were soon coming over illegally downriver.

Revolutionary sentiment spilled over the border with the refugees. In the Rio Grande valley of Texas, the traditional ranchero world was giving way to Anglo commercial agriculture. Commercial farmers took over county governments and instituted laws segregating public accommodations and schools. Frustrations erupted into violence. In 1915 a group of Tejano rancheros and businessmen met in the small town of San Diego, Texas, on the Nueces River—not far from the spot where the Mexican War had begun seventy years before—and issued a proclamation calling for armed insurrection by a "Liberating Army" of the oppressed castes of the Southwest—Latinos, Asians, African Americans, and Indians. Several hundred (perhaps several thousand) Tejanos pledged themselves to *El Plan de San Diego*, as this quixotic manifesto was known. Armed and mounted Tejano raiders attacked farms and railroads, burned bridges, and sabotaged irrigation systems, in the process killing several dozen Anglos. Texas authorities responded with what historian Walter Prescott Webb described as "an orgy of bloodshed." Anglo vigilance committees lynched suspected insurrectionists while the Texas Rangers conducted punitive raids against Tejano communities.

Revolutionary violence may have *pushed* Mexicans across the border, but they were also *pulled* by the growing demand for labor in the orchards and fields of the new Southwest. Clearly, encouraging Mexican immigration—and thus increasing the supply of labor and lowering wages—was in the interest of the powerful farmers' associations. By the 1920s Mexican migrants made up about three-quarters of the more than one million farm laborers in the American West.

The proximity of Mexican migrants to their communities of origin made them unique among the immigrant groups who settled the West. When Mexico ceded the territory to the United States, many Latino families were divided, and there was regular movement back and forth across the untended border. Thus began a pattern of continuous cross-border migration. Typical Mexican farmworkers of the early century might follow the harvest cycle of the Southwest, then return to their Mexican villages for the winter. During the mass exodus of the Mexican Revolution, however, thousands of families decided to settle permanently in the United States. They founded new *colonias* in the dozens of farm towns servicing the intensive agricultural districts—usually on the rough side of the tracks, often on the site of former Chinatowns, abandoned during earlier bouts of vigilante violence. Newcomers headed for *tenemos familiares*, places where extended family or former neighbors lived; colonias often had strong links with one or two villages back home. These connections encouraged migrants to think of themselves as members of what historian Sarah Deutsch calls a "regional community." *Sin fronteras*—a world without borders—that was the Mexican migrant's watchword.

Growers were fond of assuring themselves that Mexicans were simple peasants, unlikely to cause labor trouble. While it is true that most Mexicans remained loyal to the country of their birth, equating this ambivalence about citizenship with docility was wishful thinking. Children were taught to admire grandfathers who had fought with Benito Juárez when he resisted French occupation in the 1860s, as well as fathers who had stood with Emiliano Zapata and mothers who had been *soldaderas* in the army of Francisco "Pancho" Villa during the Mexican Revolution. Indeed, most migrants came from precisely those areas where the Mexican Revolution had been most intensely argued and fought, and many had participated in peasant rebellions or union struggles.

Working conditions in the fields and orchards of the Southwest tested loyalty to those traditions. One migrant Mexican worker remembered that the growers considered the Mexican workers slaves, treating "the horses and the cows better." According to a report of the California Department of Immigration and Housing, most migrant farmworkers were forced to provide their own accommodations, some creating "a rude shelter from the limbs of trees." Little better were the grower-owned labor camps, where California investigators found "filth, squalor, and [an] entire absence of sanitation." To make matters worse, the wages of farmworkers began to fall in the mid-twenties and kept falling during the years of the Depression. In 1935 a typical migrant worker earned only $280 per year (the equivalent of about $4,000 in 2005 values). Belying their reputation as docile and submissive, Mexican farmworkers responded by organizing unions and battling growers for better working conditions and higher wages. "We would have starved working," declared one organizer, "so we decided to starve striking."

Historians have documented 160 major farm labor strikes in California alone during the 1930s, most of them prominently featuring Mexican workers and organizers. High tide came in 1933 when growers were hit with 37 strikes involving forty-eight thousand workers and affecting two-thirds of the state's agricultural production. In the words of Carey McWilliams, who served as chief investigator for California's Department of Immigration and Housing in the late thirties, these strikes were "the most extensive in the farm labor history of California and the United States; in scale, number, and value of crops affected, they were quite without precedent." Many of the strike organizers were veterans of the Mexican Revolution.

These attachments to Mexico could inspire, but they could also be a barrier to progress. When the strikes were broken, as all eventually were, it was not because of the absence of worker resolve, for there was an abundance of that, nor because of grower violence, although there was plenty of that, too. No, most of the strikes were ended by the intervention of Mexican consular officials who arranged meager deals with growers under the assumption that the Mexican state represented the interests of Mexican migrants. "The Mexican consul played a major role in California's labor struggles of the 1930s," writes historian Gilbert Gonzáles, "providing a prominent bulwark against working class radicalism." It was an important lesson, encouraging Mexicans to stop thinking of themselves as movers and to consider the implications of becoming stickers, to be Mexican *Americans*.

Chapter 13 **The Urban Frontier**

 The historic West of popular imagination is a region of scattered populations and rural isolation, an "area of free land" whose settlement the historian Frederick Jackson Turner famously identified as "the really American part of our history." Turner was beginning his career at the University of Wisconsin when he declared this "frontier thesis" in 1893. Only six years later another young historian, Adna Weber of Columbia University, published a study that fundamentally challenged Turner's ruling assumption. Weber demonstrated that in the western states, more people lived in cities than anywhere else in the country except in the North Atlantic states. The West was more urban than rural.

In the nineteenth century, many eyewitness participants noted the importance of cities in the westward movement. "Without transition you pass from a wilderness into the streets of a city," remarked Alexis de Tocqueville after traveling through the trans-Appalachian West in the early 1830s. The urban character of westering intensified in the trans-Mississippi West, where the aridity dictated a low density of rural population, and the extractive economy encouraged the development of industrial urban centers. The result confirmed an old American pioneer proverb: "Give me a rich country, and I'll soon give you a large city."

Towns and cities were a critical part of the trans-Appalachian West. Town-builders platted Lexington and Louisville in Kentucky years before the great migration that filled the Ohio valley with American settlers. Even as the battle raged for control of the region, eastern developers laid out the town of Cincinnati as the administrative capital of the Old Northwest. In the Old Southwest, the entrepôts of Nashville and Memphis in Tennessee and Natchez in Mississippi were essential to the development of the planter economy. These towns "were the spearheads of the frontier," writes Richard Wade. "Planted far in advance of the line of settlement, they held the West for the approaching population." These incipient western cities became ruthless competitors for the trade of their extensive agricultural hinterlands. Urban merchants sought to capture the business of thousands of farmers who were moving beyond subsistence and devoting more of their time and energy to the production of a surplus for market.

The first clear victor in this struggle for western urban supremacy was Cincinnati, founded in 1789 and grown into an important market center by 1800. "I could scarcely believe my own eyes," a visitor from New Jersey wrote home, "to see the number of people and wagons and saddle horses and the quantities of meat, flour, corn, fish, fowl, and sauce [preserves and jams] of all kinds that were offered and actually sold." It was the steamboat, however, that made Cincinnati a regional power. In 1816 the first side-wheeler was launched to carry heavy cargoes in the relatively shallow waters of the upper Ohio. Taking advantage of its location at the center of the nineteenth-century "corn belt," Cincinnati's merchants concentrated on the slaughter and packing of pork ("corn on four legs") for shipment downriver to New Orleans, from where it was distributed to butchers along the Atlantic coast. From the mountains of slaughterhouse refuse, enterprising capitalists created new industries—producing leather, brushes, glue, soap, and chemicals—and on this economic base Cincinnati rose to become the first industrial city west of the Appalachians. Cincinnati also triumphed as the cultural center of the early trans-Appalachian West, with numerous academies and "commercial colleges," scores of magazines, dozens of newspapers, and many publishing houses that printed and distributed hundreds of books.

Another western metropolis developed in Saint Louis, founded by French traders from New Orleans in 1762 at the strategic junction of the Missouri and Mississippi rivers. The town long served as the headquarters of the Rocky Mountain fur trade, but it was the trade in lead—essential for ammunition—that accounted for its rise as one of the great cities of the Mississippi valley. When steamboats began operating on the Mississippi after the War of 1812, control of the nation's lead trade enabled Saint Louis to free itself from the economic dominance of Cincinnati, establishing a hinterland of its own along the Mississippi corridor north of the city.

Cincinnati and Saint Louis were the urban success stories of the early-nineteenth-century West. But the competition for hinterlands was more frequently a destroyer rather than a builder of towns. On a trip down the Ohio River, Frederick Law Olmsted was startled by the number of forlorn and abandoned towns he saw: "These mushroom cities mark only a night's camping-place of civilization." What explained the rise of some western cities and the fall of others? In general, western urban boosters believed in the "doctrine of natural advantage," in which the best location would win out. As one booster put it, "God has marked out by topography the lines of commerce." But the truth was, the "great tracings of the Almighty's finger" played a far less significant role than the "invisible hand" of eastern capital.

The rise of Saint Louis, for instance, was made possible by New York and Boston investors who were attracted by the profits that local entrepreneurs were making in the shipping business. Many capitalist firms from the East established branch offices in the city. "The counting-rooms, the stores, the mills, and the machine shops," wrote a reporter in Saint Louis, were "filled by New Englanders and New Yorkers." The city's commercial future was determined not by God, but by Wall Street and State Street bankers.

The importance of eastern control became clear during the mid-1850s, when Saint Louis was thrown into turmoil by the border war over the future of slavery in Kansas. Proslavery mobs threatened eastern merchants, attacks that were front-page news in the East. Francis Hunt, a Bostonian doing business in Saint Louis, admonished his local associates that unless the attacks ceased, the "source of their prosperity shall be cut off." With the open hostility toward Yankees unabated, Hunt soon closed his doors and joined the flight of eastern businessmen from the city. Almost overnight, the city's economy collapsed.

The controversy crippled Saint Louis at precisely the moment of its greatest challenge by the upstart city of Chicago. Little more than a swampy outpost on the southwestern shore of Lake Michigan in the 1830s, Chicago was the creation of eastern capitalists in collaboration with the state of Illinois. While speculators invested in unimproved city lots, driving up property values, the state undertook an ambitious program of lakeshore harbor improvements and canal construction, connecting Chicago with both eastern markets and the surrounding countryside. During the 1840s the city captured the grain trade of northern Illinois and southern Wisconsin. Chicago's fortunes boomed just as eastern investors were pouring capital into railroad construction, and by the early 1850s a number of eastern railroad companies had selected Chicago as their western terminus, while several western companies were constructing lines radiating outward from the city into the adjacent countryside. One of the most important was the westbound Chicago and Rock Island Railroad, which became the first railroad to bridge the Mississippi in 1854.

When a Saint Louis steamboat crashed into the bridge two years later, its owners sued the railroad. It was a showdown between the two cities. "If we are beaten," warned the Saint Louis Chamber of Commerce, "the commercial position of St. Louis, which is now the pride and boast of its citizens, would be counted among the things that were." And so it was. The jury deadlocked, the judge dismissed the suit, and Saint Louis was forced to concede the loss of the upper Mississippi. One Chicago newspaper crowed that now "Omaha eats Chicago groceries, wears Chicago dry goods, builds with Chicago lumber, and reads Chicago newspapers." Chicago's triumph did not result simply from the "natural advantage" of its geography. Rather, it was the combined result of location, savvy investing, an innovative new mode of transportation, cutthroat competition, and the political crisis that marked the coming of the Civil War.

Chicago became headquarters for the late-nineteenth-century colonization of the trans-Mississippi West, what geographer Andrew Frank Burghardt calls a *gateway city*, that is, the link between the settlements and resources of the West and the cities, factories, and commercial networks of the Northeast. Chicago lumber merchants set thousands of men to work cutting the pine forests of the Great Lakes, and shipped westward the billions of board feet of lumber needed for the construction of the railroad system as well as for countless homes, towns, and cities on the Great Plains. Chicago entrepreneurs built dozens of grain elevators and devised the practice of commodity trading on the city's Board of Trade, providing a world market for the thousands of farmers who converted the grassland into a fruited plain. Chicago meatpackers financed the western cattle industry, and the southside stockyards became the city's largest employer, drawing tens of thousands of immigrant workers from Ireland, Germany, Bohemia, Poland, and Slovakia. Much of the fabulous wealth produced by this western empire went into the hands of the eastern investors who bankrolled the system. But great accumulations also built up in the accounts of Chicago's own capitalists, who used it to build an urban industrial economy that by 1880 had made theirs into the nation's "second city."

Chicago stood atop a western urban hierarchy that included some two dozen cities in the trans-Mississippi West, each with its own immediate hinterland, but each also in a tributary relationship to Chicago. The "railroad capitalism" of the late nineteenth century concentrated decision making in great urban centers and created a pecking order for lesser cities. For the West, that great center was Chicago. This interconnected urban system, writes historian Gilbert Stelter, "reflected the basically colonial nature of western life."

William "Buffalo Bill" Cody told a story that illustrates the point. As young buffalo hunters supplying meat for construction crews on the Kansas Pacific Railway in the 1860s, Cody and a friend went into partnership to develop a town they called Rome at a spot on the prairie where the railroad planned to locate its repair shops. They staked out lots, and soon merchants, saloon-keepers, and ordinary settlers arrived and built on them. But returning from a hunt one afternoon, Cody discovered that "the town was being torn down and carted away." Officials in some far-flung corporate office had decided to relocate the repair facilities to Hays City, and Rome was unbuilt in a day.

Denver narrowly avoided duplicating Rome's sudden fall. When the Union Pacific Railroad bypassed the town in 1867, many of Denver's businessmen panicked and rushed north to Cheyenne in Wyoming on the rail line. A number of the city's more determined and optimistic citizens, however, organized a railroad company of their own called the Denver Pacific, used their Washington connections to win a land grant and subsidy from Congress, and ran tracks north to link up with the transcontinental line. Claiming a place of prominence in the emerging urban system demanded aggressive promotion.

When the transcontinental Union Pacific line was built north of Salt Lake City in 1869, Mormon leaders financed a line connecting the city with the depot at Ogden. Over the next decade, the Mormons undertook a program of industrial development that transformed the city into a manufacturing center. The twin cities of Minneapolis and Saint Paul, Minnesota, took advantage of the cheap water power available at Saint Anthony Falls on the Mississippi River and built an energetic lumber and flour milling industry. Using their own capital, local millers financed a rail line into the Dakotas to capture the wheat trade. By 1880 the combined output of companies such as Pillsbury outpaced Milwaukee, Saint Louis, and Chicago in the production of flour. In Denver, local capitalists invested in smelting and processing the ores produced by the region's many mines, and by 1900 Denver's 134,000 residents were producing commodities valued at more than $50 million. As a rising regional power, Denver was able to circumvent Chicago and establish direct connections with New York financiers, becoming a regional command post for great mining interests controlled by the Rockefeller and Guggenheim families.

Houston's remarkable rise as one of the great cities of twentieth-century America dates from the huge oil gusher unloosed in 1901 at the Spindletop oilfield, in nearby Beaumont, Texas. Spouting more than one hundred feet high, the gusher blew off one hundred thousand barrels a day for ten days, creating a lake of oil at its base. Other similar spills would catch fire and burn for weeks. Within months, engineers tapped other vast oilfields along the Gulf Coast. Local companies with the now-familiar names of Gulf, Texaco, Shell, and Humble (later Exxon) built refineries and established headquarters in Houston. With federal funding, the city deepened the channel at Buffalo Bayou, permitting access for enormous oil tankers. Petroleum became the foundation for a diversified industrial economy as other enterprises were drawn to the area: chemicals, machine tools, and warehousing. By 1910 Houston's economy had moved into the stage of self-financed growth. The growth of regional cities like Houston, Denver, Salt Lake City, and Minneapolis meant serious competition for Chicago, which by 1900 had relinquished the status of gateway city of the West.

San Francisco was the first regional city of the trans-Mississippi West to achieve first-class status, although like all western cities, it began as a colony of the East. During the city's first decade, nearly all the principal merchants and bankers were agents or associates of Boston and New York firms, and a survey of the city's lawyers found that 40 percent had been licensed to practice by the New York State bar association. But the fabulous wealth of the mines led to the early creation of a powerful group of local capitalists, providing an opportunity for independence that other western cities could only envy. Perhaps the event signaling San Francisco's arrival as one of a handful of elite American cities was the capture, by its bankers and "Silver Kings," of the unprecedented wealth of Nevada's Comstock Lode in the late 1860s. From their headquarters on San Francisco's Nob Hill, writes historian Rodman Paul, "Comstock millionaires underwrote many a new venture in the American West and abroad."

Henry George, San Francisco's radical journalist, was one of the first to note the city's rise to gateway status. "Not a settler in all the Pacific States and Territories but must pay San Francisco tribute," he wrote. "Not an ounce of gold dug, a pound of ore smelted, a field gleaned, or a tree felled in all their thousands of square miles, but must add to her wealth." By 1880 San Francisco's commercial hinterland stretched from Panama to Alaska, from the sugar plantations of the Hawaiian Islands to the mining districts of northern Idaho. It was also the first industrial city in the trans-Mississippi West. In 1880 approximately thirty thousand workers produced output valued higher than the combined total of all the other urban centers of the West.

In the 1870s San Francisco investors began to buy up thousands of arid acres in the undeveloped southern portion of the state. With a population of only ten thousand, Los Angeles was still a mere village compared with San Francisco, but San Franciscans were betting on an explosion of interest when the Southern Pacific and the Santa Fe railroads linked Los Angeles to the national rail network in the 1880s. The boom came when the two rail lines were completed in 1887 and was provoked by a fare war between them that drove down the price of a ticket from Saint Louis to as little as five dollars. That brought an estimated two hundred thousand tourists, curiosity-seekers, and land speculators who thrilled to the pitch of boosters, as had generations of previous westering dreamers. Like Kentucky and Texas in earlier years, southern California was a land unmatched for its fertility and beauty. "There are calla lilies by the acre," read one typically overblown guidebook, and "roses of a thousand varieties, by the million, it being no rare thing to see a hundred thousand, two hundred thousand, or more, buds and blossoms and full blown roses on a single bush at the same moment."

The resulting frenzy of buying and selling sent real estate prices through the roof, and in a little less than two years, southern California developers laid out more than sixty new towns on nearly eighty thousand acres. The smart money got out before the inevitable bust of 1889, which destroyed thousands of paper fortunes. "I had a half a million dollars wiped out in the crash," cried a character in Theodore Van Dyke's novel of the boom, *Millionaires of a Day* (1890), "and what's worse, $500 of it was cash." Yet the episode left Los Angeles with a population of more than fifty thousand and whetted the expectations of the local business elite. Few would have disagreed with the vice president of the Santa Fe Railway who predicted that "people will continue to come here until the whole country becomes one of the most densely populated sections of the United States."

Before that could happen, however, severe constraints had to be overcome. Los Angeles had no adequate harbor along the nearby Pacific coast, and without one, a local booster warned, the city was destined to "become a backcountry to San Diego." Moreover, southern California lacked sufficient water to support the swelling masses of a great city. Indeed, so unpropitious was the location, many have wondered why a city was being built there at all. But in the twenty years following the initial boom, the leaders of Los Angeles took on these problems and solved them. The harbor question was taken to Washington, D.C., and after a concerted campaign, Congress voted in 1897 to "improve" the anchorage at the village of San Pedro, a part of greater Los Angeles. Over the next decade, the Army Corps of Engineers invested millions to convert San Pedro into one of the world's great ports, or in the words of Robert Fogelson, "to duplicate at Los Angeles what nature created gratuitously at San Francisco."

Meanwhile, the city's establishment was on the prowl for new sources of water. In 1905 and 1907 the Los Angeles Board of Water Commissioners proposed, and the voters approved, more than $25 million in bonds to finance the construction of an aqueduct diverting the flow of the Owens River, some two hundred miles northeast on the flank of the Sierra Nevada, and channeling it to the city. It was a project comparable to the construction of the Erie Canal or the transcontinental railroad. The water arrived in 1913, providing Los Angeles with more than enough capacity to quench the thirst of its approximately 350,000 residents, enough indeed to sustain a population numbering in the millions. What the citizens of Los Angeles had not been told, however, was that a syndicate of wealthy citizens—including government insiders—had previously bought up more than one hundred thousand acres in the adjacent San Fernando valley, where Owens River water was stored in reservoirs. "Anyone who knew this, and bought land in the San Fernando Valley while it was still dirt-cheap," writes historian Marc Reisner, "stood to become very, very rich." The syndicate made an estimated profit of $100 million. In an era of aggressive western promotion, the elite of Los Angeles set a new standard for urban buccaneering.

One of the most prominent members of that elite was Henry E. Huntington, nephew and heir of Collis P. Huntington of the Southern Pacific Railroad, one of the legendary Big Four. Huntington invested his abundant family capital in Los Angeles trolley companies and real estate, and by 1900 he had become southern California's single largest landowner and majordomo of the interurban rail system known as the Pacific Electric. Huntington built dozens of new trolley lines, connecting his undeveloped tracts to the city center. He had his land subdivided into lots and planted with pepper trees from Peru, jacaranda from Brazil, and palm trees from Asia or Africa; had the streets surveyed and paved; and even had the utilities laid out in advance of building. He thus helped create the conditions for what became the southern Californian preference for detached, single-family homes with private, landscaped yards—decades before this became the ideal elsewhere in the country. Huntington helped invent a new kind of dispersed urban landscape, what a later generation would call *urban sprawl*.

Thus Los Angeles was ready-made for the automobile and became the first city in the nation to enthusiastically embrace the car culture. The country's first filling station appeared there in 1909, the same year that California became the first state to authorize a bond issue for a paved state highway system. Autos accelerated the process of decentralization that Huntington began. In the twenties, builders developed some thirty-two hundred new subdivisions with 250,000 new homes in outlying areas. Los Angeles, as Carey McWilliams famously observed, has from its beginnings been "a collection of suburbs in search of a city."

Early-twentieth-century Los Angeles was primarily an urban service center for the booming agricultural hinterland of southern California. The production of citrus fruit, for example, was spread widely throughout the foothills and valleys of the southland, but the association that organized the picking, packing, and national distribution of "Sunkist" oranges was located in the city. Real estate and tourism provided other sources of economic strength. But the low level of industrialization in early-twentieth-century Los Angeles was remarkable. James M. Cain, who moved to the area in the twenties to work as a Hollywood screenwriter, was appalled at "the piddling occupations" of his neighbors, and in *The Postman Always Rings Twice* (1934), his classic noir novel of southern California, a character remarks that the "whole goddam country lives selling hot dogs to each other."

Southern California leaders such as Huntington, however, were empire builders, and they anticipated a great future for their city. "Los Angeles is destined to become the most important city in this country, if not the world," Huntington wrote. "It can extend in any direction as far as you like; its front door opens on the Pacific, the ocean of the future." Huntington stood at the modern end of a long line of westering prophets.

During the second half of the nineteenth century, the direction of American expansion shifted from the countryside to the city. For one thing, the farm crises of the 1870s and the 1890s caused tens of thousands of families to abandon their farms and ranches and head for urban areas. But even prosperity produced out-migration in the countryside. As pioneers settled rural districts, eventually the number of farms or ranches approached the maximum number the land could support. Landowners sought to increase their productivity through mechanization, and those who were successful invested their returns by buying the farms of less-fortunate neighbors, who moved on. Compare this pattern of economic development to that of the city, where innovations in manufacturing led to the creation of new opportunities and new jobs, what economists call a *multiplier effect*. But in the countryside, economic development inevitably meant depopulation. Rural counties in the Great Plains states had begun to lose residents by the end of the nineteenth century, and over the course of the twentieth century their populations fell from 35 to 50 percent. Today, there are more than six thousand ghost towns in the state of Kansas alone.

This movement from farm to city is relatively well known. Less so is the fact that for every twenty farm boys, as many as twenty-five or thirty farm girls moved from the rural West to the cities. One historical study of rural households in late-nineteenth-century Illinois, Iowa, and Minnesota details the "defeminization" of the countryside, with six in ten daughters of typical families leaving the area while seven in ten sons remained. Many of these young women headed for the cities. By the 1880s in most western cities, native-born young women had begun to outnumber native-born young men.

What explains the greater rates of female migration to the city? In the opinion of many contemporaries, young women were pushed out of the countryside by constricted opportunities and the lingering legacy of patriarchy. In order to assess the views of country women, in 1913 the Department of Agriculture surveyed several thousand farm wives. The results confirmed the worst. The consensus among women was that they were overworked, that they had limited educational and vocational options, and that "old-fashioned" male attitudes kept them at home and prevented their full participation in public and community life.

Women may also have been fleeing male violence. Historian David Peterson del Mar finds a good deal of provocative evidence in the records of the divorce courts in rural Oregon. One man, defending himself against the charge of battering his wife, explained to the judge that he had used only the violence "necessary and reasonable to enforce rightful obedience," and swore he would hit his wife again "if she did not do to suit." Del Mar concludes that "husbands commonly used physical force on their wives." Other kinds of evidence also suggest that domestic violence was commonplace in the West. Readers of Mari Sandoz's biography of her homesteader father, *Old Jules* (1935), may be shocked at his violent treatment of women. Yet Sandoz makes it clear that her father was no different from the other men she knew growing up in Nebraska. A woman was something to exploit, to work, and to bear children.

Probably most women came to the city with high hopes. Urban employment offered them a means of determining their own affairs, of making incomes of their own—something hard to come by in the country where just about the only paid work for women was teaching school. Historians have neglected the fascinating and important story of these female migrants. Concentrating on the changing "manners and morals" of middle-class women during the early twentieth century, they have ignored the fact that it was mostly urban working women—many of them fresh from the country—who as early as the 1890s were charting a course for "the new woman," one that included a measure of economic independence and the possibilities for life apart from family. Why does the country girl come to the city? asked social worker Frances Donovan in 1920. Because "it is her frontier, and in it she is the pioneer." These young women should be given their appropriate place, side by side with the forty-niners and migrating families in the drama of the moving American.

Western cities also attracted thousands of immigrants from abroad. In 1880 foreign-born residents made up a third or more of the populations of Salt Lake City, Portland, Sacramento, and Omaha. Indeed, in 1880 San Francisco had the highest proportion of foreign-born residents (45 percent) of any city in the nation, more than either New York (40 percent) or Chicago (42 percent). During the first decades in San Francisco, immigrant groups carved out their own neighborhoods along the crowded, hilly streets. Consider the Italians. In a city with little manufacturing, they moved into fishing and skilled craftwork and started small businesses. Italian workers rose to leadership in the city's powerful labor movement, and Italian names were prominent in the city's business community.

One of them, Amadeo Peter Giannini, a lumbering, deep-voiced, stubborn tyrant of a man, spent his early years in the family wholesale produce business, selling crates of lettuce and peaches in San Francisco's foggy predawn light. But in his thirties he switched to banking, opening the Banca d'Italia in North Beach. After the devastating earthquake of 1906, he carted out of the burning city $80,000 hidden under the fruit crates of his old produce firm; and while the city still smoldered, he was the first banker to reopen for full operations. In an era when banks were austere places frequented only by capitalists and businessmen in dark suits and starched shirts, Giannini invented the idea of consumer banking, offering small loans to ordinary people at reasonable rates of interest and opening friendly "branch banks" in urban and ethnic neighborhoods. In 1930, the year he renamed his institution Bank of America, he claimed some 280 branches scattered throughout the West.

The most unique of San Francisco's ethnic communities—and the one most distinctively western—was Chinatown, a bustling district of tenements, boarding-houses, small factories, restaurants, and shops. In the 1880s approximately twenty-five thousand Chinese, nearly 10 percent of the city's population, squeezed into Chinatown's eight or twelve city blocks in the shadow of the millionaire enclave on Nob Hill. By rigid custom, San Francisco's Chinese were not permitted to live outside Chinatown. At the margins of their neighborhood, Chinese men and women were greeted by the singsong taunts of children: "ching-chong-Chinaman." Chinese fishermen, whose walk to the wharves took them through Irish or Italian neigh-borhoods, were frequent targets of abuse. But anti-Chinese violence was even more widespread in the rural West, and during the late nineteenth century, most Chinese fled to the cities. They concentrated in Chinatowns like San Francisco's, where at least they could practice their own customs and enjoy a certain security in numbers.

During the first three decades of San Francisco's history, Chinatown's chil-dren were excluded from the city's public schools. The city's school superintendent declared that the idea of educating them was "almost hopeless." Then in 1884 a Christian Chinese couple, Mary and Joseph Tape, sued the Board of Education to admit their daughter to the local elementary school. "Is it a disgrace to be born Chinese?" Mary wrote to the board. The Tapes won their suit, the court deciding that discrimination in education was unconstitutional, but the city circumvented the ruling by establishing a separate school for Chinese children in Chinatown. Segregated and excluded from the mainstream, the Chinese in San Francisco lived in a world of their own, one of the least assimilated immigrant groups ever to exist in America. Chinatown was a city within the city.

In contrast to San Francisco, relatively few European immigrants settled in early-twentieth-century Los Angeles. The city's white population was drawn mostly from the farms and small towns of Indiana, Illinois, Nebraska, Iowa, and Kansas. A large proportion of these emigrants were elderly (go West, *old* man) and joined other older folks in one or another of the several dozen "state societies" of southern California. Crowds estimated at 150,000 people or more attended the annual Iowa Society picnic.

After World War I, the character of emigration to Los Angeles changed as the city began a period of rapid industrialization. Stimulated first by the enormous expansion of federal spending during the war and then fueled by the discovery of vast local petroleum fields, the industrial revolution in southern California moved into high gear. Oil was discovered in the 1890s, but the really big fields were opened after the war, the first in 1920 at Huntington Beach (one of Henry Huntington's many developments), followed by several more in quick succession. Almost overnight, the region was supplying nearly 10 percent of the nation's fuel oil and gasoline. California overtook Texas and Oklahoma as the largest oil-producing state during the twenties, and by 1930 refining was the state's largest industry. The multiplier effects of the petroleum industry allowed Los Angeles between the wars to become the West's largest industrial center—the nucleus of the nation's oil equipment and service industry, the second largest tire-manufacturing center, and the largest producer of steel, glass, chemicals, aircraft, and automobiles in the West. Perhaps the most visible sign of economic development was the fabulous growth of the motion picture industry, which by the end of the twenties was employing more than fifteen thousand people.

As word of the city's economic miracle spread eastward, Los Angeles began to experience unprecedented population growth. More than one hundred thousand new residents—many of them poor folks in search of work—arrived each year during the early twenties from states like Arkansas, Oklahoma, and Texas. The migration to southern California included thousands of African Americans, Mexicans, and Japanese, who by 1930 made up approximately half of the unskilled workforce at the base of the region's industrial economy.

The rapid rise in the proportion of these groups in the population—from 6 percent in 1910 to nearly 16 percent in 1930—caused considerable alarm among many of the county's white residents. There was a great deal of overt hostility. Local chapters of the Ku Klux Klan staged nighttime rallies in public parks and organized auto caravans through minority neighborhoods. White residents harassed Japanese families moving into white areas. Even more effective, however, were the silent "restricted covenants" written into the deeds of homes in most sections of the city, excluding "Negroes, Mongolians, Indians, and Mexicans" from occupancy. By the twenties, 95 percent of the city's housing had been declared off-limits to racial minorities. Minority home buyers brought suit to challenge the legality of these deed restrictions, but local courts continued to uphold them until 1948.

Mexican Americans made up the largest and fastest growing of the minority communities in Los Angeles, climbing from only six thousand in 1910 to nearly one hundred thousand in 1930. Their experience illustrates another dimension of the centuries-long conflict over acculturation and assimilation that lies at the heart of the history of the American West. The Mexican immigrants arriving in the city during the 1910s and 1920s first settled in the old city center, near the nineteenth-century Catholic cathedral. But as that area filled up, they began spilling eastward, over the Los Angeles River and into the area that has since become known as East L.A., Mexican American capital of the West. By the late twenties, East L.A. was developing into a stable community, a place where, as historian George Sánchez discovered, 44 percent of Mexican families owned homes.

The Great Depression hit Los Angeles hard, and with a third or more of the county's workforce unemployed by 1931, there was growing clamor in the city for the deportation of Mexicans. President Herbert Hoover ordered the roundup of illegal aliens. In several neighborhoods of the Los Angeles barrio, immigration agents went door-to-door, demanding that residents produce papers proving their legal residency, summarily arresting and jailing those unable to do so, many American citizens among them. "It was for us the day of judgment," one resident wrote in 1931 in the pages of the local Spanish-language newspaper, *La Opinión.* "The deputies rode around the neighborhood with the sirens wailing and advising people to surrender themselves to the authorities. They barricaded all the exits to the *colonia* so that no one could escape." There are no reliable statistics on the total number of Mexicans deported from Los Angeles, but one study estimates that at least one million Mexican citizens from the Southwest were repatriated during the thirties.

Many young Mexican Americans, impatient with their immigrant parents, yet outraged by racism and segregation, became *pachucos,* a defiant cultural style that included dressing in the long coats and pegged pants of the zoot suiter, joining gangs, and "rumbling" in the streets. In 1943 hundreds of sailors from the port of Long Beach invaded East L.A., assaulting young Mexican Americans and African Americans, stripping them of their clothes, and beating them senseless as the police stood by and white bystanders cheered. For the Mexican American community, which sent its sons to fight in the war in greater proportion than any other group in the West, the "Zoot Suit Riots" would remain a bitter memory.

Perhaps injustice was most evident in the history of the Japanese American community in Los Angeles. Crowded into "Little Tokyo" in the downtown section of the city, the immigrant Issei and their Nisei children seemed willing to ignore discrimination and dedicate themselves to hard work and prosperity in the American style. "Scratch a Japanese American," writes scholar Harry Kitano, "and find a white Anglo-Saxon Protestant."

Two months after the attack on Pearl Harbor, in early 1942, President Roosevelt signed Executive Order 9066, suspending the civil rights of both citizens and aliens of Japanese background in the western states and authorizing the confiscation of their property and the "removal" of families from their homes and communities. Several thousand German Americans and Italian Americans were also subjected to restriction, relocation, and internment, but Japanese Americans were by far the most affected, with some 120,000 of them held in detention camps for up to three years. The president's order was defended on the grounds of "military necessity," a justification upheld by the Supreme Court in 1944, although in 1982 a federal commission concluded that the federal government had possessed no evidence linking West Coast Japanese Americans with espionage and that internment was the result of "race prejudice, war hysteria, and a failure of political leadership." The residents of Little Tokyo in Los Angeles and Japanese throughout the West were rounded up and sent to one of ten camps set up across the trans-Mississippi West. Many ended at the Manzanar War Relocation Center in the Owens valley of California, which had been left an arid waste by the diversion of water for urban Los Angeles. Manzanar was "the scene of a triple tragedy," says Richard Stewart, a Paiute Indian who leads tours around the abandoned site of the camp. First, native Paiutes and Shoshones lost their homes there, then farmers and ranchers lost their water there, and finally Japanese Americans lost their rights there.

"The evacuation and establishment of relocation centers were actions without precedent in American history," wrote Dillon S. Myer, director of the War Relocation Authority, which was in charge of the operation. What would the Cherokees or the Creeks, the Shawnees or the Nez Percé say to such an assertion? "Has the Gestapo come to America?" one Japanese American wondered in 1942. No, this was not some alien idea invading America, but the culmination of an old American fear of "the other," the alien, the red-skinned savage, the greaser, the chink, and the Jap. "A Jap's a Jap," declared General John L. DeWitt of the Western Defense Command. "It makes no difference whether he is an American."

Chapter 14 **Plunder and Preservation**

"The heavens are alive with pigeons!" The call echoes through the clearing where the pioneers have built their cabins. Great flocks of passenger pigeons veer and ripple in masses of blue and purple as they migrate north from their winter roosts. With rifles and pistols, the pioneers begin their attack on the birds, and feathery masses tumble to the field; but so preoccupied are the hunters with the slaughter that none bothers about the kill. Two men even deploy a little cannon, and loading it with shot, fire haphazardly into the sky, bringing down pigeons by the dozens with each report. At the edge of the carnage stands an old scout clad in buckskin. "This comes of settling a country," says old Leather-Stocking, spitting out the words in disgust. "It's wicked," he murmurs, "wicked." And shouldering his rifle, he walks sadly into the woods, taking care not to tread on the quivering birds that litter his path.

This scene appears in James Fenimore Cooper's *The Pioneers* (1823), the novel that introduced the American reading public to Natty Bumppo, or Leather-Stocking, the tragic frontier character who leads the settlement of the wilderness, bringing on the destruction of the world he loves. Cooper's depiction of the war waged on the passenger pigeon, however, was no fiction. In the nineteenth century, billions of these birds inhabited eastern North America, and "market hunters" slaughtered them by the tens of thousands, selling them as squab for thirty to fifty cents a dozen. By the end of the century, the species had been driven to extinction in the wild. The last known passenger pigeon died in the Cincinnati Zoo about mid-day on September 1, 1914.

Although the record of this demise is unusually detailed, historians are less well informed about the extinction of other indigenous North American species. Scientists have, however, compiled a list of approximately seventy known to have gone belly-up over the past two centuries, including the Labrador duck, the New England heath hen, the Carolina parakeet, the eastern sea mink, the eastern elk, the Wisconsin cougar, and the Great Plains wolf. By the early twentieth century, the only grizzly bears left in California were the ones on the state's bear flag. The beaver disappeared from most of its habitat by the 1840s, although it managed a revival. The sea otter and the fur seal of the northwest coast were on the verge of extinction when saved by an international ban on commercial hunting early in the twentieth century. The buffalo perished by the tens of millions, of course, and by 1890 only eight hundred remained in several isolated herds. The number of western mule deer, antelope, and bighorn sheep, once counted in the millions, fell by 95 percent. Americans blasted their way across the continent, says historian Donald Worster, leaving in their wake "a landscape littered with skulls and bones, drenched in blood."

Wildlife perished not only by gun and trap, but more insidiously by the destruction of habitat. Wetlands were drained and woodlands cleared. In their heyday, hunters could walk through stands of beech and maple trees stretching so broad and so deep that they might not see the sun for days. But even by the early nineteenth century, the great trans-Appalachian deciduous and evergreen forests were dwindling under the assault of civilization. Eventually, the woodlands east of the Mississippi were reduced to only about 2 percent of their former extent. With the rise of industrial logging in the mid-nineteenth century, the forests of the Great Lakes states came under attack. Some logging companies purchased huge stands from state and federal governments, while others perpetrated enormous frauds by paying their employees to enter phony homestead claims. Loggers systematically cut over massive areas. By the 1890s the logging industry had almost used up the available timber of the Great Lakes region and was moving on to the South and to the old-growth forests of the Pacific Northwest.

The development of the mining industry was particularly destructive. The use of high-pressure water jets to wash down mountains of deposits in the search for gold was cheap and effective, but it took no account of the havoc wrought to streams and valleys below as tons of mud and rocks buried plant life, including crops, like a chronic avalanche. Farmers with clogged irrigation systems and inundated crops fought bitter legislative battles against mining companies. But by the time a federal judge declared hydraulic mining a public nuisance and issued a permanent injunction in 1884, an estimated twelve billion tons of earth had been blasted and eroded away, and the resulting silt had reduced the depth of San Francisco Bay by three to six feet. Even greater destruction to the bay came from the mercury mines in the foothills surrounding the town of San Jose. Mercury was essential for separating gold from quartz rock, and those mining operations dumped tons of mercury into the streams that fed the bay, leaving a legacy that still poisons the fish there.

Petroleum drilling also could be powerfully destructive. The oil from gushers polluted soil and water, and if they caught fire, sent up heavy clouds of acrid smoke. Like the Spindletop gusher of 1901, one Texas gusher of 1911 spewed out

116,000 barrels a day for nine days before it was capped. Plunder and pollution were component parts of the frontier economy, attributable to the desire for rapid exploitation, an economic system that awarded the highest premium to the fiercest competitor, and a laissez-faire government thoughtless of the common good. Above all, the American people adhered to what naturalist William Vogt called "the cornucopian faith" of ceaseless abundance. North America was indeed rich in resources—rich enough to double the world's annual production of gold in 1849, rich enough to grow wheat sufficient to feed the world. Fish, furs, timber, oil—all were available in unending supply, it seemed. There was no need to worry.

Americans began to challenge the myth of inexhaustibility in the mid-nineteenth century. The first to note the disappearance of fish, birds, and animals were the people who hunted and fished for sport—and they were also the first to do something about it. This may come as news to today's environmentalists, some of whom accuse hunters of "animal murder," but as John Reiger puts it in his study of the origins of the conservation movement, "sportsmen led the way." The depletion of favorite trout streams and hunting ranges pushed fishers and hunters to organize, pressing state legislatures for laws limiting and regulating the take of wildlife. The campaign for hunting laws began after the Civil War, and by the end of the century a majority of states and localities established fish and game commissions, defined fishing and hunting seasons, and set licensing requirements and bag limits. These were the first modern organized efforts to regulate the use of the environment.

A prominent leader of this national movement was George Bird Grinnell, a patrician New Yorker who in 1887 with Theodore Roosevelt called together a group of wealthy sportsmen to establish the Boone and Crockett Club, named for two of the nation's legendary backwoodsmen. The club quickly became the nation's most influential environmental lobby, working for the protection of threatened species and the creation of a system of wildlife refuges.

A second and complementary interest in the environment originated in romanticism, the dominant intellectual and aesthetic movement of the nineteenth century. The romantics worried over the limiting and corrupting effects of too much civilization, and they celebrated the restorative power of immersion in nature. The sentiment remains the most prominent rationale for the preservation of wilderness.

The physical drama, the sheer grandeur of western mountains and rivers, argued for protection to keep their primeval beauty intact for later generations. The first serious proposal concerned the glacier-carved Yosemite valley in the central Sierra Nevada of California. The combination of granite cliffs, lofty waterfalls, verdant meadows, clear streams, and huge redwoods made Yosemite the perfect subject for romantic art of the sublime and picturesque, exemplified in the awe-inspiring paintings of Albert Bierstadt, which were widely distributed as engravings and chromolithographs. In 1864 a group of prominent citizens, including Frederick Law Olmsted, designer of New York City's Central Park, persuaded Congress to grant the valley to the state of California for "public use, resort and recreation." The reservation was very small, only ten square miles; no thought was given to preserving the entire ecosystem, just the monumental scenery. To prevent "destruction by settlement" of other spectacular sites in the West, a number of writers began to call for the creation of more "nature reserves." These proposals gained powerful support when the Southern Pacific Railroad noted a significant increase in tourist traffic along the rail lines leading to Yosemite.

Railroad tourism dated from the advent in the late 1860s of Pullman sleeper cars—rolling hotels, paneled in mahogany and with lights shaded with Tiffany glass—which could bring travelers comfortably to the great western tourist destinations. Western railroad interests thus became involved in the creation of federal parks, and the first was established in the headwater region of the Yellowstone River, high in the Rocky Mountains. Yellowstone was legendary among fur trappers for its iridescent pools, cobalt-encrusted springs, roaring waterfalls, and mirror lakes reflecting peaks between glistening glaciers. The descriptions were considered western tall tales until a party of scientists and local boosters hiked into the area in 1870 and confirmed the existence of Yellowstone's "curiosities" and "wonders." The next year, University of Pennsylvania geologist Ferdinand V. Hayden, founder of the U.S. Geological Survey, led a scientific party that included pioneer western photographer William Henry Jackson and landscape artist Thomas Moran. Hayden's report—and particularly Jackson's photographs and Moran's watercolors—generated considerable interest. But things didn't really begin to happen until financier Jay Cooke, mindful of the profits that tourist traffic would generate for his Northern Pacific Railway, proposed that Congress declare Yellowstone "a public park forever—just as it has reserved that far inferior wonder, the Yosemite Valley." His rhetoric marked the beginning of competition among railroads for the western tourist dollar.

Unlike Yosemite, however, Yellowstone was located in federal territory (Wyoming, Montana, and Idaho were not granted statehood until 1890), and hence this reserve would have to be a federal creation. Assured that the area was too high and too cold for agriculture, and that consequently its designation as a park would do "no harm to the material interests of the people," in March 1872 Congress set apart more than two million acres on the Yellowstone River as "a public park or pleasuring ground for the benefit and enjoyment of the people." Defining and preserving lands as "pleasuring grounds" was unprecedented, and the measure provoked vociferous opposition. One congressman snorted at the proposed entrance of the government into "show business." Fortunately, the majority followed the Missouri senator who asserted the benefits of a "great breathing-place for the national lungs." Yellowstone remained the only national park until 1890, when the Southern Pacific succeeded in lobbying for federal legislation creating a wilderness sanctuary in the area surrounding the Yosemite valley, and another to protect the groves of immense sequoias in the southern Sierra Nevada.

The first national parks thus had everything to do with commerce and enterprise. In the public mind, however, there was a single person most responsible for these developments—John Muir, an American original and the country's most effective propagandist for wilderness. Born in Scotland and raised on a hardscrabble Wisconsin farm, Muir left home at a young age for a lifelong study of the natural environment. He tramped from Canada to Mexico and sailed from Alaska to the South Seas, writing about his experiences. A fervent disciple of Transcendentalism, Muir once invited Ralph Waldo Emerson, who was touring California, to "worship" with him at Yosemite. Emerson accepted, but instead of sleeping with Muir under the stars, he chose to bunk in one of the park's tourist hotels, explaining that the wilderness was "a sublime mistress, but an intolerable wife." For Muir, nature was all—wife, mistress, offspring, even God (the forests, he wrote, were "God's first temples"). Muir's wilderness philosophy was anchored in the romantic contrast between sacred nature and what he called "the galling harness of civilization."

In truth, there was no such clear line of demarcation between wilderness and civilization. From the beginning, the national parks were exercises in compromise. Tourism demanded the construction and maintenance of roads, trails, and buildings; park visitors required hotels, restaurants, campgrounds, and garbage dumps, as well as water, sewage, and power systems. Moreover, the mandate to retain the parks' "natural conditions" was interpreted to mean the cultivation of landscapes that conformed to the *public's* notion of wilderness. Officials at Yellowstone worked hard to encourage what one park superintendent called "the type of animal the park was for." To protect browsing herds of elk, moose, deer, and bighorn sheep, park managers went to war against wolves, mountain lions, and coyotes. To save the last bison herd from extinction, they created a ranch on which the animals were fed park-grown hay. To improve the fishing, they introduced trout in the streams. And to protect this concocted "wilderness," they struggled to suppress the forest fires that were a normal part of nature's cycle. This was what critic Alston Chase would later characterize as "playing God in Yellowstone." The dilemma has been a part of the history of the national parks since their beginnings.

John Muir understood better than most the practical side of the national parks, and without hesitation he joined with the efforts of the railroads to generate more tourist business. He worked with the Northern Pacific, lobbying for the creation of Mount Rainier and Glacier national parks in 1899, and with the Southern Pacific in 1906 to persuade California to cede the state park at Yosemite valley back to federal jurisdiction. To monitor federal administration of the parks and counter new threats to the mountain environment, in 1892 he began the environmental organization called the Sierra Club—an organization that to this day would "make the mountains glad"—and served as its president for the next twenty-two years. Muir was an idealist and a romantic. But he was also an environmental politician.

Curtailing the massive assault on the nation's forests by loggers proved more difficult than creating national parks. The first expression of official concern came when the report of the 1870 census documented the appalling deforestation that had taken place in the Great Lakes region. But Congress was in no mood to restrict access to western resources. Instead, it passed the Timber Cutting Act of 1878, which made it even easier for private citizens and companies to cut timber on federal land.

To be fair, Congress also called for "further study." Those federal studies had little effect on lawmakers, but they aroused many in the intellectual community. Scientists were beginning to consider the web of connections among living things, a subject already known as ecology. An important contribution to this thinking was the book *Man and Nature* (1864), written by American amateur scientist George Perkins Marsh. Deforestation and erosion, Marsh implied, had contributed to the fall of Old World civilizations and might produce the same result in America. Soon, other Americans were repeating his warnings, and by the 1880s the American Forestry Association (founded in 1875) was calling for a moratorium on the sale of all public forest lands.

The fledgling forestry movement found itself in a race with loggers, who were rapidly moving the center of their operations to the Pacific coast. By 1890 the easily accessible forests of Douglas fir, spruce, and redwood along the California, Oregon, and Washington coasts had already fallen to the ax, their ancient logs sawed into boards and shipped to San Francisco or Los Angeles for the booming home-construction market. Loggers had penetrated the mountainous backcountry, using "steam donkeys" to open hauling trails, clear-cutting huge patches of forest, and shipping out the harvest of logs on precarious narrow-gauge railroads. In regions too rugged or isolated for rails, they built mountain "splash dams" where they dumped their logs; when the ponds were full, they blasted the dams to kingdom come, producing floods that washed the logs downstream to the sawmills. These floods changed watercourses and scoured river bottoms, ripping away salmon spawning beds, destroying their eggs, and leaving fish flopping on gravel bars. The extinction or near extinction of salmon was the inevitable result.

In 1891, as Congress considered a complete revision of the nation's land laws, friends of forest reform cleverly slipped in an amendment—later known as the Forest Reserve Act—providing the president with the authority to carve "forest reserves" from the public domain. The expectation seemed to be that this power would be used sparingly, but over the next decade, presidents Benjamin Harrison, Grover Cleveland, and William McKinley used it to withdraw more than forty-seven million forested acres. Preservationists hoped—and loggers feared—that these reserves would be closed forever to commercial exploitation. But Congress in 1897 made it clear that the reserves were not intended for the *preservation* but rather the *use* of the forests. The Forest Management Act declared that the reserves should "furnish a continuous supply of timber for the use and necessities of citizens of the United States." The executive branch was directed to establish regulations for the management of the reserves, auctioning to the highest bidder the right to harvest timber in them.

This legislation was a triumph for Gifford Pinchot, whom President McKinley named chief forester of the United States in 1898, at the age of just thirty-three. Born to a wealthy family, Pinchot had been interested in woodcraft from a young age. His classmates at Yale described him as "tree mad." After college, he went to Europe to pursue advanced studies in forestry. When Theodore Roosevelt became president in 1901, Pinchot quickly became his closest adviser on environmental policy. Both men, members of the Boone and Crockett Club, were outdoorsmen and lovers of what Roosevelt called "the strenuous life."

"Conservationism," the name Roosevelt and Pinchot chose for their approach to the environment, was an ideology for postfrontier America. Roosevelt recognized that America was filling up and old thinking had to change. No longer, he said, could the nation allow "the right of the individual to injure the future of us all for his own temporary and immediate profit." The nation now required an activist federal government to manage the western environment. Roosevelt's administration featured an unparalleled array of environmental activity. The president encouraged Congress to create several new national parks, and he used his presidential power to set aside sixteen national monuments of unique natural and historical value, including Devil's Tower in Wyoming, the Olympic peninsula in Washington, and the Petrified Forest and the Grand Canyon in Arizona. He established more than fifty wildlife preserves and refuges. He transferred the forest reserves (renamed "national forests") from the Department of the Interior to Pinchot's National Forest Service in the Department of Agriculture. In his first directive to the agency, Pinchot laid out the "wise use" environmental perspective that he shared with Roosevelt: "All the resources of forest reserves are for *use*, and this use must be brought about in a thoroughly prompt and businesslike manner, under such restrictions only as will insure the permanence of these resources." Pinchot's words remain Forest Service gospel to this day.

The approach of *utilizers* such as Roosevelt and Pinchot differed considerably from that of *preservationists* like John Muir. The president once joined Muir on a camping trip into Yosemite. The two men slept under the stars, awaking under a blanket of fresh snow. Later, around the campfire, Muir challenged Roosevelt's love of hunting, asking him when he was going to "get beyond the boyishness of killing things." Muir communed with nature, but Roosevelt wanted to ride it like a bucking bronc. Another time, Pinchot toured the western forests with Muir. As they conversed, their differences emerged. Muir challenged the federal policy of allowing sheep (which he called "hoofed locusts") to graze on the public domain, and when Pinchot allowed that he held no animus toward sheep, Muir lost his patience. "I don't want anything more to do with you," he sputtered. For Muir, "the hope of the world" was "fresh, unblighted, unredeemed wilderness." Compare this to Pinchot's favorite aphorism: "Wilderness is waste." The distinction between conservation and preservation goes back to the very beginnings of national environmental policy.

The truth is, neither Roosevelt nor Pinchot spent much time worrying about their differences with Muir; they were too busy putting their conservation programs into operation and fending off more dangerous attacks from critics who wanted to dismantle federal authority over the forests. Ironically, they found their most important allies in the large logging companies, which saw distinct advantages in establishing a cozy relationship with the National Forest Service. By the early twentieth century, these corporations had gained control of nearly 50 percent of the nation's standing timber, and locking up an additional 35 percent in the national forests suited them just fine, for it stymied the competition of smaller loggers. In exchange, Pinchot expected companies to apply the principles of scientific management to their forests. The Weyerhaeuser Company—the world's largest private owner of standing timber, controlling resources equal to half the entire national forest system—instituted impressive programs of reforestation. Historian William Robbins persuasively argues that corporate loggers used the Forest Service "as a tool to achieve stability," to avoid overproduction, glutted markets, and low prices in their industry. But on the positive side, they also rejected the old logging practice of "cut and get out."

It was the small loggers who opposed federal regulation. In 1907 they won congressional repeal of the president's authority to declare national forests by executive order. Before Roosevelt signed the legislation, however, he and Pinchot pored over maps of the West and selected more than 16 million acres of new forest reserves. Independent loggers were outraged by these "midnight reserves," which increased the size of the national forests to more than 150 million acres. Pinchot stayed on at the Forest Service when Roosevelt left office in 1909, but he found the administration of President William Howard Taft far less friendly to conservation. Secretary of the Interior Richard Ballinger represented western anticonservation interests that wanted federal resources transferred to the states to facilitate their private development, a policy antithetical to the chief forester's plan of rational development under federal management. The two men tangled, and Taft eventually dismissed Pinchot. By the time he left office, however, Pinchot had built the Forest Service into a proud organization of more than fifteen hundred employees.

To the American public, the Forest Service was personified by the forest ranger, the mounted officer in military garb—khaki shirts and jodhpurs, knee-high riding boots, and the flat-brimmed Stetson "campaign" hats that have since become the rangers' most notable symbol. The American public fell in love with the hearty masculine figure of the ranger. Such men were the embodiment of what President Roosevelt extolled as "the great virile virtues." Now they were to guard the forests. Rangers offered a modern substitute for frontier heroes such as Boone and Crockett.

With such a masculine institutional culture, it comes as a surprise that in its very early years the Park Service also employed women as park rangers. Horace Albright, the first civilian superintendent at Yellowstone, hired at least ten women for his force of rangers. When the chief inspector of the Department of the Interior came to Yellowstone in 1926, he was shocked. Nosing around, he found male rangers who complained about these "posy pickers" and "tree huggers." But Albright forthrightly defended his policy. "Women can do just as well or better than men," he wrote, especially interacting with the public. Not a man on his force could give a lecture, "even if his life depended on it." But Albright's retirement in 1933 marked the end of this bold experiment. Within a few years, the Park Service was looking back on the days of the female ranger with considerable loathing. It was important for the service, insisted one official, that rangers maintain their image as "the embodiment of Kit Carson, Buffalo Bill, Daniel Boone, the Texas Rangers, and General Pershing." It wasn't until the 1970s that women rejoined the service.

By 1920 the great assault on the forests had moderated. The forested area of the United States stabilized at around 730 million acres, approximately 32 percent of the nation's land, about where it has remained in the years since. Although conservation, and especially the work of Roosevelt and Pinchot, was vitally important, the primary reason for the stabilization of the country's forests was the nation's declining need for farmland. The proportion of land devoted to growing crops had grown from 5 percent in 1850 to 20 percent in 1920, and at least half of this increase had come at the expense of forests. By the second decade of the twentieth century, however, American agriculture was well into a mighty transformation characterized by the development of high-yield hybrid crops, the use of chemical fertilizers, and the introduction of labor-saving machinery. The increases in agricultural productivity were so great that there was little need for opening additional land, though there remained plenty of need for water.

The nation was confronted with a new problem—a *surplus* of crops and farmers—that would require new ways of thinking. Yet Theodore Roosevelt and Gifford Pinchot focused on the problem of scarcity, not surplus. This was most evident in another environmental program adopted during the Roosevelt administration: the federal support for western irrigation that would fundamentally reshape the twentieth-century West. By 1900 public and private projects were watering some eight million arid acres in the western states, but it was clear that further development would require massive dams, substantial reservoirs, and long-distance canal systems, investments beyond the means of corporations, municipalities, or even the states. Federal support for irrigation would open new lands and "furnish homes for the homeless and farms for the farmless," declared one congressman; such a plan would be "a great pacificator," promised another, offering a safety valve in times of "great social disturbances in the great cities." Not only was this nonsense, it was old nonsense; yet it remained politically potent nonsense.

In 1902 Congress passed the Reclamation Act, which established the Bureau of Reclamation in the Department of the Interior to administer a vast federal effort in the states of the trans-Mississippi West to make the deserts bloom. "Reclamation" is a curious term, however, since the West was naturally arid and the lands were not really being reclaimed at all but transformed. And this transformation of desert land would disrupt many rural westerners. Water development often involved the destruction of traditional ways of life that had served residents for generations. Elephant Butte Dam on the Rio Grande in central New Mexico created a system of modern reservoirs and canals that replaced the ancient complex of *acequias* (ditches) watering hundreds of Hispano subsistence farmers, and forced them to become agricultural laborers. Western water projects also ran roughshod over Indians. Although in 1908 the Supreme Court declared that Indians retained an inviolable right to the waters of their homelands, over the next half-century the Department of the Interior—the very agency entrusted with protecting Indian rights—approved dozens of projects that flooded reservation lands and drained reservation rivers, but provided little or no benefit to reservation people.

Perhaps this was to be expected. But the positive effects of reclamation on the lives of white farmers is also debatable. The Reclamation Act included provisions restricting the use of irrigation water to resident (not absentee) farmers with plots of 160 acres or less. From the program's beginning, however, bureaucrats found it inconvenient to enforce these limitations, and generally ignored them. Agribusiness, not the small farmer, was the big beneficiary of federal irrigation. The men and women laboring in the irrigated fields and orchards were not independent proprietors but migrant farmworkers. Moreover, reclamation projects meant to benefit rural residents were sometimes hijacked by urban interests, most famously when the city of Los Angeles commandeered the Owens River project, which was supposed to benefit local farmers. "It is a hundred or thousandfold more important and more valuable to the people as a whole," Roosevelt avowed when he announced federal funding for the city's plan, if water was "used by the city than if used by the people of the Owens Valley." As western writer Mary Austin watched the Owens River run dry, turning the farms and orchards around her into desert sands, she wondered, "is all this worthwhile, in order that Los Angeles should be just so big?"

Frequently, rivers were dammed and valleys flooded with little concern for the loss of ecosystems or natural wonders. The most infamous example was the Hetch Hetchy valley in Yosemite National Park, whose sharp glacial walls and meadowed floor John Muir described as "a grand landscape garden, one of Nature's rarest and most precious mountain temples." Some two hundred miles to the west, San Francisco engineers in search of a dependable urban water supply fastened upon Hetch Hetchy as the best place to impound city water. Muir went on the attack and composed an essay containing these famous lines: "Dam Hetch Hetchy! As well dam for water-tanks the people's cathedrals and churches, for no holier temple has ever been consecrated by the heart of man." Roosevelt vacillated, passing the matter on to his successors when he left office. Finally, in 1913, the project won approval by the Wilson administration. It would be Muir's last stand. He died a year later, deeply saddened by his defeat. The granite temple of Hetch Hetchy would disappear under hundreds of feet of water, and preservationists would never forget this cautionary tale. But today, their efforts may well restore the Hetch Hetchy valley to its predammed state.

These negative effects should be weighed against the success of the Reclamation Bureau, which during its first three decades completed twenty-two western projects. By that time, irrigation was watering some fourteen million acres of western land, on which were grown major portions of the nation's fruits, vegetables, sugar beets, alfalfa, and cotton. Yet that very success was, in a way, the program's greatest weakness, for reclamation only added to the growth of agricultural surpluses. Following World War I, when demand collapsed and farm prices plummeted, individual farmers responded to lower prices in the only way they knew how, by growing more in the hope of increasing their revenue. Predictably, this drove the price of farm commodities further downward. By 1929 average farm income had fallen to 64 percent of its level ten years before, and this was *before* the stock market crash and the onset of the Great Depression. When the nation's industrial economy went into a tailspin, agricultural markets literally collapsed. By 1932 farm income was a mere fifth of its postwar high. What future was there in a program designed to increase the nation's cropland when the nation could not market the crops it was already producing?

The victory of Franklin D. Roosevelt in the presidential election of 1932 brought to the White House a leader committed to tackling the farm problem. In one of his first acts, Roosevelt signed the Agricultural Adjustment Act, authorizing the government to fix production quotas, purchase surplus crops at a guaranteed price, and store those surplus commodities in government granaries for sale during years of crop failure. It was a version of the program western Populists had proposed a half-century before, and it would remain the foundation of federal agricultural policy for the rest of the twentieth century. Gradually, farm prices climbed back to profitable levels. Yet the program only assisted farmers with large operations; it did little or nothing for small producers, who continued to lose their farms at an alarming rate. It also had the effect of tossing tenants and sharecroppers off their rented land, since those plots were frequently the very ones landlords retired from production. A displaced Oklahoma tenant described his family's options starkly: "move or starve."

The turmoil of farm bankruptcy and tenant eviction created another epic western migration, but this time with pioneers traveling by automobile rather than covered wagon, as does the Joad family in John Steinbeck's vivid novel *The Grapes of Wrath* (1939). California seemed a new promised land. "By God, they's grapes out there, just a-hangin' over inta the road," says Steinbeck's Grandpa Joad. "I'm gonna pick me a wash tub full a grapes, an' I'm gonna set in 'em, an' scrooge aroun', an' let the juice run down my pants." But instead of an agrarian dream, the family finds an industrial nightmare: California's factories in the field. Like the Joads, tens of thousands of "Okies" and "Arkies" found work as fruit or vegetable pickers, but even more joined the ever-increasing human flood into greater Los Angeles or other western urban centers.

The states of the Pacific coast received more than 750,000 migrants during the 1930s. They came not only from Oklahoma and Arkansas but from the Dakotas, Kansas, and Texas, all areas where the agricultural crisis of the Great Depression

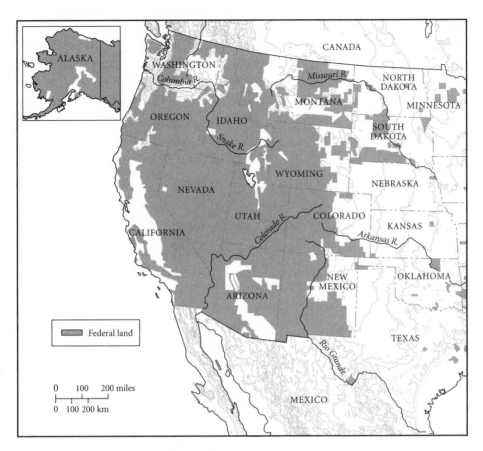

Federal Lands in the Twentieth-Century West

was compounded by the extraordinary environmental crisis known as the Dust Bowl. Drought gripped the entire nation during the thirties, but it had its worst effects on the Great Plains. Huge dust storms began sweeping across the prairies in the early spring of 1932. The next year the dust rose so high it was sucked up by the jet stream and came down like snow on Chicago, Washington, D.C., and even ships out in the Atlantic. With each passing year, the storms grew more fierce, until the drought finally loosened its grip late in the decade, the rains returned, and the dust storms subsided. There had been small dust storms during previous dry cycles, but nothing in recorded history approached the ferocity of the Dust Bowl. The difference was the extent of the grassland that had been lost since the 1890s, especially because of the excessive plowing and grazing of the 1920s that denuded millions of acres of their natural vegetation. Dry prairie winds scoured the unprotected topsoil, turning some twenty-four million acres into barren desert by 1938.

The rural West thus faced not only economic collapse but environmental catastrophe. Franklin Roosevelt responded with the most environmentally oriented administration since that of his distant cousin Theodore in the early century. For secretary of the interior (or secretary of the West, as some called the position), he appointed Harold Ickes. "We have reached the end of the pioneering period of 'go ahead and take,'" Ickes declared upon assuming his duties; "we are in the age of planning for the best of everything for all." Ickes and Roosevelt moved on several fronts to establish better environmental management of the Great Plains. Thousands of young men in the Civilian Conservation Corps were set to work planting trees by the hundreds of millions in "shelterbelts," designed to provide windbreaks, retard soil erosion, and create habitat for wildlife. The Taylor Grazing Act of 1934 brought the public range lands under new regulation with the mandate of preventing overgrazing. The Soil Conservation Service, established the following year, returned more than eleven million acres to grass.

The New Deal marked a watershed in the history of the West. "Our last frontier has long since been reached and there is practically no more free land," Roosevelt declared during the campaign of 1932. "There is no safety valve in the form of a Western prairie to which those thrown out of work by the eastern economic machines can go for a new start." Americans were faced with "the soberer, less dramatic business of administering resources . . . , of distributing wealth and products more equitably." No president had ever said such a thing. In 1935 Roosevelt made good on this declaration with an executive order that withdrew all remaining public lands from entry and placed them under federal conservation authority. The termination of the federal policy of selling off or giving away the public domain—a program that began with the first Land Ordinance in 1784—truly marked the passing of the nation's long era of frontier settlement.

The frontier era was over, and the West had been left an economic basket case. During the 1930s westerner Bernard DeVoto voiced the old western complaint of colonial exploitation. The East had created the West as a colonial dependency, he argued, plundered its natural resources, and didn't give a damn for its economic development. The New Dealers were largely in agreement with this analysis. "Economic disadvantage creates a backward country," wrote Thurman Arnold, a lawyer from Laramie, Wyoming, who served in the Department of Justice. The Northeast and the Midwest had developed into economic powerhouses, but the rural West and South remained essentially colonial economies. Only by building up the whole country could the nation avoid future catastrophes. One of the most enduring legacies of the New Deal was Roosevelt's decision to build an industrial infrastructure in these underdeveloped regions. The New Deal's program of public investment was unlike anything seen previously in American history, and it transformed the West.

The program focused on multipurpose river development. During the twenties, many westerners began arguing for river projects that would provide hydroelectric power. Wherever electricity was cheap and plentiful, prosperity seemed to follow. But private utilities failed to see a market in rural electrification, and vast districts of both the rural West and South remained unconnected to the nation's growing power grid and thus essentially blocked from economic development. In 1928 a coalition of southern Democrats and western Republicans ("the alliance of cotton and corn") succeeded in passing the first multipurpose river bill—a huge dam and hydroelectric complex at Boulder Canyon on the Colorado River, designed to provide irrigation, flood control, public water supplies, and hydroelectric power to the states of Arizona, Nevada, and California. They next attempted to secure federal funding for projects on the Tennessee and Columbia rivers but were blocked by the Hoover administration.

Roosevelt, however, was an enthusiastic supporter of multipurpose river development. During his campaign for the presidency, he came out in favor of the Columbia project, and even before he took office, he announced the model New Deal river project, the Tennessee Valley Authority (TVA). Congress approved the TVA in the spring of 1933, and over the next several years New Dealers in Congress won approval of similar projects for the Columbia, the Sacramento and San Joaquin in California's Central Valley, and dozens of smaller rivers throughout the West. The Rural Electrification Act connected tens of thousands of rural households to the nation's power grid. "I want my people out of the dark," Congressman Sam Rayburn of Texas told his colleagues. "Can you imagine what it will mean to a farm wife to have a pump in the well and lights in the house?"

The projects themselves employed tens of thousands of workers and helped launch some of the West's biggest corporations. The consortium of western contractors that built Hoover Dam on the Colorado was led by Henry J. Kaiser, an energetic, smiling German American known as the New Deal's "favorite businessman." He went on to build the superstructure at Grand Coulee Dam on the Columbia (three times the size of Hoover Dam) and the gigantic cement pilings for the San Francisco Bay Bridge. Kaiser and other New Deal contractors in the West were largely financed by San Franciscan Amadeo Peter Giannini's Bank of America, which in turn was funded by the New Deal's Reconstruction Finance Corporation.

In the 1930s, the federal government typically invested more in development projects in the West than in any other region. The river projects proved enormously successful, generating far more power than anyone anticipated and sharply lowering energy prices throughout the country. Cheap electricity from government-built dams stimulated the industrialization of the Tennessee and Columbia basins and propelled California forward as the nation's leading industrial state during World War II. Indeed, it can be argued that victory in the war was made possible by the New Deal strategy of industrial development. New western aluminum and steel mills provided the materials that western shipyards and aircraft plants needed. Nuclear weapons were developed at industrial complexes supplied by power generated by dams on the Tennessee, Columbia, and Colorado rivers. In short, the New Deal transformed the West into a powerful industrial economy.

The New Deal conviction that the frontier era had ended was also reflected in its Indian policy. When Roosevelt took office, the total Indian land base stood at forty-seven million acres—only a third of what it had been when allotment was proclaimed as the solution to further Indian dispossession. Indians had become the most impoverished group in the United States. Those who demanded that Indians assimilate had assumed the superiority of Anglo-American culture. But intellectuals connected with the New Deal were strongly influenced by a new perspective known as "cultural pluralism," which argued that each culture should be considered from within the framework of its own values and assumptions. John Collier, a leading spokesman for the pluralist ideal, became the new commissioner of Indian affairs. Indians, he announced "whose culture, civic tradition, and inherited traditions are still strong and virile, should be encouraged and helped to develop their life in their own patterns." The Indian Reorganization Act (1934), the so-called "Indian New Deal," represented the most radical shift in Indian policy in American history. It inaugurated an unprecedented era of Indian cultural freedom. Collier issued a directive proclaiming religious freedom on all reservations. Boarding schools were phased out and replaced by reservation day schools with bilingual textbooks. And Indian people began to take a more prominent role in the running of the Bureau of Indian Affairs (BIA).

The Indian New Deal also ended the policy of allotment. Individual Indians with allotments were encouraged to voluntarily exchange those lands for shares of common stock in Indian corporations. The BIA also established a fund from which tribes might borrow to repurchase land and pursue projects of economic development such as tribally owned stock raising. Encouraged by Collier's BIA, the number of Indian cattle ranchers doubled and the value of Indian cattle sales increased more than tenfold, reaching $3 million by 1939.

Under the auspices of the Indian Reorganization Act, 181 tribes voted to organize new forms of representative self-government, and during Collier's tenure about half of those tribes adopted written constitutions and elected leaders. To be sure, the BIA continued to have extraordinary authority in the affairs of reservation Indians, retaining veto power over the decisions of tribal councils and supervising the fiscal and economic arrangements of Indian nations. Nevertheless, the New Deal was the first time in American history that a presidential administration endorsed Indian sovereignty over their own affairs. Through the next several decades, the federal government itself would frequently violate this principle, but it established a critical precedent. Upheld by a series of important federal court decisions after World War II, Indian sovereignty would become the most fundamental principle of Indian law in the second half of the twentieth century.

Chapter 15 **The Myth of the Frontier**

 In the year or two before Daniel Boone died in 1820 at the age of nearly eighty-six, a steady stream of visitors beat a path to his home in Missouri. Frequently, they brought copies of *The Adventures of Col. Daniel Boon* (1783), the account written by Kentucky promoter John Filson, who claimed to have used the authentic first-person voice of Boone himself. A comparison of the text with Boone's letters suggests that few of the words were Boone's own. But for Filson's account, Boone had nothing but praise: "All true! Every word true! Not a lie in it!"

Filson's book had made Boone famous as an American original, the archetypal frontier hero, the leading man in a unique narrative tradition that would come to be known as the "Western." He is a man most at home in the wilderness, a world he understands and loves as the Indians do. And that intimate knowledge of the Indians enables him to confront and defeat them. Boone delighted in the honor that his accomplishments brought to the family name. Yet he did not hesitate to reveal to his visitors the fact that his life had taken some disappointing turns. He had pioneered the land of Kentucky, but then came the lawyers and the speculators, and eventually he lost everything. Legend portrayed him as an Indian fighter, but "I am very sorry to say that I ever killed any," he avowed to the shock of his visitors, "for they have always been kinder to me than the whites." If forced to choose, Boone concluded, he would "certainly prefer a state of nature to a state of civilization."

Boone's life story, appearing as it did during the formative years of the early republic, was one of the foundation stones for what Richard Slotkin calls "the myth of the frontier." In our debunking age, the word *myth* has become a synonym for erroneous belief. Slotkin, however, employs the term in an anthropological way to mean the body of tales, fables, and fantasies that help a people make sense of their history. Myth, like history, tries to find meaning in past events. But when transformed into myth, history is reduced to its ideological essence. The Western—the characteristic story form of the frontier myth—is essentially a tale of progress, a justification of violent conquest and untrammeled development. Boone's story was a prominent piece of that triumphant tale. Yet it raised troubling questions. If the western country had been wrested from the Indians by men like him, why had the rewards been swept up by the merchants and lawyers? Why were poor people who lived in the backwoods dispossessed of their lands, just as the Indians had been? Was that the real meaning of the term *civilization*? Because myth is composed in the figurative language of metaphor and symbol rather than the logical language of analysis, it may incorporate such doubts without actually confronting them. As Slotkin writes, "the most potent recurring hero-figures in our mythologies are men in whom contradictory identities find expression." Thus the progressive narrative of the Western is consistently subverted by the presence of pathfinders who are also critics of civilization, outlaws who are Robin Hood or Jesse James, and prostitutes who have hearts of gold. Americans are drawn to characters of paradoxical impulse, to "good-badmen," or army scouts who identify with the Indian enemy. Things are simple in the Western, but not always as simple as they seem.

During the generation following Boone's death, the character of the frontiersman became a ubiquitous presence in American culture. Of primary significance was the work of American novelist James Fenimore Cooper, who created Natty Bumppo, an enduring literary version of the Boone character variously identified as Leather-Stocking, Hawk-eye, the Pathfinder, or the Deerslayer in a series of five novels known as "The Leather-Stocking Tales." Cooper did not, however, intend Leather-Stocking as the hero. According to the literary conventions of the day, heroes had to be men of genteel birth. Thus Cooper's plots feature well-bred officers romancing pale ladies who swoon when the going gets rough. Most readers now have little interest in the leading characters of novels like *The Last of the Mohicans* (1826). It is the supporting cast that fascinates: strong and resourceful Cora, condemned by her mixed-blood heritage; noble Indian warrior Uncas, instinctively understanding Cora's worth and loving her for it; brave and honest Hawk-eye, nature's aristocrat.

The two groupings of characters allowed Cooper to stage a conflict between civilized restraint and natural freedom. On the surface, his stories make a case for "the march of our nation across the continent." Nonetheless, Cooper allows Leather-Stocking to make a powerful argument against civilization. "The garden of the Lord was the forest," declares the old hunter, and was not patterned "after the miserable fashions of our times, thereby giving the lie to what the world calls its civilizing"—a paraphrase of one of old Boone's lines. Cooper's sentimental attachments lie with "forest freedom," compelling his readers to dwell on the price of progress. Ambivalence about progress resonated with a deeply felt American regret about the loss of wilderness as an imagined place of unbound freedom.

The frontier settler soon entered the broader realms of American popular culture. David Crockett published his own life story—the story of a bragging, buckskin-clad frontiersman elected to Congress—in 1834, the first autobiography of a western American. Although the book considerably stretched the truth, it was written in Crockett's authentic voice and introduced frontier tall tales to a wide popular audience. Soon, there were many imitations, including a long-running series of the *Davy Crockett Almanac*, supposedly recounting Crockett's ongoing feats in his own words, although the stories saw their heyday long after their protagonist had been killed at the Alamo. "I can walk like an ox, run like a fox, swim like an eel, yell like an Indian, fight like a devil, and spout like an earthquake, make love like a mad bull, and swallow a nigger whole without choking if you butter his head and pin his ears back," thunders the Davy of the almanacs.

Crockett was also a character in the first of the "dime novels," cheap paperbacks with sensational themes that began appearing in the 1840s. The publishing house of Beadle & Adams first began issuing them in large numbers, applying the techniques of mass production to publishing. Their first great success, *Seth Jones; or, The Captives of the Frontier* (1860), tells the story of a white girl captured by Mohawks. In a stirring finale, she is rescued by Seth Jones, a lovable scout in buckskin, who turns out to be a gentleman in disguise, thus neatly combining the roles of frontier scout with well-born hero. The book sold 450,000 copies in just six months and established Beadle & Adams as a publishing powerhouse. The books were bought and read by Americans of all stripes, but particularly by men and women of working-class background. More than two-thirds of the 3,158 titles published between 1860 and 1898 were set in the West. Hunter-scouts like Seth Jones gradually gave way to outlaw, ranger, and cowboy heroes, and the requirement of genteel parentage was eventually dropped.

In the developing standard plot, savage redskins, vicious greasers, or heathen Chinee were laid low by conventional white heroes. By this time, the relatively gentile Boone had given way to more violent characters—Indian-fighting Kit Carson, or big Jim Bowie, with a chip on his shoulder to match the massive knife in his belt. Beadle & Adams's writers loved to focus on real westerners, like Wild Bill Hickok or Billy the Kid. The stories also took subversive turns. In the early 1880s the James gang, then terrorizing banks and railroads on the Missouri border, became a favorite subject. Week after week, Jesse and Frank James defied the law and got away with it in the dimes—until respectable outrage finally forced the postmaster general to ban the series from the mails.

Female characters were central to many recurring dime-novel fantasies. The very first Beadle & Adams novel, *Malaeska: the Indian Wife of the White Hunter* (1860), retold America's oldest frontier legend—the Pocahontas story. An Indian maiden rescues a white frontiersman, marries him and bears his child, is exiled from her own land, and suffers a lonely death in an urban slum. Another persistent dime-novel fantasy was the "woman with the whip"—the western gal who acts a man's part but is all the more alluring for it. *The Mustang-Hunters; or, The*

Beautiful Amazon of the Hidden Valley (1871) features a cross-dressing heroine, "a marvelous mixture of feminine gentleness and masculine firmness."

Dozens of similar dime-novel "she-males" followed, most famously Calamity Jane, introduced in Edward L. Wheeler's *Deadwood Dick on Deck; or, Calamity Jane, the Heroine of Whoop-Up* (1878), based on the life of a real western woman, Martha Jane Canary. In dime novels, fact and fancy came indiscriminately mixed. But Beadle & Adams warned its authors to avoid "repetition of any experience which, though true, is yet better untold." It remained "better untold," for example, that Martha Jane Canary had turned tricks in the end-of-track helldoradoes of the plains, or that she had ridden with General Crook's troops and was banished from camp for swimming nude with the enlisted men. Dime novelist Wheeler turned prostitute Canary into kindhearted Calamity. In an age when women's freedom was inhibited by genteel conventions, Calamity Jane captured the public imagination by demanding and receiving equal rights in a man's world. While readers surely had little trouble recognizing the dime novels as fictions, the inclusion of authentic details encouraged a suspension of their disbelief. All true! Just think of it!

The ideal of authenticity also powerfully influenced the art of the frontier. All the major exploring and surveying expeditions mounted by the federal government included artists assigned to record and document the land, animals, and peoples of the West. Their art fused romanticism with realism. As William Goetzmann writes about Heinrich B. Möllhausen, who documented the route of one of the Pacific railroad surveys of the 1850s, he "never allowed facts, or the demands of literalism, to interfere with his romantic imagination." Riding with the Frémont expeditions of 1845 and 1848 were the brothers Edward and Richard Kern, artists who proved willing to bend what they saw to fit what they wanted. Making permanent copies of his field sketches, for example, Richard repositioned an Indian pueblo in order to create an illusion of space and order missing from real life.

A similar mix of documentary and artistic impulses characterized the work of frontier painter George Catlin. As a young man he once saw an Indian delegation in Philadelphia and was so impressed with those "lords of the forest," he resolved that "nothing short of the loss of my life shall prevent me from . . . becoming their historian." In 1832 he enthusiastically worked his way up the Missouri River to the mouth of the Yellowstone, sketching practically every Indian he met on the way. He asked the public to view his works "as *true* and *fac-simile* traces of individual life and historical facts." To the backs of his work Catlin attached certificates signed by Indian agents or army officers certifying that the drawings were "painted from the life."

Yet in truth, Catlin aimed at more than mere record; he sought to express a point of view through his art, as well as his writing. "The bane of this *blasting frontier* has regularly crowded upon them," he wrote of the Indians, "and like the fire in a prairie, which destroys everything where it passes, it has blasted and sunk them." Catlin was on a mission of deliverance. "I have flown to their rescue—not of their lives or of their race (for they are '*doomed*' and must perish), but to the rescue of their looks and their modes." There is much to admire in Catlin's sentiments, especially when they are placed within the Indian-hating context of his times. And clearly, the Indians could inspire great art. The men and women of his Indian portraits never fail to impress. But he was oblivious to the cultural transformations that in fact would ensure the survival of Indian people.

More successful, perhaps, at capturing images of Indians as people of culture was Karl Bodmer, a Swiss painter who toured the upper Missouri country in 1833 and 1834. A fine draftsman and colorist, Bodmer is notable for the abundance of ethnographic detail he packed into his images, as in his celebrated study of a Mandan family relaxing around the central hearth of their earth lodge, showing shields, lances, and medicine symbols, the cooking pots and basketry of the women, the framing timbers and the solidity of the lodge itself. But like Catlin, Bodmer missed the evidence of cultural interaction. For both artists, the mission was to portray images of Indians in their "pristine" condition.

Alfred Jacob Miller was the painter who best captured the cultural mix of the frontier. In 1837 Captain William Drummond Stewart, a Scottish nobleman, hired Miller to accompany him on a trip to the Rockies. Miller's watercolors and drawings of this expedition feature Indians and mountain men setting traps, spinning tales around campfires, and resting peacefully together in the midday shade. More than any other nineteenth-century artist of the West, Miller paid close attention to Indian women—preparing skins and meat, tending children, racing horses, even hunting buffalo. His work provides powerful visual support for the central place of women in fur trade society. Yet many of Miller's images of women reflect his colonial assumptions. They are frequently unclothed in his work, bringing to mind, as William Goetzmann suggests, the Tahitian works of Paul Gauguin. The eroticism of an image like the beautiful *Snake Girl Swinging* (1837) was certainly intended for the private male reveries of Miller's patron.

Missouri artist George Caleb Bingham brought to his images of frontier settlers the documentary concerns that animated these painters of Indians. Art, Bingham declared at the onset of his career, should be history's "most efficient hand-maid." He depicted everyday life, settlers at work and at play, at home with their families or in town participating in politics. His most famous series of canvases featured flatboatmen on the Missouri and Mississippi rivers. But Bingham's paintings were not documentary in any narrow sense. Indeed, his images are so tranquil that they seem to depict a world in which time stands still. This is especially notable in his masterwork, *Daniel Boone Escorting Settlers through the Cumberland Gap* (1852). At the head of a column of settlers stretching back through the dark and forbidding pass, Boone leads his family into the clear light of Kentucky. He symbolizes immense courage, unconquerable faith in hard work, and the coming of civilization to a raw West. Executed in the aftermath of the Mexican War, the high tide of American empire, the work is a quintessential celebration of pioneering.

Bingham studied in Düsseldorf, Germany, with Emanuel Gottlieb Leutze, an eminent painter of American historical themes, best known for *Washington Crossing the Delaware* (1852). Leutze's *Westward the Course of Empire Takes Its Way* (1862), which graces a wall of the Capitol in Washington, D.C., was equally monumental in scale, filling six hundred square feet. It depicts a group of pioneers mounting the summit of a mountain range and celebrating their arrival in the golden West. In a landscape of Leutze's romantic imagining, the pioneers are a mélange of stereotypes: frontiersmen shouldering their rifles, a young man with a bloody bandage on his forehead (a wound, perhaps, from fighting Indians), a stoic pioneer bride, a dead loved one being buried by a grieving family. At the summit is a buckskinned Boone-like frontier farmer, joyously indicating the destination to the recumbent mother and child sheltered in his arms. Completed during the Civil War, Leutze's work offered an allegorical visualization of expansionist plans for the postwar West.

The artist who best captured the public taste for the monumental was Albert Bierstadt, an American who also studied in Düsseldorf. Returning to the states, he joined a government survey headed west and found in the Rockies "the best material for the artist in the world." He sketched his way through the Wind River Mountains, then returned to his studio in New York City to paint a number of huge finished works. *The Rocky Mountains, Lander's Peak* (1863) created an immediate sensation. On a canvas measuring six by ten feet, Bierstadt created a panoramic and infinitely receding landscape of valley, lake, and mountains, replete with a busy Indian encampment in the foreground. Dramatic interplays of shadow and sunlight highlight the distant peaks and overwhelm the human subjects. Bierstadt took the canvas on a triumphant tour through the United States and Europe, then sold it for the unprecedented sum of $25,000 (the equivalent of about $400,000 in 2005 values). He had the picture engraved and sold by subscription, netting him thousands more. The painting, he assured buyers, had "a geographical and historical value such as few works by modern artists have obtained." In truth, Bierstadt concocted the landscape in *The Rocky Mountains*, redistributing peaks and valleys and foreshortening distances for dramatic effect. Bierstadt suffered considerable criticism for this kind of artistic manipulation. Mark Twain once described one of his Yosemite landscapes as having "more the atmosphere of Kingdom-Come than of California." But Twain missed the point of Bierstadt's art, which aimed not at *documenting* the western landscape as much as *transforming* it into something otherworldly, a place of mystery and magic.

Another great late-nineteenth-century painter of monumental western landscapes was Thomas Moran, an artist as well steeped in English romanticism as Bierstadt was in its German form. Longing for dramatic western vistas appropriate for emerging impressionistic currents, in 1871 Moran joined the Yellowstone survey party of Ferdinand V. Hayden, which included photographer William Henry Jackson. After completing the expedition, Moran produced a series of watercolors that were engraved for reproduction. Together with Jackson's photographic prints, these images were instrumental in persuading Congress to create Yellowstone National Park.

Moran and Bierstadt encouraged the public to think of the western landscape as a spectacular emblem of America. Bierstadt's West was like a Gothic cathedral, attuning awe-struck men and women to the infinite beauty of western nature. Moran's paintings were like stained-glass windows, each small piece of color transmitting an aura of mystical reverence. Yet Moran in 1892 also painted *Smelting Works at Denver*, in which huge smokestacks belch toxic wastes into the crisp air, the sky dissolving into a haze of yellows, browns, and blacks. Moran's mature painterly interests could find artistic possibilities not only in the towers and pinnacles of Yellowstone, but also in the cityscapes of the emerging industrial West.

During the long cycle of economic hard times and farmer-worker protest that began with the Panic of 1873 and lasted until the late 1890s, many Americans became concerned about the "close of the frontier." In his influential book *Progress and Poverty* (1879), Henry George argued that the nation's economic progress had depended on western expansion. "But our advance has reached the Pacific," he warned. "Further west we cannot go." It seemed the country was being thrown in on itself. In 1889 fifty thousand people participated in a frenzied rush to stake claims on two million acres of "unoccupied" land in Indian Territory, almost overnight creating the territory of Oklahoma. That year and the next, six new western states entered the union—North and South Dakota, Montana, Washington, Idaho, and Wyoming—and over the next dozen years, the admission of the final four—Utah, Oklahoma, Arizona, and New Mexico—completed the process of state-making in the nation's contiguous area. Worry over the closing frontier echoed in government reports, scholarly treatises, and ministers' sermons. Humorist and western editor Bill Nye spoke for ordinary folks: "There ain't no frontier any more."

These apprehensions seemed confirmed by the conclusions of statisticians and cartographers who examined the returns of the 1890 federal census. "At present," they wrote, "the unsettled area has been so broken into by isolated bodies of settlement that there can hardly be said to be a frontier line." These words fired the imagination of young Wisconsin historian Frederick Jackson Turner. In his 1893 essay "The Significance of the Frontier in American History," delivered at a meeting of historians at the World's Columbian Exhibition in Chicago, Turner made this famous declaration: "Up to our own day American history has been in large degree the history of the colonization of the Great West. The existence of an area of free land, its continuous recession, and the advance of settlement westward, explain American development." But now, Turner concluded, "four centuries from the discovery of America, at the end of a hundred years of life under the Constitution, the frontier has gone, and with its going has closed the first period of American history."

There were some serious problems with the notion of a closed frontier. Far more land in the trans-Mississippi West, both public and private, was taken up in the years after 1890 than in the years before. Western settlements continued to expand after 1890, yet on the census maps of 1900 and 1910, the "frontier line" made a mysterious reappearance. Geographer Frank Popper, reporting on "the strange case of the contemporary American frontier," points out that using Turner's own population definition of "unsettled," there were at the end of the twentieth century 149 "frontier" counties in the West. The cartography that so inspired Turner, it turns out, was less a work of science than of the imagination. A century later, the West had yet to fill up.

The closing of the frontier became part of the myth of the frontier. After reading Turner's frontier essay, Woodrow Wilson wrote that with the continent occupied "and reduced to the uses of civilization," the nation must inevitably turn to "new frontiers in the Indies and in the Far Pacific." Theodore Roosevelt agreed, arguing that American colonies in the Caribbean and the Pacific were the logical and necessary extension of continental westering. He likened Filipinos to Apaches and condemned anti-imperialists as "Indian lovers." If the United States was "morally bound to abandon the Philippines," he blustered during the debate on annexation after the Spanish-American War of 1898, "we were also morally bound to abandon Arizona to the Apaches." Just as expansionists of the 1840s had marshaled public enthusiasm for westering to justify a war against Mexico, so imperialists of the 1890s exploited fears of the end of frontier opportunity in order to build support for the creation of an American overseas empire.

Simultaneous with Turner's promotion of the frontier thesis, three prominent easterners were doing their part to bring the myth of the frontier to popular attention: politician Theodore Roosevelt, artist Frederic Remington, and writer Owen Wister. Born into prominent families during the Civil War era, educated at Harvard or Yale, at a critical point in their early twenties each of these men went west seeking personal regeneration. Historian G. Edward White persuasively argues that these sojourns convinced each of them that only by coming to grips with the experience of westering—with the myth of the frontier—could Americans preserve important aspects of their culture that were being swept away by the rush of industrialization. Most importantly, they sought to encourage a rugged version of American manhood. Their heroes were all, in Remington's phrase, "men with the bark on," tough and shaggy.

Roosevelt's encounter with the West followed the devastating death of his young wife (in childbirth) and his mother (from disease) on the same dark day in 1884. The young man abandoned New York and for three years lived on a Dakota cattle ranch, "far off from mankind." For Roosevelt, this western sojourn became a critical test of his manhood. At first, the cowboys ridiculed him as an effete easterner, but things turned around once he stood up to a bully and floored him with a lucky punch. Roosevelt learned to hunt. He joined a posse and participated in the capture of a gang of desperadoes. He returned to New York in 1886, a rough-and-tumble westerner. This experience would inform all his subsequent work—as author of hunting memoirs and a multivolume history of the West; as president of the Boone and Crockett Club; as conservationist, sports hunter, and advocate of "the strenuous life"; as Rough Rider during the Spanish-American War; and as America's first "cowboy president." What was good for the American male was good for the country.

Frederic Remington went west in 1883 to escape a domineering mother who ridiculed his artistic ambitions. Writing that he wished to "cut women out of his life altogether," he used a small inheritance to purchase a Kansas ranch, where he found western men who were "untainted by the enfeebling influences of luxury and modern life." Simultaneously, Remington rediscovered his talent and joy for art and like Catlin and Bingham before him, resolved to capture on paper the last days of the frontier. Magazines began to accept his sketches. Captivated by Remington's work, Roosevelt asked him to illustrate his forthcoming *Ranch Life and the Hunting Trail* (1887). It was the beginning of a lucrative career as the day's most successful commercial illustrator. Soon, oils and bronzes were also pouring from his studio and commanding top dollar. Remington rivaled his friend Roosevelt in his devotion to the cult of masculinity. True manliness, he believed, developed in the struggle with raw nature, the individual pitted against drought and wind. His works include dozens of images of men battling against a barren landscape.

Owen Wister, a classmate of Roosevelt's at Harvard, in 1885 exchanged a career as a Boston businessman for a position as manager of a large Wyoming cattle ranch. Like Roosevelt and Remington, Wister self-consciously conceived of his western experience as a test of his manhood. He slept outdoors with the cowboys, bathed in an icy creek, drank his steaming coffee from a tin cup, and joined in the roundup, reinventing himself as "kin with the drifting vagabonds who swore and galloped by his side." Returning east, his writing about cattle country culminated in *The Virginian* (1902), a runaway best seller and the most influential and widely read of all western novels. The mythical country of the open range—the classic setting of the Western—was entirely masculine, restoring health and re-creating American men as self-reliant individuals. Wister staged *The Virginian* as a series of tests of manhood. The hero rides at the head of a posse that captures and lynches a group of cattle rustlers, including his own best friend. He confronts the threatening outlaw Trampas—"When you call me that, smile!"—and in the prototype of the western duel, shoots him dead in the dusty main street of Medicine Bow. By dint of intelligence and industry, he rises from cowboy to foreman, eventually becoming "an important man, with a strong grip on many various enterprises." But the central test is the Virginian's courtship of the eastern schoolmarm. In a series of arguments, the cowboy persuades the lady to abandon sentimental attachments and accept his moral code, the rule of honor. "Can't you see how it is about a man?" he implores as he rejects her pleas to leave town and avoid the final confrontation with Trampas. She cannot see—but in the end she accepts. After all, she had come west because she "wanted a man who was a man."

If Turner, Roosevelt, Remington, and Wister brought intellectual respectability to their version of the frontier myth, "Buffalo Bill" Cody was the man who turned that myth into America's most bankable commercial entertainment. Born in Iowa in 1846, William Frederick Cody grew up on the frontier. As a teenage boy he tramped to the Colorado gold rush and rode for the Pony Express. He scouted for the frontier army in campaigns against the Comanches, Sioux, and Kiowas, and earned his nickname hunting buffalo to feed railroad construction gangs. In 1869 dime novelist Ned Buntline wrote Cody up in the fanciful *Buffalo Bill, King of the Bordermen* (1869) as "the greatest scout of the West." Honor motivated all his actions, whether protecting public virtue or rescuing white women from dastardly attacks by Indians. Before Cody's death in 1917, he had been the subject of no fewer than fifteen hundred dime novels.

Cody was such a showman, such a ham actor, that he tried his best to live the role in which Buntline had cast him. He went on the stage playing himself and organized a troupe of cowboy and Indian actors who reenacted actual events in western history. In 1882 Cody organized the greatest of his shows, "Buffalo Bill's Wild West," which toured America and the world for the next three decades. The performance began with an overture played by thirty-six "cowboy" musicians wearing flannel shirts and slouch hats. Laced throughout were exhibitions of shooting and riding. Annie Oakley, the sweetheart of the show, entered trippingly, throwing kisses. Then her rifle would begin to crack as she dispatched glass balls, clay pigeons, and little three-by-five-inch cards embossed with her picture, thrown high, sliced by her bullets, then thrown to the delighted audience. Buck Taylor, King of the Cowboys, clung to bucking broncs and led a group in square dances and Virginia reels on horseback.

The show always included a large contingent of Indians, mostly Sioux, performing their dances and displaying life as they had lived it on the plains. Sitting Bull joined the tour for the 1885 season, but when the great Sioux chief appeared in his ceremonial feathers, the audience hissed at him and he refused to tour for another season. Reformers complained that Cody exploited his Indian performers, but most of the historical evidence suggests that the Indians enjoyed the work and considered themselves well treated. Black Elk, a young Oglala dancer who later became a famous spiritual leader, came down with a bad case of homesickness while touring with Cody in England in the early 1890s. Cody gave him a ticket home and ninety dollars. "Then he gave me a big dinner," Black Elk remembered. "Pahuska [Long Hair] had a strong heart."

Authenticity through historic reenactment was the highlight of the Wild West show. Hunters chased buffalo, Indians attacked the Deadwood stage, and the Pony Express once again delivered the mail to isolated frontier outposts. The climax was a staging of "Custer's Last Fight," with Buffalo Bill arriving just after Custer's demise, the words "Too Late" projected by lantern slide on a background screen. In the grand finale, Cody led a galloping victory lap of all the company's players—"The Congress of Rough Riders of the World"—with the American flag proudly flying in

Early depictions of Californian cities typically emphasized their relationships to their environments. *Top:* First view of Los Angeles published after the American conquest; from *Reports of Explorations and Surveys, to Ascertain the Most Practicable and Economical Route for a Railroad from the Mississippi River to the Pacific Ocean*, vol. 5 (1855). *Bottom:* "Snow and Palms at Pasadena, California," Detroit Photographic Company (c. 1900).

The development of the American West depended on the exploitation of the environment. *Top:* Sugar beet fields in Longmont, Colorado, north of Denver, with the sugar refining plant in the background, an example of what journalist Carey McWilliams called "factories in the fields." From a brochure promoting irrigation, *The Call of the West* (1907). *Left:* Old-growth spruce in the Pacific Northwest supplied lumber for the construction of cities and suburbs throughout the Far West. Photograph by Darius Kinsey (1906).

The New Deal program of economic development for the West was founded on multipurpose river development. *Top:* Bonneville Lock and Dam on the Columbia River; photograph by the Bonneville Recreation Association (1937). *Right:* Federal support for highway construction, including famous Route 66 from Chicago to Los Angeles, encouraged the migration of hundreds of thousands of new western residents as well as the development of western tourism. Pamphlet published by the National U.S. 66 Highway Association (c. 1940).

A mix of documentary and artistic impulses characterized the painters of the American West. *Clockwise from top:* Carl Bodmer's depiction of the Buffalo Dance of the Mandans, from Maximillian, Prinz von Wied, *Voyage dans l'intérieur de l'Amérique du Nord,* 3 vols. (1840–43); George Catlin's self-portrait of the artist at work, from Catlin, *Illustrations of the Manners, Customs, and Condition of the North American Indians* (1848); Alfred Jacob Miller's eroticized watercolor of Snake Indian girls, from "William Drummond Stewart Expedition Paintings" (1837).

The work of artists and photographers helped create the public sentiment that resulted in the establishment of the world's first national parks. *Top:* Yosemite valley from Inspiration Point, photograph by Carlton E. Watkins (c. 1865). *Bottom:* Castle Geyser, Yellowstone National Park, chromolithograph of a painting by Thomas Moran, from F. V. Hayden, *The Yellowstone National Park* (1876).

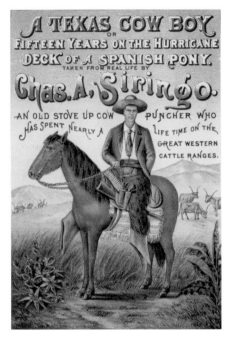

The West became a consuming subject of popular culture during the late nineteenth century. *Clockwise from top left: Deadwood Dick* dime novel, showing Calamity Jane, the first dime-novel heroine, cover (1879); Charles Siringo, *A Texas Cow Boy*, cover (1885); Buffalo Bill and Sitting Bull, photograph by W. R. Cross (1891); Theodore Roosevelt as frontier hunter, from Roosevelt, *Hunting Trips of a Ranchman* (1886).

Westerns were the most popular Hollywood genre from the beginning of the twentieth century until the 1960s. *Top:* Lobby card for "The Covered Wagon" (1923), which reenacted the great overland migration; *bottom:* poster for "Cheyenne Autumn" (1964), the last Western made by director John Ford, the acknowledged master of the genre.

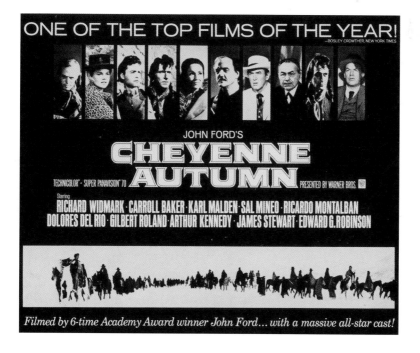

The legacy of colonialism and ethnic diversity was a continuing challenge for the West in the twentieth century. *Clockwise from top left:* Broadside ordering the relocation of Japanese Americans during World War II (1942); leaflet supporting the United Farm Workers' boycott of nonunion grapes (1970); traditional Sioux leader John Fire Lame Deer symbolically reclaiming the Black Hills at Mount Rushmore, South Dakota, photograph by Richard Erdoes (c. 1970).

the van. The whole spectacle, in the words of the souvenir program, was designed to illustrate "the inevitable law of the survival of the fittest."

In the early twentieth century, Cody began to feel competition from the movies. *The Great Train Robbery* (1903) was the first motion picture to tell a complete story, the first movie Western. Director Edwin S. Porter based his one-reel film on the 1901 holdup of the eastbound Union Pacific by an outlaw gang known as the Wild Bunch, led by Butch Cassidy and the "Sundance Kid." The plot built on the Wild West formula pioneered by Cody: a dastardly attack, a dramatic chase, and a violent climactic shoot-out. In the film's final image, one of the outlaws points his gun directly at the audience and fires. People were thrilled. *The Great Train Robbery* marked the birth of the American motion picture industry, which from its beginnings was preoccupied with western stories. Over the next sixty years, at least a third of all the films made in the United States were Westerns.

The first movie actor to assume the mantle of the western hero was Max Aronson, a traveling salesman from Arkansas whose first screen role was playing one of the outlaws in *The Great Train Robbery*. Under the stage name of Bronco Billy Anderson, he starred in some four hundred astoundingly popular western two-reelers, all with essentially the same plot—Bronco Billy as a good-badman redeemed by the love of a virtuous woman or the disarming cuteness of a helpless child. The public next fell for Tom Mix, a veteran of Wild West shows who was a master of trick riding and fancy shooting. In his snow-white ten-gallon Stetson, hand-tooled boots, and dandified cowboy clothes, Mix cut a fantastic figure, and by the 1920s, in addition to dozens of cheap films, he was being featured in a regular weekly radio program and his own series of comic books.

Bronco Billy and Tom Mix played comic book characters, but other filmmakers went to lengths to emphasize the authenticity of their Westerns. Director Thomas Ince and actor William S. Hart made a series of pictures celebrated for their accurate portrayal of the West. The appeal and influence of a picture like *Hell's Hinges* (1916) was Hart's good-badman character and the verisimilitude of its mise-en-scène—the wonderfully mangy prairie towns populated by authentic-looking western types, many of them rodeo cowboys or ranch hands picking up a few extra dollars by performing stunts or filling out the cinematic ranks of outlaw gangs and vigilante posses. Until the 1920s, plenty of places within a few hours of Hollywood retained the look and feel of the late-nineteenth-century West—the old gold rush town of Sonora in the Sierra Nevada or the arid Owens valley, frozen in time by the construction of the Los Angeles aqueduct.

The concern for authenticity inspired the production of a number of "epic" Westerns during the twenties. Hart directed and starred in *Tumbleweeds* (1924), an ambitious and gritty depiction of the Oklahoma land rush of 1889. *The Iron Horse* (1924), directed by John Ford, told the story of the construction of the transcontinental railroad. Perhaps the most impressive of this set of nationalistic celebrations of the western adventure was *The Covered Wagon* (1923), the story of an overland migration. The film was shot on location in Wyoming and included several hundred Indians from nearby reservations as well as dozens of men, women, and children from local ranches, who also supplied the wagons and oxen, lending the film a documentary look that remains startling today.

Authenticity thus continued as one of the most powerful attractions of western image-making. There was, however, more artifice than honesty in western films. Most were adaptations of the patterned western stories being published in the "pulps," weekly or monthly magazines printed on cheap paper made of wood pulp. The most successful writer of western pulp fiction was Zane Grey, a midwestern dentist who hit the big time with his novel *Riders of the Purple Sage* (1912), in which the lightning-fast gunman hero rescues his lover from Mormon perfidy. Filled with violence, intrigue, cross-dressing, hard-riding women, and plenty of sex, the novel was a blockbuster, eventually selling nearly two million copies. Over the next twenty years, Grey published fifty-six Westerns and sold at least seventeen million books; his name was rarely absent from the best-seller list. Between the world wars, more than one hundred Hollywood films were based on Grey's novels.

Taking cues from men like Roosevelt, Remington, and Wister, western movies became a primary source for twentieth-century images of American manhood. For sheer masculinity, probably no movie star before World War II was more powerful than Gary Cooper, who appeared in at least a dozen Westerns by 1940, including a number of Zane Grey adaptations. In the role that made him a star, Cooper played the greatest western hero of them all, *The Virginian* (1929). Part of the appeal of Westerns undoubtedly lies in the psychological realm. Feminist film critics argue persuasively that Hollywood pictures impose a male-oriented perspective—"the male gaze"—that encourages women, and men, to view women on the screen as the objects of male pleasure. But surely an actor like Cooper—lithe and sexually smoldering—was equally the object of an admiring "female gaze." The strong man with a gun certainly has sexual connotations, and as the roles of women changed and broadened in the twentieth century, some women, and some men, may have looked on images of male dominance with a shiver of nostalgia. But there seems little doubt that the primary audience for Westerns was male. The masculine world of the cowboy was especially attractive to boys feeling constrained by the authoritarian controls of childhood.

The myth of the frontier came under serious question during the Depression. No one happily celebrated the jalopy migration of Okies and Arkies, although they moved for reasons not dissimilar to the covered wagon pioneers of the mid-nineteenth century. Instead, their trek was commemorated in John Steinbeck's *Grapes of Wrath* (1939) or in the hard-edged documentary photographs of Dorothea Lange. At the same time, the major Hollywood film studios stopped making "prestige" Westerns. Perhaps, as historian Robert Athearn suggested, "viewers were uncomfortable with the idea of watching the triumphal westward march of American civilization on the screen while it was falling apart just outside the door."

The genre was abandoned to a group of "poverty row" production companies that turned out cheap "B-Westerns" by the dozens, often as serials.

But on the eve of World War II, the big Hollywood studios turned once again to making Westerns. *Union Pacific* (1939) and *Western Union* (1941) repeated the saga of the transcontinental railroad, while *Dodge City* (1939) and *Frontier Marshall* (1939) chronicled the coming of law and order to the western town. *Jesse James* (1939) retold the story of the James gang as a Populist tale in which the James brothers are driven to lawlessness by evil railroad capitalists. But director John Ford's *Stagecoach* (1939) was the most impressive and influential Western of the late thirties. A dangerous stagecoach journey through Apache country during Geronimo's uprising throws together a colorful cast of characters drawn directly from dime novels and pulp fiction: a good-badman seeking revenge (John Wayne, in the role that made him a star), a prostitute with a heart of gold, an alcoholic doctor, a respectable army wife, an aristocratic southerner, and a venal banker. The film included scenes shot in spectacular Monument Valley on the Navajo Reservation, with its fantastic buttes towering above the desert—a site fully worthy of Bierstadt's art. There is a wonderful stunt sequence in which renegade Apaches (played by local Navajos) chase the stagecoach through the desert until the day is saved by the last-minute arrival of the cavalry. But Ford manipulates and recombines these conventional elements into a film that amounts to considerably more than the sum of its parts. He skillfully reveals the "civilized" members of the party as snobs, hypocrites, or crooks and recruits audience sympathy for the outcasts, who become the heroes of the melodrama. The film celebrates westering while it simultaneously debunks the civilization brought to the West by the East. In the end, the good-badman and the prostitute ride off to spend their lives together on a ranch in Mexico, "saved from the blessings of civilization," as one of the characters puts it. *Stagecoach* is able to have it both ways, which is the way the Western has always wanted to tell the story of America.

Chapter 16 The Frontier and West in Our Time

In the midst of the Great Depression, young James A. Michener received an offer to teach in Colorado. Anxious about leaving his Pennsylvania home, he asked one of his former professors at Swarthmore College for advice. "You'd be making the biggest mistake in your life," the man told him. "The sands of the desert are white with the bones of promising young men who moved West." But without other prospects, Michener decided he had no choice. Much to his surprise, he fell in love with the West. He was awed by the landscape of majestic buttes and mountain valleys and astounded by the irrigation systems that turned deserts into fields of melons and sugar beets. But what struck him most forcefully were the people: "A new type of man was being reared in the West," he wrote. "He was taller, ate more salads, had fewer intellectual interests of a speculative nature, had a rough and ready acceptance of new ideas, and was blessed with a vitality that stood out conspicuously to a stranger from the East." Over a long career as one of the most successful American novelists of the twentieth century, Michener traveled to many exotic places, but he always treasured his western sojourn. "One of the good things about my life was that I spent the formative years in Colorado and got away from an insular Eastern-seaboard perspective," he reflected.

Michener's excitement about the West was typical of post–World War II America. Millions of newcomers poured into the region. Economic development—jumpstarted by the historic projects of the New Deal—reordered the relations between East and West. Certainly, the postwar West could no longer be considered a colonial periphery, what Bernard DeVoto called a "plundered province"; but the country's "westward tilt," in journalist Neil Morgan's phrase, not only applied to migration but to a national shift of attitude. The West often became the economic, cultural, and political pacesetter of postwar America. Indeed, this shift was so fundamental, it signaled an end to the era of sectional politics in American history. In a variety of ways, the whole country became a lot more "western" during the second half of the twentieth century. *Western* remained a key word in the American lexicon, but it signified more about cultural style than regional identity.

Frontier also remained a concept of singular importance. The mass migration of Americans into the West from the East was matched by an equally large migration of immigrants from Mexico, Central America, and Asia. Millions poured across borders to join in the making of one of the world's most multicultural societies. Indian peoples were very much a part of this diverse world. Against all odds, the Indian nations survived, regaining important elements of their sovereignty and reclaiming the proud heritage of their traditions. Not only did the frontier persist, it began to seem like the wave of the future. "Young and eager, cocky and eternally hopeful," as Neil Morgan put it in 1963, "the West seethes with the spirit of *why not.*"

World War II was the most significant event in the economic transformation of the modern West. The New Deal had set out to build an industrial infrastructure in the West, and those efforts laid the foundation for what was to come. But the tidal wave of federal investment during the war telescoped decades of development into a few years. Worried about the vulnerability of the Atlantic coast to German attack, military planners sought to disperse vital industries throughout the West. Then, with the Japanese assault on Pearl Harbor, the West became the staging area for the whole Pacific operation. During the war the federal government supplied 90 percent of the capital for western industrial growth, directly investing at least $70 billion in industries and military installations. The aircraft industry expanded spectacularly in Texas, Washington, and California; aluminum plants sopped up the hydroelectric power of the Northwest's great rivers; and steel foundries arose in Texas, Utah, Oklahoma, and southern California.

In April 1942 Henry J. Kaiser broke ground for a huge steel mill in the quiet rural town of Fontana, east of Los Angeles. The priority was winning the war, and with federal loans Kaiser built the world's most modern and efficient facility for the production of steel. The Fontana mill turned out mammoth prefabricated plates for the hulls of wartime merchant ships. Many of them went to Kaiser's new shipbuilding plants at Los Angeles harbor and to Richmond on San Francisco Bay; Portland, Oregon; and Puget Sound near Seattle. By the end of the war Kaiser was launching a new "Liberty Ship" every ten hours, making him the largest shipbuilder in American history. He drew his workforce—including a large percentage of minorities and women—from all over the country, luring them not only with high wages but with child-care facilities and subsidized medical care. The pioneering Kaiser-Permanente Health Plan was one of the first health maintenance organizations in the nation, and remains one of the strongest.

Kaiser's most important financial partner—aside from the federal government

—was San Francisco banker Amadeo Peter Giannini, owner of the Bank of America. Giannini believed in the future of the West, and he invested in western enterprises, like the studios of United Artists and Walt Disney in Hollywood and the construction of the Golden Gate Bridge. By 1945 the Bank of America had become the largest commercial and savings institution in the world. "The West hasn't even started yet," Giannini declared shortly before his death in 1953. The Bank of America continued as an innovator, the nation's first bank to computerize, to introduce direct deposit, and in 1958 to distribute consumer credit cards, the BankAmericard (later renamed Visa).

Howard Hughes, a tall Texan who inherited a Houston petroleum fortune, was another westerner who touched many of the most important themes in the economic history of the postwar West. He built Hughes Aircraft Corporation into one of the giants of western industry. He won lucrative government contracts during the war, and in the subsequent Cold War years developed weapons-guidance systems, satellites, and other secret projects for the Central Intelligence Agency. He invested in Trans World Airlines, sold his holdings for a half-billion dollars in 1966, and founded Hughes Air West, a carrier specializing in short hauls of passengers and freight. He underwrote some of Hollywood's dramatic growth, and after the war bought RKO Pictures and diversified its operations by buying into television stations and broadcasting old movies. Hughes was also one of the great eccentrics of twentieth-century America, his fear of germs and disease causing him to withdraw almost completely from society. But his investing continued unabated. By the time he died in 1976, he had become one of the wealthiest men in the world.

These biographies are only the foam on the surface of an ocean of phenomenal industrial expansion. The dams and public works of Henry Kaiser had counterparts in the huge construction firms of Stephen Bechtel and John McCone that moved from building dams in the thirties to constructing military bases and freeways during and after the war. The Bank of America was only the largest of a number of powerful western banks; in Los Angeles, for example, Security First National would finance much of the home-construction boom in postwar southern California. Hughes was but a bit player in Hollywood's growth as the capital of the nation's culture industry, and the gamblers he looked down upon from his hermetically sealed Las Vegas penthouse were part of a growing tourism industry that stretched from the ringing slot machines of desert casinos to the dude ranches of Phoenix, from the ski slopes of the Rockies to the surfing beaches of southern California. Hughes was also just one of a group of western aerospace capitalists that included John Northrop, Allan Lockheed, Donald Douglas, and William Boeing. In the late 1950s, both Boeing and Douglas created worldwide markets for their new passenger jets.

The West excelled in high-technology industries. The foundation was laid by the powerful petrochemical industries of Texas and California, and the superstructure was completed during the war. One model was the atomic laboratory at Los Alamos, New Mexico, where the University of California brought together one of the most impressive groups of scientists in the world to build the first atomic bomb. At Hanford, Washington, forty thousand scientists and technicians produced plutonium for such bombs, an assignment that would not have been possible but for the power they drew from the hydroelectric system of the Columbia River. At Pasadena, in southern California, the Jet Propulsion Laboratory of the California Institute of Technology conducted fundamental research in rocketry that later gave it a leading voice in space technology.

Defense spending obviously was critical to this growth. In Seattle, where Boeing Aircraft dominated the local economy, military expenditure accounted for 40 percent of job growth in the postwar period. In Denver, the military facility at Rocky Flats and the federal Rocky Mountain Arsenal employed more than twenty thousand people. Forty percent of all federal aerospace contracts after the war went to firms operating in California, an annual subsidy to the state's economy that amounted to approximately $20 billion. Federal military demand accounted for two-thirds of the state's manufacturing growth from 1945 to 1965.

In the 1950s, Stanford University encouraged a consortium of science and industry in the nearby Santa Clara valley, and new electronics companies such as Hewlett-Packard created the critical mass for what became known as Silicon Valley, a place where startups such as Intel, a computer chip maker founded in 1968, could prosper and grow into giants. In the 1970s, Steve Jobs and Steve Wozniak, two college dropouts tinkering in a Silicon Valley garage, developed an easy-to-use desktop computer they called the Apple. Five years later they were marketing thousands of personal computers and had provoked the eastern computer giant IBM into entering the growing PC market. Microsoft, a company based in Redmond, Washington, organized by westerners Paul Allen and Bill Gates, won the contract to provide the operating software that ran those IBM machines and became one of the great success stories of late-twentieth-century capitalism. By the 1990s, Gates had become the wealthiest person in the world, his net worth estimated at $50 billion.

In 1950 only 10 percent of the nation's two hundred largest corporations were headquartered west of the Mississippi. By 2005 that proportion had climbed to more than 37 percent. The West was home to some of the nation's largest corporations: in computers and computer software (Hewlett-Packard, Dell, Microsoft, Intel, Cisco Systems, Apple, Oracle), aerospace (Boeing, Northrop Grumman), petroleum refining (Exxon-Mobil, Chevron, ConocoPhillips, Marathon, Tesoro, Murphy Oil), wood products (Kimberly-Clark, Weyerhaeuser), and commercial banking (Wells Fargo). The West's long colonial dependence on the East had finally ended.

Other westerners, however, felt that eastern masters had simply been traded for new ones in the high-rise office towers of Houston and Los Angeles or the corporate "campuses" of Seattle. At the beginning of the new century, much of the farming, ranching, and mining West remained tied to a cycle of boom and bust. During the period of economic stagnation that began in the early 1970s and extended into the 1980s, the combined effects of tight money and double-digit inflation created the worst depression in western extractive industries since the 1930s. Tens of thousands of people were thrown out of work. Rural westerners by the thousands lost their lands. Over the second half of the twentieth century, the number of independent western ranchers and farmers fell by half, while corporate "factories in the fields" became commonplace. Radical depopulation occurred in dozens of interior counties as people left the countryside for the urban centers of Texas, California, or the Pacific Northwest. The rise of the West as a national economic power was largely confined to the region's great cities and suburbs.

One of the most powerful forces of western economic expansion was the population boom. Disproportionately large since at least 1900, after World War II it was staggering. From 1945 to 1970, more than thirty million people moved beyond the Mississippi, the most significant redistribution of population in the nation's history. California surpassed New York to become the nation's most populous state in 1964, and in the early 1990s Texas pushed into the second spot, passing New York. This growth is predicted to continue. In the census bureau's projections for the first quarter of the twenty-first century, fifteen states are expected to grow by rates of more than 30 percent—and all but two are in the West.

Most of this past and projected growth is metropolitan. The statistics are stunning. Between 1940 and 1980, the urban proportion of the trans-Mississippi population jumped from 43 to 78 percent. During the 1980s, all but one of the thirty fastest growing cities were in the West, and eighteen were in California. By 2005 the West claimed seven of the nation's fifteen largest metropolitan areas: Los Angeles (number 2), Dallas (number 5), Houston (number 7), San Francisco (number 12), Riverside–San Bernardino (number 13), Phoenix (number 14), and Seattle-Tacoma (number 15). Fully 86 percent of the population west of the Mississippi lived in cities, making the West America's most urban region. The state of Utah has a higher percentage of urban dwellers than the state of New York.

Today's West is dominated by a few large urban oases, the centers of economic and political power, with huge dependent hinterland districts. Think of them as modern-day city-states. "Imperial Texas" centers on the Houston–Dallas–San Antonio triangle and dominates a massive region extending from the Gulf Coast to the oilfields of Oklahoma, from the cattle range of the southern plains to the industrial transborder zone surrounding the twin cities of Brownsville-Matamoros and El Paso–Ciudad Juárez. In the Pacific Northwest an empire with its capital at Seattle includes much of Washington, eastern Oregon, Idaho, and Montana, swinging north along the coast to pull in Alaska. The granddaddy of these western empires is "Greater California," based at Los Angeles, the largest and most diversified urban economy in the nation. So powerful is the southern California economy that it has swept into its orbit not only the state's other urban centers (including rival San Francisco), but satellite cities such as Phoenix and Tucson, Arizona; Las Vegas and Reno, Nevada; Portland, Oregon; and Honolulu, Hawaii.

Each of these economic regions is strengthened by world-class harbors on the Pacific or Gulf Coast. Without such access, the landlocked Rocky Mountain and

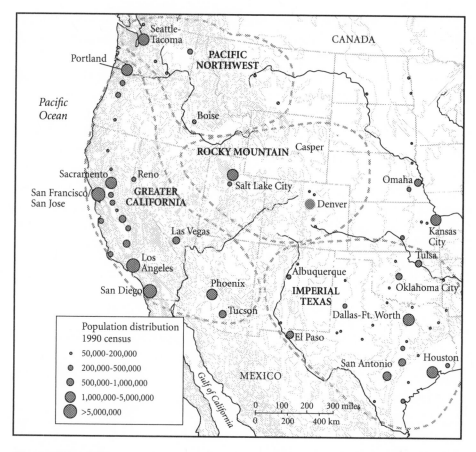

Western Cities, 1990

Great Plains states are forced into subordinate economic relationships. But at the end of the twentieth century—in an emerging era of high-tech air transport—the western interior has begun a comparable economic take off. This new empire is centered at Denver, with its state-of-the-art jetport, and is based on the export by air transport of processed foods (pasta, boxed steaks, and frozen chicken) to foreign markets in Russia, Latin America, and the Far East. During the 1990s, one of the nation's fastest growing population centers was the corridor along Interstate 25 that connects the front range cities of Pueblo, Colorado Springs, Denver, and Fort Collins.

Much of the West's urban growth originated in the search for open space, for a freer, cleaner, less encumbered life, especially in an appealing climate. These were the attractions of the Sunbelt. The enormous swath of arid country stretching from Texas to southern California became the postwar destination of millions of Americans, and almost overnight there appeared thousands of tracts of detached homes, each framed by ample lawns with clusters of palm, avocado, or banana trees, and perhaps a swimming pool in the backyard.

The best known Sunbelt mecca was southern California. Builders there created the modern home-construction industry, moving beyond the innovations of Henry E. Huntington in the early part of the century to consolidate subdivision, construction, and sales into single operations. In the late 1930s, builders invented the techniques of tract construction, in which specialized teams of workers moved sequentially through the project, grading, pouring foundations, framing and sheathing, roofing, and completing the finishing work. With the boom in wartime industry, developers rushed to meet an enormous demand for housing, which was subsidized by federal loans and income tax deductions for home mortgage interest. The combination was explosive, and the resulting development intensified beyond all experience the sprawl of southern California. During the 1950s, profits in southern California homebuilding averaged an impressive 21 percent annually, while the steady inflation of real estate prices turned a generation of homeowners into speculators. The area from Santa Barbara, California, to the Mexican border was converted into a single megalopolis.

Americans embraced this new kind of urban living with enthusiasm. Despite the objections of social critics, families delighted in the opportunity to own their own detached house and yard on a cul-de-sac miles from the central city. But with sprawl came a series of bedeviling problems—abandoned inner cities, polluted air, congested freeways. Many cities vainly tried to avoid the sprawl of Los Angeles, but with little success.

Urban sprawl, congestion, and overdevelopment were not just western problems, of course. In the postwar period, subdivisions ate up the countryside on the edges of every major American city. In exploring this trend, most historical accounts begin with Levittown, the famous Long Island subdivision that opened in 1947; but in fact Levittown was built on the model pioneered in southern California. And not only western construction techniques but western home styles went national after the war. Not everyone moved West, but millions of postwar Americans looked forward to living in a western ranch house, which sought to capture the feeling of western wide open spaces with its horizontal orientation, low-slung roof, rooms flowing one into the other, picture windows, and sliding glass doors inviting residents outdoors to the patio (a western loan word) and the barbecue grill.

The ranch style in domestic architecture was just one of the many things western that went mainstream in the second half of the twentieth century. Consider the growing popularity of comfortable western clothes. After the war, Levi's became the everyday choice of young Americans from coast to coast. By the 1980s, not only jeans but western shirts, belts, boots, bandanas, and even Stetson hats were gracing bodies all over the country. Meanwhile, there was the growing popularity of "country and western" music, pickup trucks, and four-wheel drive vehicles, many named for Indian tribes or western places. Television commercials for Durangos and Dakotas, Comanches and Cherokees frequently featured the vehicles driving through the splendors of western locales such as Monument Valley.

↤ ⊰⊱ ↦

Politics ranks high in the list of ways that the country grew more like the West after the war. Consider the eleven presidents who served from the end of World War II to the beginning of the new century: seven of them—Harry Truman, Dwight Eisenhower, Lyndon Johnson, Richard Nixon, Ronald Reagan, George H. W. Bush, and George W. Bush—were westerners. Add to this list the names of midwestern and western also-rans: Henry Wallace of Iowa, Barry Goldwater of Arizona, George McGovern of South Dakota, Ross Perot of Texas, and Robert Dole of Kansas. Of the twenty-four major party candidates who stood for election between 1948 and 2004, half of them hailed from the West.

No politician exploited western imagery better than Ronald Reagan, a mid-century Hollywood actor who starred in a number of Westerns and loved nothing better than spending time on his ranch in the southern California foothills. Reagan discovered his real talent when he became a leader of the Screen Actors Guild in the late 1940s. Politically, he turned right during the McCarthy era, adding a pro-business perspective to his anti-communism when he became a spokesman for General Electric. He burst onto the national scene in 1964 in a televised speech endorsing Arizona Republican Barry Goldwater's presidential bid. Two years later, he was elected governor of California. Although he did little to cut taxes during his two terms as governor, Reagan successfully rode a national tax revolt into the White House in 1981.

His advisers were masters of appearances. An excellent horseman, Reagan was accustomed to dressing in jodhpurs and riding boots but was told that this wouldn't wash with the American public; instead, he had to act the part of the cowboy. Costumed and frequently photographed in a Stetson hat, Levi's jeans, and Justin boots, Reagan inherited Teddy Roosevelt's mantle of "cowboy president," a distinction he wore with pride. Reagan not only walked the walk, he talked the talk. His oratorical use of the mythic West reached a perfect pinnacle in his second inaugural address: "History is a ribbon, always unfurling; history is a journey. And as we continue on our journey we think of those who traveled before us. . . . The men of the Alamo call out encouragement to each other; a settler pushes west and sings a song, and the song echoes out forever and fills the unknowing air. That's our heritage, that's our song. We sing it still. For all our problems, our differences, we are together as of old." Of course, Reagan didn't write those lines himself (speech-writer Peggy Noonan did), but he had the political savvy to know how well they would play with the American people.

But, as a later cowboy president discovered, western imagery could cause trouble. Although George W. Bush was born in Connecticut, he was raised in Texas, and throughout his political career—as Texas governor, then as the first president to assume office in the twenty-first century—he assiduously cultivated his image as a Texan. He drew on it most overtly after the terrorist attack of September 11, 2001, when he declared that he wanted Osama bin Laden "dead or alive." And he used it during the invasion of Iraq, daring Iraqi insurgents to "bring it on." Confronted by the international and domestic criticism of such "cowboy" talk, Vice President

Richard Cheney of Wyoming was unapologetic. "The notion that the president is a cowboy," Cheney told a reporter, "that's not necessarily a bad idea. I think the fact of the matter is he cuts to the chase. He is very direct and I find that very refreshing." But five years after 9/11, with bin Laden still at large and civil war breaking out in Iraq, Bush was forced to face the limits of his rhetoric. His "tough talk," he admitted, had "sent the wrong message to people. . . . It was misinterpreted." Not everyone found cowboy talk so refreshing.

Political evocations of the frontier myth were bolstered by the dramatic popularity of Westerns for Americans of both Reagan's and Bush's generations. In the postwar period, Westerns were the most popular genre in American fiction, with paperbacks flying off the racks in the 1950s at the rate of thirty-five million copies a year. Western movies were even more popular. From 1945 through the mid-1960s, Hollywood studios produced an average of seventy-five western features each year, a quarter of all films released. Likewise, Westerns dominated television programming during the fifties and sixties. In 1958, for example, twenty-eight primetime Westerns provided more than seventeen hours of gunplay each week. The administration of justice on these shows was always swift. Lawyers and judges were rarely seen on camera. The Western didn't give a hoot for civil liberties.

Westerns thus had their political side. Most clearly, they were a vehicle for promoting America's role during the Cold War. Metaphors of western violence— showdowns, hired guns, last stands—permeated the language of postwar politics. "Would a Wyatt Earp stop at the 38th Parallel in Korea when the rustlers were escaping with his herd?" a conservative commentator whined in 1958. "Would a Marshal Dillon refuse to allow his deputies to use shotguns for their own defense because of the terrible nature of the weapon itself? Ha!" The analogy continued into the Vietnam era. President Johnson, a Texan, once said that Vietnam was "just like the Alamo" and he sent troops there because "somebody damn well needed to go to their aid." American troops carried these metaphors off to war. The primary object of the fighting, one veteran later recalled, was "the Indian idea: the only good gook is a dead gook." Reporter Michael Herr wrote of being invited to join an army company on a "search and destroy" mission. "'Come on,' the captain hailed, 'we'll take you out to play cowboys and Indians.'"

The connection between Westerns and political ideology is perhaps best demonstrated by the precipitous demise of the genre amid the general cultural crisis of the 1960s and 1970s. Consider the case of filmmaker John Ford. Not since Buffalo Bill Cody had an artist better assembled the components of frontier myth as popular entertainment. But in the final Westerns of his career, Ford's vision of frontier history turned sour. *The Searchers* (1956) is an uncompromising study in the devastating effects of hating Indians, and *Sgt. Rutledge* (1960) is a pathbreaking depiction of the black Buffalo Soldiers in the frontier army. In *The Man Who Shot Liberty Valance* (1962), Ford called attention to the good things lost in the civilizing process, and in his final western, *Cheyenne Autumn* (1964), he finally presented the case for the Indians, exposing the American side of the frontier as murderous and corrupt. Ford's doubts about the meaning of frontier history became commonplace in the mid-sixties, evident in a flood of films exploiting the widening gap between old images and new ideas, most prominently in the Italian "spaghetti" Westerns that featured the young actor Clint Eastwood as a completely amoral gunfighter. This cynical approach quickly wore thin, however, and by the late 1970s Westerns were no longer a Hollywood staple.

Yet the genre persisted. The 1989 television broadcast of the miniseries *Lonesome Dove*, based on Larry McMurtry's Pulitzer Prize–winning novel about the first cattle drive to Montana, was a ratings triumph and a pop culture phenomenon. In Hollywood fashion, it was followed by a herd of western projects: big-budget studio features, TV movies and miniseries, even a "Westerns Channel," which since 1994 has been replaying old western movies and western TV series. Viewers could catch a classic Western on cable, but few of the new productions were in the same league as *Lonesome Dove*. An exception was Clint Eastwood's *Unforgiven*, which won the Academy Award for Best Picture of 1992. The two films share a revisionist perspective on the Western while at the same time paying tribute to the genre. *Lonesome Dove* details the heroic efforts of the men to get their cattle to the "cattleman's paradise" of Montana, but closes with the surviving hero bitterly reflecting on the toll it has taken in human life. *Unforgiven* fills the screen with violence but strips it of all pretense to honor, romance, or nobility. "It's a hell of a thing, killing a man," says Eastwood, in the role of a hardened old gunfighter. "You take away all he's got, and all he's ever gonna have." These Westerns ask viewers to consider the costs of westering.

Perhaps the most successful Western of our time was Kevin Costner's *Dances with Wolves* (1990). In the film, Indians play the "good guys," and the arrival of the cavalry is treated as a disaster. The picture was a big moneymaker and also won an Academy Award for Best Picture. Its success suggested changing American attitudes toward Indians. At the beginning of the twentieth century, the assumption had been that Indians and their cultures would vanish; but at the end of the century, they ranked as one of the fastest growing ethnic groups in the country. The Native American population rose from some 350,000 in 1950 to more than two million in 2000. How do demographers explain such growth? For one thing, there has been a clear trend for more and more people to self-identify as American Indians. "It's the *Dances with Wolves* syndrome," said demographer Ross Baker. "It has sort of become neat to be an Indian." Such feelings did not emerge spontaneously but were the result of fifty years of concerted Indian activism.

It was not an easy struggle. During World War II, 25,000 Indians served in the armed services and another 125,000 in the war industry. Pointing to this patriotic record, at war's end the National Council of American Indians (NCAI)—representing many of the nation's 554 tribes—argued that the time had come for the country to make a fair reckoning with Indians for stolen lands and broken treaties.

Congress responded by creating the Indian Claims Commission, empowering it to fully investigate tribal claims and award monetary compensation. By the time the commission finished its work, more than thirty years later, it had heard and considered a total of nearly four hundred cases and awarded more than $800 million in damages (much of which remained in the hands of lawyers). There was, however, an important caveat. The settlement of claims would "terminate" official relations between tribes and the federal government. That would mean the end of all remaining treaty obligations, and the limited sovereignty previously guaranteed to tribes would be revoked. Termination, as the program became known, was made official by an act of Congress in 1953. Only a few tribes actually were terminated, but for those that were, the effects were disastrous. The program worked in an insidious manner, striking at the three most important things to reservation people—sovereignty, land, and culture.

Fear and anger led to a broad movement of pan-Indian activism. In 1961 the NCAI passed a "Declaration of Indian Purpose," calling on the federal government to end termination and begin a new era of "Indian Self-Determination." Endorsed first by President John F. Kennedy, this goal became national policy when President Johnson declared an official end to termination in 1968. In 1975 Congress passed the Indian Self-Determination Act, a measure that strengthened tribal governments by giving them the opportunity and the funds to administer their own programs to promote education and welfare, to oversee natural resources, and to improve reservation infrastructure.

Termination, meanwhile, had accelerated the migration of young Indians to the cities. Indian reservations during the postwar period were some of the most depressed places in America, with a well-established litany of problems from unemployment to alcoholism, a situation termination did nothing to improve. Like other rural westerners, Indians increasingly looked to western urban oases for employment. During the second half of the century, the proportion of American Indians living in urban areas rose from 13 to 60 percent. Large Indian communities developed in all the major metropolitan areas of the West. A new pan-Indian identity grew increasingly important.

The best-known pan-Indian activist organization of the postwar period, the American Indian Movement (AIM), captured the imagination of young urban Indians with the successful occupation of San Francisco Bay's Alcatraz Island in 1969. With its slogan of "Red Power," AIM expanded throughout the urban Indian communities of the West. In 1973, led by Russell Means, an Oglala Sioux, AIM involved itself in the internal politics of the Sioux reservation at Pine Ridge, South Dakota, the most impoverished place in America. Frustrated by a conservative tribal government, AIM activists and reservation supporters armed themselves and occupied a church at the site of the Wounded Knee massacre of 1890. It was a brilliant bid for national media attention at a place many Americans had recently learned about from historian Dee Brown's bestselling *Bury My Heart at Wounded Knee* (1970). They were besieged by FBI agents and federal marshals armed with

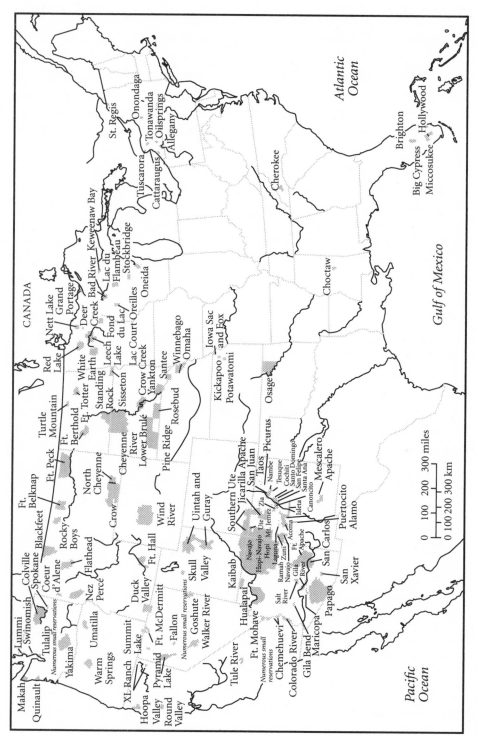

Indian Reservations

automatic weapons, tanks, and helicopters, but opinion polls showed that the public sympathized with the Indians rather than the "cavalry." After seventy-one days, the occupiers finally surrendered with federal promises of negotiations. But afterward, AIM was hounded to extinction by the FBI, and many tribal Indians considered the occupation a disaster.

More effective change came through the struggles of tribal governments to stimulate economic development on the reservations. During the 1980s and 1990s, tribal and Indian-owned businesses in the East and the West grew by a rate nearly five times the national average. Western Indian tribes control a vast resource base: 30 percent of the coal deposits west of the Mississippi, 50 to 60 percent of the country's uranium, 5 percent of the proven oil and gas reserves, fifteen million acres of timber and watershed, and extensive fish and wildlife habitat. At the end of the twentieth century, there was great optimism that the source of development capital might come from Indian gaming, perhaps the most significant assertion of Indian self-determination in American history. The Seminoles first opened a high-stakes bingo parlor near Fort Lauderdale, Florida, in 1978. Florida sued, but a federal appeals court ruled in favor of Seminole sovereignty, and soon tribes around the country were opening gaming operations of their own. In 1988 Congress passed the Indian Gaming Regulatory Act, which required tribes and states to agree on ground rules. By 2005, 39 percent of the nation's 562 federally recognized tribes were doing a gross annual business of nearly $20 billion, about a fifth of the nation's total gaming revenue. But prosperity depended on location. Ten tribes, those within easy reach of major metropolitan areas, accounted for more than 50 percent of the take. Pine Ridge, hundreds of miles from a major urban center, remained the poorest community in the country. And Pine Ridge was all too typical.

Despite ongoing problems and controversies, the Indian nations had made a remarkable comeback. During the last third of the twentieth century, tribes founded twenty-seven reservation colleges that annually enrolled more than twenty-five thousand students. This was part of a cultural renaissance and a resurgence of pride among both reservation and urban Indians. Russell Means, still a controversial figure, offered a sensible summary: "We're still here, and we're still resisting. John Wayne did not kill us all."

Frontiers are what happen when cultures collide and attempt to work out ways of living together. By this measure, our own time deserves prominence in the annals of American frontier history. Not only were Indians resurgent, but Mexican Americans and African Americans mounted an impressive challenge to the social order that had been established during the nineteenth century—the ethnic labor system, the segregation of minorities, and their exclusion from the political process. World War II marked the decisive transition to this new era.

Booming wartime industry in western cities, particularly on the Pacific coast, encouraged the migration of African Americans from the rural South and Mexican Americans from the rural Southwest. Men and women from both groups found jobs building ships, airplanes, and new housing. Jobs were abundant, but assurances of equitable treatment were few. Signs warning "We Cater to White Trade Only" were common in business establishments. African Americans and Latinos were refused service in restaurants and hotels, required to sit in separate sections in theaters, and excluded from public facilities such as parks and swimming pools (except perhaps for a single weekday, usually just before pools were drained and cleaned).

After the war, returning combat veterans were determined not to return to the "bad old days." The late Edward Roybal, who in 1949 became the first Latino elected to the Los Angeles City Council since 1888, remembered how he had learned to confront racism during his time in the army. In his barracks was a man who continually cursed Mexicans. "Then one day he cursed me," Roybal said. "So, I turned around and socked him." To his surprise, Roybal found that his commanding officers approved. They wanted no expressions of bigotry—"not because they loved us, but because they wanted things to run smoothly. It dawned on some of us for the first time that the Anglos were divided. And if we united, we could win concessions." After the war Roybal was one of the founders of a Los Angeles group called the Community Service Organization that registered fifteen thousand new Mexican American voters.

The mobilization of minority voters was one of the most important of postwar struggles. In 1961 Henry B. Gonzáles of San Antonio became the first Mexican American elected to Congress. The next year he was joined by Roybal, elected to represent East L.A. That same year voters in South Central Los Angeles sent Augustus Hawkins, an African American who had migrated from Louisiana to escape "the ruthlessness and ugliness of segregation." In Texas, most African Americans could not participate in electoral politics until the Supreme Court declared the poll tax unconstitutional in 1966. Six years later, voters elected to Congress Barbara Jordan of Houston, the first African American to represent the state in Washington, D.C.

There were also challenges to segregation. The case of Felix Longoria, a young Mexican American serviceman killed in action in the Philippines, provided an early symbol. The Longoria family was outraged to discover that the local funeral home in Three Rivers, Texas, would not allow his remains to lie in state in the chapel because "the whites would not like it." The American G.I. Forum, an activist group of Mexican American veterans, appealed to Senator Lyndon Johnson, who arranged to have Longoria buried in 1949 with full military honors at Arlington National Cemetery. It was one of the first challenges to Jim Crow in Texas.

Perhaps the most important struggle was the fight to integrate public education. Immediately after the war, the League of United Latin American Citizens (LULAC) offered legal assistance to a group of frustrated Mexican American parents whose children were confined to a separate "Mexican school" in the southern California citrus town of Westminster. In a 1947 landmark decision, the California Supreme Court found for the parents. The Westminster schools were integrated, and other southern California districts soon followed. The victory inspired others to think that the West might be the best place to challenge the national system of segregation. In 1952 a group of black parents in Phoenix won a state court ruling against the segregation of public schools in Arizona. At the same time, black parents in Topeka, Kansas—represented by attorneys that included descendants of Exoduster pioneers—filed suit in federal court. In *Brown v. Board of Education of Topeka* (1954), the Supreme Court unanimously ruled that separate schools were inherently unequal.

As important as these victories were, however, they were foiled by intractable patterns of residential segregation. In southern California, restrictive neighborhood covenants barred "non-Caucasians" from an estimated 95 percent of all the housing constructed during the immediate postwar period. In 1947 James Shifflett, a leader of the African American community in Los Angeles, moved his family to a bungalow in an all-white district of the city. Shifflett's neighbors filed suit to enforce the white-only covenant. The case went to the Supreme Court, which ruled that such restrictions were "unenforceable as law and contrary to public policy"—yet the practice continued behind the scenes for many years. The right of owners to refuse to rent, lease, or sell to anyone they chose was confirmed in 1964 when California voters, by a margin of two to one, approved an initiative known as Proposition 14. The resulting pattern was that most African American and Mexican American newcomers crowded into existing ghettos and barrios, which expanded into fringe neighborhoods as whites fled to outlying suburbs. Historian Charles Wollenberg concludes that by the 1970s more schools were segregated than in the 1940s.

Such patterns of discrimination created an ethnic and racial powder keg. As factory jobs moved to new industrial parks in the urban fringe, unemployment rose among minorities in the central city. Cars were scarce in black neighborhoods, and by bus it took almost four hours to get to major industrial plants. Southern California was the most industrialized region in the country yet blacks were left without work. More than 40 percent of African American families in Los Angeles lived at or below the poverty level. The inevitable explosion was touched off one hot, smoggy August evening in 1965 by a minor traffic accident and a botched arrest in Watts, the most impoverished of the black neighborhoods of Los Angeles. For six successive days, thirty thousand angry people fought with police and the National Guard, looting stores and burning hundreds of buildings within a forty-mile radius. Thirty-four people were killed during the Watts Riot. Over the next five years, black urban uprisings occurred in many of the major cities of the West.

Although many Mexican Americans found employment in the booming industrial economy of the postwar West, thousands continued to labor in the fields as agricultural workers. It was not until the 1960s that they found their champion in César Chávez. Once as a boy in a California desert town, Chávez and his brother were refused service at a diner, the waitress rejecting him with a laugh—"We don't sell to Mexicans." Chávez left in tears. That laugh, he said, "seemed to cut us out of the human race." A few years later he was arrested for refusing to move from the white-only section of a movie theater. It was his introduction to political activism. Chávez worked first for the Community Service Organization in San Jose, then focused his attention on organizing farmworkers.

The Mexican deportations of the thirties and wartime mobilization had left growers short of farmworkers. Pressing the federal government for relief, they secured the passage of legislation permitting the entrance into the country of temporary Mexican farmworkers, or *braceros*. But the Bracero Program outlasted the war. Growers used the guest worker program as the means of keeping the lid on wages and preventing strikes. The program also had the unintended effect of stimulating a huge increase in the number of migrants who came across the border illegally. By the early 1950s, the Border Patrol was apprehending more than half a million illegal immigrants each year, and estimates were that perhaps two or three times that many came across successfully. Chávez argued that the presence of a large pool of politically powerless aliens severely hampered the effort to unionize farmworkers who were American citizens. Mobilizing both Mexican Americans and liberals, Chávez's first success came when Congress eliminated the Bracero Program in 1964.

Chávez and fellow organizers like Dolores Huerta, a dynamic young Hispana from an old New Mexican family, organized the United Farm Workers (UFW), and in 1966 they launched their first strike (*huelga*) against grape growers in California's Central Valley. To pressure growers, the UFW launched a nationwide boycott of grapes that had widespread effects. Governor Reagan of California was reduced to pleading with Americans to eat more grapes, and President Nixon ordered the Department of Defense to buy tons more than it needed, sending planeloads to the troops in Vietnam. But Chávez's charismatic and inspirational leadership proved stronger. In 1970 the growers relented and began signing union contracts. With the sympathetic support of Governor Jerry Brown, who succeeded Reagan, the UFW was able to raise wages and living standards. It was a historic achievement, capping decades of struggle in California's factories in the field.

Chávez and the UFW were part of a broad political and cultural renaissance among Latinos in the Southwest. In New Mexico, a volatile leader named Reies Tijerina organized an alliance, or *alianza*, of twenty thousand Hispanos demanding an investigation of the wholesale theft of land that had occurred after the Mexican War. Frustrated at the inaction of authorities, he and his followers occupied federal lands at gunpoint in 1966, declaring an independent Hispano nation. Two officers were wounded during the confrontation and exchange of gunfire that followed, and Tijerina was sent to prison for two years. In south Texas, the Raza Unida Party was established in 1970 and scored a series of impressive victories in local elections. Among young people throughout the urban Southwest, there was a surge of enthusiasm for *mexicanismo*. Amid cries of *"Viva la Raza!"* activists celebrated the memory of pachucos and zoot suiters and began calling themselves *Chicanos*, embracing with pride a slang term Mexican Americans had used to denigrate Mexican newcomers. New slogans were heard on the streets—*"Somos Uno Porque*

America Es Una" (We Are One Because America Is One) and *"Somos Un Pueblo Sin Fronteras"* (We Are One People Without Borders).

In 1965 Congress reformed the immigration laws, abolishing the system of quotas based on national origins enacted in 1924. In the years after, a massive new wave of immigration brought nearly ten million Latinos and more than eight million Asians to the country. The majority settled near the major immigrant gateways of the West: Los Angeles, San Francisco, and Houston. The Mexican American population of the Southwest increased by 379 percent from 1970 to 2000, when it stood at more than twenty million. Over the same period, the Asian population increased more than eight times, with more than five million living in the West by 2000. Demographers project that during the first quarter of the twenty-first century, western cities will attract another thirty million Latinos and seven million Asians.

The number of migrants entering the United States illegally also increased enormously. At the turn of the twenty-first century, about half of the illegal migrants crossed into the country from Mexico. In the words of one commentator, they had "an economic gun at their backs." For others, the gun was all too real, for armed conflict in Central America created thousands of refugee Salvadorans, Guatemalans, and Nicaraguans. Tragedy frequently occurred at the border: greedy middlemen, known as *coyotes*, extorted high fees for guiding illegal migrants into the country; violent *banditos* lay in wait to rob vulnerable individuals of their valuables; migrants by the hundreds, perhaps the thousands, died by drowning or exposure. Despite the construction of walls and barricades along the border, in the first years of the new century, the Border Patrol along the Mexican border was apprehending and expelling more than one million illegal migrants each year.

Yet by the thousands the people kept coming, drawn by the availability of jobs Americans declined to fill because the wages were so low—jobs as textile workers, farm laborers, gardeners, nannies, and housekeepers. Most studies suggested that undocumented workers contributed substantially to economic growth and paid their fair share in taxes, but they were blamed for everything from unbalanced budgets to shoddy schools. In 1994 California voters approved Proposition 187, which would have denied illegal aliens and their children access to public services such as education and health care, but a federal judge declared the measure unconstitutional. It was an old story—Mexican workers have been a critical component of the southwestern economy for more than one hundred years, but they make convenient targets for nativist anxiety and anger.

In the last quarter of the twentieth century, southern California became the most ethnically diverse metropolitan area in the world. Los Angeles became home to immigrants from 140 countries, including the largest communities of Mexicans, Salvadorans, Guatemalans, Koreans, and Filipinos outside their homelands, as well as the country's largest concentrations of Japanese, Cambodians, and Iranians. The 2000 census found Los Angeles County to be 45 percent Latino, 12 percent

Asian, 10 percent African American, and only 31 percent Anglo (a category including people from a variety of European backgrounds). In 2005 city voters elected Antonio Villaraigosa to be the first Latino mayor since 1872. Thus does the wheel turn. "Our modern metropolis is returning to the enduring Pueblo de Los Angeles of years past," declared California state senator Art Torres.

It was but one dramatic scene in a larger drama. In a great arc from the Gulf Coast to the Pacific, the Southwest was gradually turning "majority minority": New Mexico in 1996, California in 2000, Texas in 2005, Arizona by 2010. Urban westerners of the new century would need to learn how to live in a multicultural world. But adjustment was slow. Anglos constituted only 31 percent of the population of Los Angeles, but they made up 70 percent of the registered voters and controlled 90 percent of the fixed wealth. Although the economic gap between whites and minorities was narrowing nationally, it was growing in the Southwest.

The starkest evidence of the problem came with the devastating 1992 Los Angeles riots, the worst urban disorder of the century. For decades, African American and Latino communities had complained of systematic police brutality. Those charges seemed confirmed when an amateur videotape of four white police officers beating a black motorist was played repeatedly on television. But when an all-white suburban jury acquitted the officers of brutality, the city exploded in violence. For several days rioters swept through black, Latino, and Asian neighborhoods, looting and burning. Fifty-one people died and several square miles were torched before the National Guard restored order. More than twelve thousand people were arrested. Not only was this uprising deadlier and more destructive than the Watts Riot of 1965, it was multiethnic. Forty-one percent of those arrested were African American, but 12 percent were Anglo and 45 percent Latino. Furthermore, much of the violence was directed at the downtown community of Korean Americans, many of whom owned successful businesses in minority districts. The riot exposed the festering ethnic and racial divisions within this "world city."

Doubts about the future of the urban Southwest were reflected in the considerable out-migration from western cities at the turn of the century. During the 1990s, as many as two million more people left California than arrived there from other states, although the loss was more than counterbalanced by the influx of foreign migrants. The out-migration continued in the new century. According to the census bureau, the majority was moving to Las Vegas or Reno in Nevada, or to the Rocky Mountain West, to counties on the outskirts of Denver, Salt Lake City, or Boise. One southern Californian who had relocated to Idaho in the seventies warned of the dangers. "I've seen it all happen on the coast," he declared, and "now it's happening here—trout streams dug up for freeways, the smog, the elk herd declining." Local sentiments were summed up in the Boise bumper sticker that pleaded, "Don't Californicate Idaho!"

The controversy over the new rush to the interior West was part of an extended postwar debate over the use of the western landscape. It was a reminder

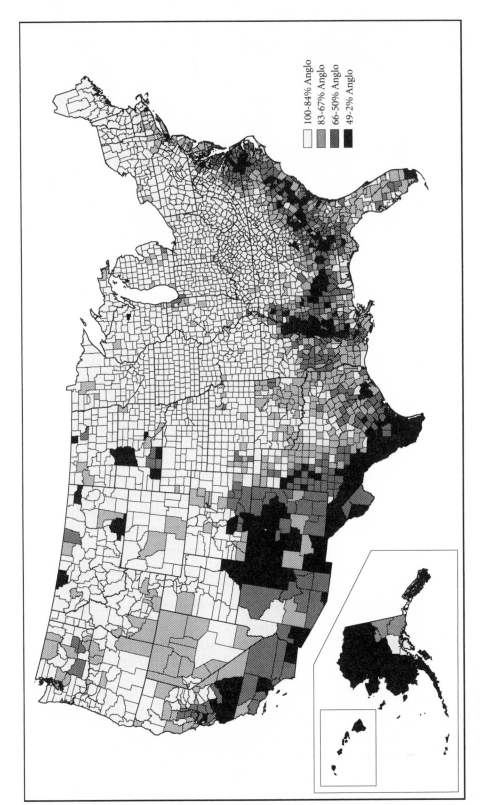

Emerging Minority Majorities

100-84% Anglo
83-67% Anglo
66-50% Anglo
49-2% Anglo

of how special the glorious western vistas were to Americans, but also how fragile. The national parks, of course, were to be protected, as jewels in the crown of western empire. During the postwar period, Congress created twenty-one new parks, increasing the territory for which the National Park Service was responsible to eighty million acres, nine-tenths of it in the trans-Mississippi West or Alaska. But the breathtaking scenery of the parks drew armies of tourists, too many people trampling fragile meadows and too many vehicles and other machines fouling fresh air. The danger of "loving the parks to death" confronted Park Service leaders with a fundamental dilemma they are still trying to resolve.

One of the most frequent arguments made for environmental preservation called upon the importance of the frontier in American tradition. Only by setting aside wilderness areas, wrote Robert Marshall, one of the founders of the Wilderness Society, could "the emotional values of the frontier be preserved." In the early 1960s, the Wilderness Society and the Sierra Club lobbied Congress for legislation that would protect large areas of country in the West from development. The resulting Wilderness Act (1964) set aside as undeveloped wilderness nine million acres of federal land; Congress increased this to ninety-five million acres by the beginning of the new century. By preserving wilderness, wrote novelist Wallace Stegner, "the hope and excitement can be passed on to newer Americans, Americans who never saw any phase of the frontier." The problem with this argument was that *frontier* could mean different things to different Americans. It could stand for untrammeled wilderness, but it could also stand for the process of development that had produced the powerful American economy, providing the standard of living that allowed Americans to vacation in the national parks.

Thus the struggle between utilizers and preservationists continued. Federal agencies administering 258 million acres of western range issued grazing permits to thousands of cattle ranchers. But by the 1980s, overgrazing had destroyed nearly 10 percent of that range. Environmentalists argued that by charging grazing fees that were only a quarter of the going rate on private range, the federal government had actually subsidized the work of destruction. Yet efforts to charge more caused a storm of controversy. In a difficult market, many small ranchers depended on low federal grazing fees and would be put out of business if they were raised. Environmentalists wanted to preserve the range, but might not there be national value in preserving the tradition of small ranching as well?

There were other controversies. The Forest Service controlled 191 million acres of forest, much of it in the West. Timber companies increasingly turned to those public forests to supply their needs. Vast areas of old-growth forest in the Pacific Northwest were clear-cut, threatening the viability of wildlife and causing serious erosion that choked streams with mud and silt. In 1991 environmentalists sued the Forest Service, citing environmental laws that mandated provision "for diversity of plant and animal communities" and using for their cause threats to the spotted owl, designated an "indicator species" for northwestern forests—a kind of "miner's canary" for the entire ecosystem. They won, and for a time the federal timber harvest was halved, although the Forest Service eventually increased output by salvaging diseased and damaged trees. But that simply put off the day of reckoning. In the long run, recreational use of the forests must be both sustainable and profitable.

The most contentious issue concerned water, the fundamental resource of the arid West. There was no doubt that the New Deal's development of the Columbia and Colorado rivers had been crucial to the spectacular rise of the West, and after the war the Bureau of Reclamation and the Army Corps of Engineers took on the Missouri, the Rio Grande, and dozens of smaller rivers, transforming their raging waters into a series of placid lakes. The most powerful western constituency supporting river development was the surging population of the cities. Los Angeles was sucking enough northern water into its reservoirs to top off the Rose Bowl every hour and a half and was drawing millions of gallons more from the Colorado. In 1963, after a long court battle, Arizona won a Supreme Court decision that cut California's share of the Colorado River. But the fact was, by the 1970s the West had in place a system of dams, aqueducts, and canals sufficient to provide for anticipated urban needs, providing the city-states adopted simple and effective conservation measures.

The biggest water user was agribusiness, which drank up more than 90 percent of western water for crop irrigation. Corporate farms enjoyed a munificent subsidy from the federal government, paying only a fraction of the real costs while cities shouldered most of the burden. Water was essential if western agriculture were to sustain its amazing ability to feed America and much of the world. But cheap federal water sustained not only the production of the nation's essential vegetable and fruit crop, but also of cotton, rice, and even alfalfa—crops far better suited to other regions. Western agribusiness grew skilled at evading the legislative provision supposedly limiting federal water to 160-acre farms, finally pressuring Congress into dropping the limitation altogether.

The struggle between utilizers and preservationists was at its starkest in the argument over development in Alaska. "Alaska is our last great frontier," President Truman declared in 1948. Twenty years later, on the far northern shores of the Arctic Ocean, petroleum engineers discovered one of the largest oil reserves in North America, and a consortium of oil companies proposed building a 789-mile pipeline across frozen tundra and monumental mountain ranges to the ice-free port of Valdez on Prince William Sound. It was a project comparable to the construction of the transcontinental railroad. Environmentalists warned that an oil spill in the fragile arctic environment would be "the greatest environmental disaster of our time." But developers were equally determined. Attempting to block the project, one Alaskan asserted, "makes as much sense to us as an attempt to block Daniel Boone from cutting a trail through Cumberland Gap." After a bitter and prolonged debate, in 1973 Congress approved the pipeline by a single vote—Vice President Spiro Agnew's tie-breaker. In 1989, after the pipeline had been operating more than a decade, the oil tanker *Exxon Valdez*, which had just loaded up at Valdez, rammed into a reef and spewed at least eleven million gallons of crude oil into Prince William Sound. The thick goo spread with the current, blackening fifteen hundred miles of shoreline; killing thousands of birds, animals, and fish; and causing damage of unknown proportions. Development had indeed produced disaster.

Thus the story of the frontier can be both positive and destructive. Occasionally in our time that story has been relegated to the status of mere myth or anachronism, no more than a refuge for conservative politicians. But it need not be so. The frontier story has always been reformulated to fit the realities of our history, providing us with a national myth not only to "match our mountains" but to match the needs and aspirations of a new century. The Indians offer heroic examples of resistance, survival, and adaptation. No story in our history is more inspiring than their tale of persistence and resurgence. Although today we may approach the pioneer story with ambivalence, that intellectual experience can be illuminating. The settlers stood alone against authority, but they also welcomed the assistance of an active government. They went their own way, but they also believed in community. They were a hodge-podge of gender and race and nationality. They approached the frontier from the south, the north, and the west, as well as the east. But beyond the ambiguity, the frontier is still the common past of us all, and it binds us together, like a continental warming blanket. The frontier may also be one blueprint of our common future. Though the struggle to build a humane and equitable society from the legacy of colonialism continues, and we have not yet resolved the dilemmas of development, the frontier remains, as writer Willa Cather expressed it, our "road of Destiny." It will not cease to chart this new century, and those to come.

Further Reading

Abbott, Carl. *The Metropolitan Frontier: Cities in the Modern American West* (1993).

Adams, David W. *Education for Extinction: American Indians and the Boarding School Experience, 1875–1928* (1995).

Armitage, Susan, and Elizabeth Jameson, eds. *The Women's West* (1987).

Aron, Stephen. *How the West Was Lost: The Transformation of Kentucky from Daniel Boone to Henry Clay* (1996).

Axtell, James. *The Invasion Within: The Contest of Cultures in Colonial North America* (1985).

Bagley, Will. *Blood of the Prophets: Brigham Young and the Massacre at Mountain Meadows* (2002).

Brooks, James. *Captives and Cousins: Slavery, Kinship, and Community in the Southwest Borderlands* (2002).

Brown, Richard Maxwell. *No Duty to Retreat: Violence and Values in American History and Society* (1992).

Butler, Anne M. *Daughters of Joy, Sisters of Mercy: Prostitutes in the American West, 1865–90* (1985).

Calloway, Colin G. *One Vast Winter Count: The Native American West before Lewis and Clark* (2003).

Camarillo, Albert. *Chicanos in a Changing Society* (1979).

Chaffin, Tom. *Pathfinder: John Charles Frémont and the Course of American Empire* (2002).

Chan, Sucheng. *This Bittersweet Soil: The Chinese in California Agriculture, 1860–1910* (1986).

Coates, Peter. *The Trans-Alaska Pipeline Controversy* (1992).

Coleman, Jon T. *Vicious: Wolves and Men in America* (2004).

Cook, David Noble. *Born to Die: Disease and New World Conquest, 1492–1650* (1998).

Cronon, William. *Nature's Metropolis: Chicago and the Great West* (1991).

———. *Changes in the Land: Indians, Colonists, and the Ecology of New England* (1983).

Cronon, William, George Miles, and Jay Gitlin, eds. *Under an Open Sky: Rethinking America's Western Past* (1991).

Crosby, Alfred W. *The Columbian Exchange: Biological and Cultural Consequences of 1492* (1972; 2003).

Davis, Mike. *City of Quartz: Excavating the Future in Los Angeles* (1992).

Deutsch, Sarah. *No Separate Refuge: Culture, Class, and Gender on an Anglo-Hispanic Frontier in the American Southwest, 1880–1940* (1987).

Deverell, William. *Whitewashed Adobe: The Rise of Los Angeles and the Remaking of Its Mexican Past* (2004).

Dykstra, Robert R. *The Cattle Towns* (1968).

Eccles, W. J. *The Canadian Frontier, 1534–1760* (1986).

Emmons, David M. *Butte Irish: Class and Ethnicity in an American Mining Town, 1875–1925* (1989).

Etulain, Richard W. *Re-Imagining the Modern American West: A Century of Fiction, History, and Art* (1996).

Faragher, John Mack. *Daniel Boone: The Life and Legend of an American Pioneer* (1992).

———. *Sugar Creek: Life on the Illinois Prairie* (1986).

———. *Women and Men on the Overland Trail* (1979).

Fenn, Elizabeth Anne. *Pox Americana: The Great North American Smallpox Epidemic of 1775–1783* (2001).

Foley, Neil. *The White Scourge: Mexicans, Blacks, and Poor Whites in Texas Cotton Culture* (1997).

Frank, Dana. *Purchasing Power: Consumer Organizing, Gender, and the Seattle Labor Movement, 1919–1929* (1994).

Goetzmann, William H. *Exploration and Empire: The Explorer and the Scientist in the Winning of the American West* (1966).

Gregory, James. *American Exodus: The Dust Bowl Migration and Okie Culture in California* (1989).

Gutiérrez, David G. *Walls and Mirrors: Mexican Americans, Mexican Immigrants, and the Politics of Ethnicity* (1995).

Gutiérrez, Ramón A. *When Jesus Came, the Corn Mothers Went Away: Marriage, Sexuality and Power in New Mexico, 1500–1846* (1991).

Haas, Lisbeth. *Conquests and Historical Identities in California, 1769–1936* (1995).

Hietela, Thomas R. *Manifest Design: Anxious Aggrandizement in Late Jacksonian America* (1985).

Hine, Robert V. *Community on the American Frontier: Separate But Not Alone* (1980).

———. *Bartlett's West: Drawing the Mexican Boundary* (1968).

Holliday, J. S. *The World Rushed In: The California Gold Rush Experience* (1981).

Horsman, Reginald. *Race and Manifest Destiny* (1988).

Hundley, Norris, Jr. *The Great Thirst: Californians and Water—A History* (2001).

Hurtado, Albert L. *Indian Survival on the California Frontier* (1988).

Hutton, Paul. *Phil Sheridan and His Army* (1985).

Hyde, Anne. *An American Vision: Far Western Landscape and National Culture, 1820–1920* (1990).

Igler, David. *Industrial Cowboys: Miller and Lux and the Transformation of the Far West, 1850–1920* (2001).

Iverson, Peter. *When Indians Became Cowboys: Native Peoples and Cattle Ranching in the American West* (1994).

Jennings, Francis. *The Invasion of America: Indians, Colonialism, and the Cant of Conquest* (1975).

Johnson, Benjamin Heber. *Revolution in Texas: How a Forgotten Rebellion and Its Bloody Suppression Turned Mexicans into Americans* (2003).

Johnson, Susan. *Roaring Camp: The Social World of the California Gold Rush* (2000).

Jordan, Terry G., and Matti Kaups. *The American Backwoods Frontier: An Ethnic and Ecological Interpretation* (1989).

Kahrl, William L. *Water and Power: The Conflict over Los Angeles' Water Supply in the Owens Valley* (1982).

Klein, Kerwin L. *Frontiers of Historical Imagination: Narrating the European Conquest of Native America, 1890–1990* (1997).

Kling, Rob, Spencer Olin, and Mark Poster, eds. *Postsuburban California: The Transformation of Orange County since World War II* (1991).

Lamar, Howard R. *The Far Southwest, 1846–1912: A Territorial History* (1970).

———. *Dakota Territory, 1861–1889: A Study of Frontier Politics* (1956).

————, ed. *The New Encyclopedia of the American West* (1998).

Lamar, Howard R., and Leonard Thompson, eds. *The Frontier in History: North America and Southern Africa Compared* (1981).

Limerick, Patricia. *The Legacy of Conquest: The Unbroken Past of the American West* (1987).

Luebke, Frederick C. *Ethnicity on the Great Plains* (1990).

McGirr, Lisa. *Suburban Warriors: The Origins of the New American Right* (2001).

McGrath, Roger D. *Gunfighters, Highwaymen, and Vigilantes: Violence on the Frontier* (1984).

McWilliams, Carey. *Southern California Country: An Island on the Land* (1946).

Merrill, Karen. *Public Lands and Political Meaning: Ranchers, the Government, and the Property between Them* (2002).

Milner, Clyde, II, Carol O'Connor, and Martha Sandweiss, eds. *The Oxford History of the American West* (1994).

Montejano, David. *Anglos and Mexicans in the Making of Texas, 1836–1986* (1987).

Moses, L. G. *Wild West Shows and the Images of American Indians, 1883–1933* (1996).

Myres, Sandra L. *Westering Women and the Frontier Experience, 1800–1915* (1982).

Nash, Gerald D. *The American West Transformed: The Impact of the Second World War* (1985).

Nash, Roderick. *Wilderness and the American Mind* (1982; 2001).

Neihardt, John G. *Black Elk Speaks: Being the Life Story of a Holy Man of the Oglala Sioux* (2000).

Nugent, Walter. *Into the West: The Story of Its People* (1999).

Ostler, Jeffrey. *The Plains Sioux and U.S. Colonialism from Lewis and Clark to Wounded Knee* (2004).

Painter, Nell Irvin. *Exodusters: Black Migration to Kansas after Reconstruction* (1976).

Peck, Gunther. *Reinventing Free Labor: Padrones and Immigrant Workers in the North American West, 1880–1930* (2000).

Pitt, Leonard. *The Decline of the Californios: A Social History of the Spanish-Speaking Californians, 1846–1890* (1966).

Pomeroy, Earl. *The Pacific Slope: A History of California, Oregon, Washington, Idaho, Utah, and Nevada* (1965).

Prucha, Francis Paul. *The Great Father: The United States Government and the American Indians* (1984).

Richter, Daniel K. *Facing East from Indian Country: A Native History of Early America* (2001).

Robbins, William G. *Colony and Empire: The Capitalist Transformation of the American West* (1994).

Rohrbough, Malcolm J. *Days of Gold: The California Gold Rush and the American Nation* (1997).

————. *The Trans-Appalachian Frontier: People, Societies, and Institutions, 1775–1850* (1978).

Ronda, James. *Lewis and Clark among the Indians* (1984).

Ruiz, Vicki. *From Out of the Shadows: Mexican Women in Twentieth-Century America* (1998).

Salisbury, Neal. *Manitou and Providence: Indians, Europeans, and the Making of New England, 1500–1643* (1982).

Sanchez, George. *Becoming Mexican American: Ethnicity, Culture, and Identity in Chicano Los Angeles, 1900–1945* (1993).

Sandweiss, Martha A. *Print the Legend: Photography and the American West* (2002).

Scharff, Virginia. *Twenty Thousand Roads: Women, Movement and the West* (2003).

Slatta, Richard W. *The Cowboy Encyclopedia* (1994).

Slotkin, Richard. *Gunfighter Nation: The Myth of the Frontier in Twentieth-Century America* (1992).

————. *The Fatal Environment: The Myth of the Frontier in the Age of Industrialization* (1985).

————. *Regeneration through Violence: The Mythology of the American Frontier, 1600–1860* (1973).

Smith, Henry Nash. *Virgin Land: The American West as Symbol and Myth* (1950).

Spicer, Edward H. *Cycles of Conquest: The Impact of Spain, Mexico, and the United States on the Indians of the Southwest, 1533–1960* (1962).

Stevens, Joseph E. *Hoover Dam: An American Adventure* (1988).

Takaki, Ronald. *A Different Mirror: A History of Multicultural America* (1993).

Taylor, Quintard. *In Search of the Racial Frontier: African Americans in the American West* (1998).

Thornton, Russell. *American Indian Holocaust and Survival: A Population History since 1492* (1987).

Unruh, John D. *The Plains Across: The Overland Emigrants and the Trans-Mississippi West, 1840–60* (1979).

Utley, Robert M. *The Lance and the Shield: The Life and Times of Sitting Bull* (1993).

———. *The Indian Frontier of the American West, 1846–1890* (1984).

Wade, Richard C. *The Urban Frontier: The Rise of Western Cities, 1790–1830* (1959; 1996).

Wallace, Anthony F. C. *The Death and Rebirth of the Seneca* (1969).

Walton, John. *Western Times and Water Wars: State, Culture, and Rebellion in California* (1992).

Webb, Walter Prescott. *The Great Plains* (1931).

Weber, David J. *The Spanish Frontier in North America* (1992).

———. *The Mexican Frontier, 1821–46: The American Southwest under Mexico* (1982).

Weber, Devra. *Dark Sweat, White Gold: California Farm Workers, Cotton, and the New Deal* (1994).

West, Elliot. *The Contested Plains: Indians, Goldseekers, and the Rush to Colorado* (1998).

White, G. Edward. *The Eastern Establishment and the Western Experience: The West of Frederic Remington, Theodore Roosevelt, and Owen Wister* (1968).

White, Richard. *It's Your Misfortune and None of My Own: A History of the American West* (1991).

———. *The Middle Ground: Indians, Empires, and Republics in the Great Lakes Region, 1650–1815* (1991).

Worster, Donald. *A River Running West: The Life of John Wesley Powell* (2001).

———. *Rivers of Empire: Water, Aridity, and the Growth of the American West* (1985).

———. *Dust Bowl: The Southern Plains in the 1930s* (1979).

Wrobel, David M. *The End of American Exceptionalism: Frontier Anxiety from the Old West to the New Deal* (1993).

Wyman, Mark. *Hard Rock Epic: Western Miners and the Industrial Revolution, 1860–1910* (1979).

Yung, Judy. *Unbound Feet: A Social History of Chinese Women in San Francisco* (1995).

Index

Arizona (*continued*)
145; mining in, 95, 107, 108, 118; San
Carlos reservation in, 117; segregation
in, 218; statehood of, 197; territory of,
85, 86; water and electricity to, 189,
224
Arkansas: farm families migrating from,
186–87; slaves in, 65
Armour, Philip, 124
Army, U.S.: and buffalo extinction, 127–28;
"Buffalo Soldiers" of, 93, 212; Corps of
[Topographical] Engineers, 63, 76, 169,
224; and Geronimo's people, 117; and
Johnson County War, 131; at Little
Bighorn, 101–2; segregation in, 93, 217;
at Wounded Knee, 155–56
Arnold, Thurman, 143, 188
Aronson, Max, 201
Articles of Confederation, 40
Asbury, Francis, 149
Ashley, William H., 58, 59–60
Assiniboine people, 88
Astor, John Jacob, 56–57, 61
Atchison, Topeka, and Santa Fe Railway,
116–17, 122–23, 168
Athearn, Robert, 6, 202
atomic bomb, construction of, 207
Austin, Mary, 185
Austin, Moses, 62, 63
Austin, Stephen F., 63, 66–67
Averell, James, 131
Aztec people, 2; and human sacrifice, 11;
legendary homeland of, 13; Spanish
conquest of, 9–12; Tenochtitlán as
capital of, 8–9, 10
Aztlán, 13

Bacon, Nathaniel, 24, 34
Bacon's Rebellion (1676), 24
Bad Ax River, massacre of, 71
Baja California, 36–37
Ballinger, Richard, 183
Bank of America, 172, 189, 206
barbed wire, invention of, 130
Bartlett, John Russell, 86
Bassett, Ann, 127
Beadle & Adams, 193–94
Beard, Charles and Mary, 111
Bechtel, Stephen, 206
Becknell, William, 66

Bent, George, 92–93
Bent, William, 92
Benton, Thomas Hart, 76, 112
Berkeley, Bishop George, 1
Bierstadt, Albert, 178, 196, 197, 203; *The
Rocky Mountains, Landers Peak*, 196
Big Foot, Sioux chief, 155
Billy the Kid, 193
Bingham, George Caleb, 199; *Daniel Boone
Escorting Settlers through the Cumber-
land Gap*, 195–96
bin Laden, Osama, 211, 212
Black Elk, Oglala dancer, 200
Black Elk, at Wounded Knee, 128, 155
Black Hawk, Oglala spokesman, 88
Black Hawk, Sauk leader, 71, 82
Black Hills: gold discovered in, 101, 102;
Homestake mine in, 107; as Indian
territory, 100, 101, 102
Black Kettle, Cheyenne chief, 92–93, 101
Bodmer, Karl, 195
Boeing, William, 206, 207
Bonaparte, Napoleon, 52–53
Book of Mormon (Smith), 77
Boone, Daniel: in Bingham painting, 195–96;
book about, 191; death of, 191; family
of, 29; and frontier myth, 46, 58, 76,
183, 184, 191, 192
Boone, Rebecca Bryan, 29, 46
Boone and Crockett Club, 178, 182, 199
Bosque Redondo reservation, 91, 92
Boudinot, Elias, 51, 69
Boulder Dam, 189
Bowie, Jim, 67, 193
Bracero Program, 219
Brackenridge, Henry Marie, 46
Braddock, Edward, 32
Brant, Joseph, 39
Bridger, Jim, 59
Britain: and American Revolution, 39–40; and
Canadian border, 71–72, 79, 81; colonial
wars with, 30–31; forts held by, 47;
French and Indian War, 31–33; in fur
trade, 18, 47, 56; Indian allies of, 33–34,
39, 40; Indian removal as goal of, 27;
investments in the West from, 107;
joint-stock companies, 22; New World
colonies of, 21–27, *21*, 30, 33; and Paci-
fic region, 57–58; Scotch-Irish settlers,
29; war between Spain and, 22; War of

47–48, 87–88, 117; Five Civilized
Tribes, 68; French and Indian War, 31–
33; gaming parlors of, 216; genocide of,
11–12, 25, 50, 83, 91, 100; Ghost Dance
movement, 154–55; gift-giving protocol
of, 33; and gold rush, 69, 99–100, 101–2,
106; government policies toward, 47–
48, 87–88, 90–93, 100, 101, 103, 128, 135,
153–54, 189–90; guns supplied to, 47,
90; horse trading, 78; hunters, 18, 28,
33, 49, 55, 87, 88, 92, 101, 102, 103, 127;
independent nations of, 68–69; kidnapped and sold, 100; land set aside
for, 34, 40, 47, 77–78, 87–88, 91, 117,
128, 152–54, 214, *215*, 216; land title
extinguished, 68–71, 154, *154*, 190; languages of, 31; lifestyles of, 2–4, 7; at
Little Bighorn, 48, 100–102; as manual
laborers, 37, 78, 99–100, 103; matriar-
chies of, 14, 15, 17, 19; movement of,
48, 214; of Pacific region, 57; pen-and-
ink frauds against, 31; populations of,
12, 15, 24, 49, 100; poverty of, 190, 214;
progressives vs. traditionalists among,
49–50; and railroads, 117; religions of,
5, 16, 48–50, 154–55; religious conversion resisted by, 15, 36; removals of,
27, 69–71, *70*, 87–88, 91–93, 152–56, 175,
189–90, 214; reparations to, 213–14;
resources on lands of, 69, 101–2, 216;
revitalization movements of, 48–51;
rights to the land, 5, 15, 16, 25, 26, 34,
40, 47, 87; Sand Creek Massacre, 92–
93, 100, 101; schools for, 153, 190, 216;
settlers helped by, 22–23, 25; sovereignty of, 190, 205, 214, 216; taken into
slavery, 14, 26, 30, 78, 100; trade with,
17, 18–19, 24, 25, 31, 55; Trail of Tears,
70, 152; treaties with, 24, 69, 87–88, 91,
101, 153; tribal locations, *4;* uprisings
of, 15, 23–24, 26, 33, 37–38, 93, 154–56,
214, 216; use of term, 2; and War of
1812, 50; wars with, 26–27, 30, 44;
water diverted from lands of, 175, 185;
women's roles, 60. *See also specific
tribes*
Indian Self-Determination Act (1975), 214
Indian Territory (Oklahoma), 152, 197
Industrial Workers of the World (IWW;
    Wobblies), 108, 144, 145

Intel Corporation, 207
Interior Department, U.S., 87–88, 185
Interstate Commerce Act (1887), 141
Iowa: farmlands in, 136; population growth in,
    75; women moving to cities in, 170–71
Iron Horse, The (movie), 201
Iroquois people: as British ally, 39; Confeder-
    acy, 18, 30, 31; declining populations of,
    48–49; Five Nations of, 18; land of, 34,
    40, 43, 47, 49; longhouses of, 17, 49; Six
    Nations of, 39, 40, 49; spirituality of, 49
Irvine, James, 106

Jackson, Andrew, 29, 69, 71, 72
Jackson, William Henry, 179, 196
James, Jesse and Frank, 118–19, 193, 203
James I, king of England, 22, 23
Jamestown, Virginia, 22–24
Japan: attack on Pearl Harbor by, 205;
    Gentleman's Agreement with, 159
Japanese immigrants: American-born *Issei*
    and *Nisei* citizens, 159, 174; farm
    workers, 145, 159; picture brides,
    159–60; prejudice against, 158–62, 173,
    174–75; removed to detention camps,
    174–75
Jefferson, Thomas: on democratic colonial
    policy, 44; on land distribution, 42, 43,
    133; Lewis and Clark expedition, 53,
    55, 62; and Louisiana Purchase, 52; on
    slavery, 80
Jesse James (movie), 203
Jet Propulsion Laboratory, California, 207
Jobs, Steve, 207
Johnson, Lyndon B., 211, 212, 214, 217
Johnson County War, 131
Joliet, Louis, 20
Jordan, Barbara, 217
Jordan, Terry, 128
Joseph, Chief, 152
Juárez, Benito, 161
Judah, Theodore, 113
Julian, George Washington, 136
Juneau, Joe, 103
Justin, Joe, 125

Kaiser, Henry J., 189, 205–6; Kaiser-
    Permanente Health Plan, 205
Kansas: African American community in,
    151–52; cattle ranching in, 102, 122–23,

logging industry, 177, 180–83, 207, 223–24
Lonesome Dove (TV), 213
Long, Stephen H., 63, 136
Longoria, Felix, 217
Los Alamos, New Mexico, atomic laboratory, 206–7
Los Angeles: automobile culture in, 169; development of, 168–70, 173, 208–10; Great Depression in, 174; home construction in, 206, 210; immigrants in, 172–75, 220–21; and Mexican War, 84; migrant workers in, 186; population growth, 173, 208; racism in, 173–75, 221; settlement of, 37; as trade center, 181; water diverted for use in, 168–69, 185, 224; Watts Riot, 218, 221
Louisiana: borders of, 72; cattle raising in, 122; Indians in, 30; naming of, 20; slaves in, 65; territory of, 52–53, 55
Louisiana Purchase, 52–53, *54*, 57, 62–63, 80, *88*, 89
Love, Nat, 126
Loving, Oliver, 124–25

mail delivery, 110–11
Malíntzin (La Malínche), 9
Mandan people, 53–54, 88
Manifest Destiny, 2, 26, 80
Man Who Shot Liberty Valance, The (movie), 212
Manzanar War Relocation Center, 175
Marquette, Jacques, 20
Marsh, George Perkins, *Man and Nature*, 181
Marshall, James, 94
Marshall, John, 69
Marshall, Robert, 223
masculinity, cult of, 199, 202
Mason, John, 26
Massachusetts, settlement of, 72
Massasoit, Wampanoag chief, 25
Masters, Edgar Lee, *Spoon River Anthology*, 157
Maverick Law (1884), 131
McCone, John, 206
McCormick Reaper, 137
McGovern, George, 211
McKinley, William, 142, 181
McLoughlin, John, 56, 79
McMurtry, Larry, *Lonesome Dove*, 213

McWilliams, Carey, 159, 162, 169
Means, Russell, 214, 216
Melville, Herman, 90
Metacomet, Wampanoag chief, 26, 27
Mexican Americans: challenge to social order by, 216–21; Chicanos, 219; cultural renaissance, 219–20; and labor unions, 162, 218–19; *pachucos*, 174; *El Plan de San Diego*, 160; populations, 220; prejudice against, 86–87, 106, 158, 160, 217–18; voters, 217
Mexican immigrants: and Border Patrol, 219, 220; and Bracero Program, 219; and citizenship, 161; legislation about, 220; migrant workers, 145–46, 160–62, 218–20; miners, 95, 98–99, 107; prejudice against, 98, 174; *sin fronteras*, 161, 220; in southern California, 173–74; undocumented workers, 220
Mexico: boundary with, 81–82, 85–86, *88*, 220; Catholic missions in, 14–16; cattle ranching in, 63, 122; independence of, 77–78; mass migrations from, 160–62; missions secularized in, 77–78; population, 12; rebellion against Spain, 63; revolution (1911), 160, 161, 162; slavery abolished in, 64, 65–66; and Southwest territory, 64–68, 81–83, *82*, 84–86; Spanish conquest of, 8–14; Treaty of Guadalupe Hidalgo, 85, 86, 98, 99; and U.S. slavery question, 88–89; war with, 81–86, *82*, 88–89, 219
Mexico City, 10, 84
Miami people, 48
Michener, James A., 204
Microsoft Corporation, 207
Míkmaq people, 2, 17
Miller, Alfred Jacob, 195
Miller, Joaquin, 76
mining, *96;* boom and bust in, 207–8; commercial effects of, 106–7; copper, 107; corporate investment in, 107, 118, 167; gold (*see* gold); and habitat destruction, 177; hazards of, 107; and Indians, 99–100, 103; labor unions, 107–8; and laws, 105–6; mercury, 177; and mobility, 104, 105, 108; and railroads, 118; silver, 97; women's roles in, 104–5
Minnesota: cities in, 167; farmlands in, 136, 137; immigrant communities in, 156;

Stewart, Elinore Pruitt, *Letters of a Woman Homesteader*, 139
Stewart, Richard, 175
Stewart, William Drummond, 195
Stockton, Robert, 84
Strauss, Levi, 96, 124, 210
Sugar Creek, Illinois, 147
Sumner, Charles, 83, 102
Sunbelt, 109–10
Supreme Court, U.S.: on desegregation, 218; on farm issues, 141; on immigrants, 158, 175; on Indian affairs, 69, 153, 185; on voting rights, 217
Sutter, John A., 78, 94, 95
Swan Land and Cattle Company, 128
Swift, Gustavus, 124

Taft, William Howard, 183
Taíno people, 7, 11–12
Talleyrand-Périgord, Charles-Maurice de, 53
Tape, Mary and Joseph, 172
Taylor, Buck, 200
Taylor, Zachary, 82, 83
Taylor Grazing Act (1934), 188
Tecumseh, Shawnee chief, 50, 82, 155
Tejanos, 63, 64, 66, 67, 68, 82, 86–87, 160
telegraph, 110
Tennessee: settlement of, 34; slaves in, 65; towns and cities in, 163
Tennessee Valley Authority (TVA), 189
Tenochtitlán, 8–9, 10
Tenskwatawa (Shawnee Prophet), 49–50, 155
Texas: African Americans in, 64–66; aircraft industry in, 205; Alamo, 67–68; annexation of, 66, 81, 85, *88;* bandits in, 86–87; borders of, 72, 85–86, 219, 220; cattle ranching in, 63, 102, 121, 122, *123,* 124, 128, 129; farm families migrating from, 186–87; farming in, 137, 144, 145, 160; Franciscan missions in, 36; immigrant populations in, 138, 221; independent republic of, 67–68; land grants in, 63; and Mexican revolution, 67–68; Mexican territory of, 62, 63–64, *64,* 66, 81; petrochemicals in, 167, 173, 177–78, 206; politicians from, 211–12; population growth in, 208; Raza Unida Party in, 219; rural electrification in, 189; segregation in, 217; settlement of, 63–64; slavery in, 65–66, 68, 74, 80;

statehood of, 45, 68, 80, 81, 87; steel industry in, 205; in Sunbelt area, 209; tall tales of, 74; voting rights in, 217
Texas longhorns, 122, 128, 132
Texas Rangers, 86–87, 129, 160, 184
Texians, 64, 66–67, 68
Thayendanegea (Brant), 39
Thoreau, Henry David, 85
Thorn, Jonathan, 57
Tijerina, Reies, 219
Timber Cutting Act (1878), 181
Timucua people, 2
Tlaxcalan people, 9–10, 13, 14
Tlingit people, 2, 103
tobacco, 23–24
Tonquin, 57, 58
Torres, Art, 221
tourism, 179, 180, 206
Toussaint, François Dominique (L'Ouverture), 53
Townes, Samuel, 65
Trail of Tears, 70, 152
Transcendentalists, 85, 180
Trans World Airlines (TWA), 206
Traven, B., *Treasure of the Sierra Madre,* 104
Travis, William Barret, 66, 67
Treaty of Guadalupe Hidalgo (1848), 85, 86, 98, 99
Treaty of Paris (1763), 33, 47
Trist, Nicholas, 85
Truman, Harry S, 211, 224
Tumbleweeds (movie), 201
Turner, Frederick Jackson, 5, 163, 197, 198
Tuscorora people, 39
Twain, Mark, 111, 196
Two Moons, Cheyenne chief, 102
Tyler, John, 81

Unforgiven (movie), 213
Union Pacific (movie), 203
Union Pacific Railroad, 111, 112, 113, 114–15, 117, 119, 166
United Farm Workers (UFW), 219
United States: ethnic diversity in, *222;* immigrant communities in, 156, *157,* 158–62; imperialism of, 198; independence of, 40; internal migration in, 147; population of, 62; post-World War II, 204; right of conquest, 40, 47; as transconti-

nental nation, 87, *88;* urban vs. rural communities, 157–58, 163; wealth gap in, 65, 158, 221

Utah: border of, 72; mining in, 107; Mormons in, 77, 149–51, 166–67; Mountain Meadows attack in, 151; polygamy in, 150–51; and slavery question, 89; statehood of, 151, 197; steel industry in, 205; territory of, 85, 89; urban development in, 166–67, 208

Vallejo, Mariano, 83
Vallejo, Salvador, 78
Vancouver Island, 79
Van Dyke, Theodore, *Millionaires of a Day,* 168
vaqueros, 78, 122, 125, 126
Vermont, settlement of, 34
Verrazano, Giovanni da, 17
Victoria, British Columbia, 79
Villa, Francisco "Pancho," 161
Villaraigosa, Antonio, 221
Virginia, settlement of, 22, 24
Virginia Company, 22–24
Vogt, William, 178
Voltaire, *Candide,* 33

Walker, Robert J., 85
Wallace, Henry, 211
Wampanoag people, 25, 26
War of 1812, 50, 57, 71
War Relocation Authority, 175
Washington, George, 32, 44, 47, 48, 196
Washington state: aerospace industry in, 205–7; farming in, 145; logging industry in, 181; Olympic peninsula, 182; statehood of, 197; urban development in, 208
Watson, Ella "Cattle Kate," 131
Watts Riot, 218, 221
Wayne, Anthony, 48
Wayne, John, 203
Weaver, James B., 142
Webb, Walter Prescott, 136, 160
Weber, Adna, 163
Wells Fargo, 111, 207
West: artistic depictions of, 194–97, 199; backcountry pioneers in, 34; cattle ranching in, 63, 78, 102, 106, 127; cities in, 163, *209;* corporations in, 172, 189, 207; cultural influence of, 204–5, 210;

distribution of land in, 40–44, *41,* 90 (*see also* land); eastern financing in, 35, 42, 43, 48, 106–7, 118, 140–41, 158, 167, 179, 188; farming in, 136–37, 144–46, 148, 160–62; federal government involvement in, 76, 87, 188–89; federal lands in, *187,* 188; gold rush in, 94–100; guns in, 125; historical meanings of, 5–6; industrialization of, 173, 188, 189, 205–7, 216; labor system in, 144; Lewis and Clark expedition to, 53–56, *54,* 62, 71, 72; mining in, *96,* 97, 100, 104–8, 118, 177; mountain men of, 46, 58–61, 76; nabobs vs. nobodies in, 65; politicians from, 211; population growth in, 47, 62, 75, 208–9; racial prejudice in (*see* racism); and railroads (*see* railroads); religion in, 148–51; restlessness in, 104, 105, 108, 147; settlers vs. Indians for control of, 39–40, 62, 102; trans-Appalachian, 163–65; trans-Mississippi, 87, 90, 197; vigilantes in, 34–35, 45, 89, 106, 119, 129–30, 131; water diverted for, 168–69, 184–86, 224. *See also specific states*

Western Federation of Miners (WFM), 107–8
Westerns: artworks, 194–97, 199; dime novels, 193–94, 200; and frontier myths, 191–93, 212–13; historic reenactments, 200–201; movies, 201–3, 211–13; political side of, 212–13; pulp fiction, 202; revisionist, 213; on television, 212; "wild west shows," 200–201
Western Trail, 124
Western Union (movie), 203
West Virginia, settlement of, 34
Weyerhaeuser Company, 183
Wheeler, Edward L., *Deadwood Dick on Deck,* 194
White, John, 22
White Bull, Sioux warrior, 102
Whitman, Marcus, 73, 74
Wilbur, Charles Dana, 136–37
Wilde, Oscar, 116
wilderness: preservation of, 178–80, 182, 223; public's notion of, 180, 182
Wilderness Act (1964), 223
Wilderness Society, 223
wildlife: extinction of, 61, 127–28, 176–78, 181; and habitat destruction, 177–78, 181;